Stealing
the
Show

Stealing the Show

the
Show

How Women Are
Revolutionizing Television

JOY PRESS

ATRIA BOOKS

NEW YORK   LONDON   TORONTO   SYDNEY   NEW DELHI

ATRIA
BOOKS

An Imprint of Simon & Schuster, Inc.
1230 Avenue of the Americas
New York, NY 10020

First Atria Books hardcover edition February 2018

ATRIA BOOKS and colophon are trademarks of Simon & Schuster, Inc.

For information about special discounts for bulk purchases, please
contact Simon & Schuster Special Sales at 1-866-506-1949
or business@simonandschuster.com.

The Simon & Schuster Speakers Bureau can bring authors to your live event.
For more information or to book an event, contact the Simon & Schuster Speakers
Bureau at 1-866-248-3049 or visit our website at www.simonspeakers.com.

Interior design by Laura Levatino

Manufactured in the United States of America

10   9   8   7   6   5   4   3   2   1

Library of Congress Cataloging-in-Publication Data

Names: Press, Joy, 1966– author.
Title: Stealing the show : how women are revolutionizing television / Joy Press.
Description: New York : Atria Books, 2018.
Identifiers: LCCN 2017032332 (print) | LCCN 2017050318 (ebook) | ISBN
9781501137730 (ebook) | ISBN 9781501137716 (hardback) | ISBN 9781501137723
(paperback)
Subjects: LCSH: Television and women—United States—History. | Women
television producers and directors—United States. | Television programs—United
States—History. | Television broadcasting—United States—History. | BISAC:
PERFORMING ARTS / Television / Direction & Production. | SOCIAL SCIENCE /
Women's Studies. | PERFORMING ARTS / Television / History & Criticism.
Classification: LCC PN1992.8.W65 (ebook) | LCC PN1992.8.W65 P74 2018 (print) |
DDC 791.456522—dc23
LC record available at https://lccn.loc.gov/2017032332

ISBN 978-1-5011-3771-6
ISBN 978-1-5011-3773-0 (ebook)

To my parents, Rebecca and Stephen Press, who kept our house stocked with books and never uttered the words "Too much TV is bad for you."

CONTENTS

CONTENTS

INTRODUCTION

Mary Tyler Moore became an icon of single working
womanhood on *The Mary Tyler Moore Show*.

Growing up in the seventies, I devoured *The Mary Tyler Moore Show* and *That Girl* reruns. I couldn't have explained why back then, but the chutzpah and ambition of those characters were a big part of it. Both shows featured young women chafing at their limits. Sometimes I felt they were winking at me, as if to acknowledge the ridiculousness of their predicaments. But as much as I loved them, *The Mary Tyler Moore Show* and *That Girl* were innocuous reflections of the ferocious changes shaking up our culture.

During the second half of the twentieth century, American women expanded their ability to control reproduction, to pursue careers, to decide when (or whether) to marry, and to end marriages gone bad. Looking back at those decades of change and turbulence, I'm amazed by how little of this translated to the TV screen—and how few women had creative control over the shows America watched. Marlo Thomas recalled that while working on *That Girl*, she was usually "the only girl in the room." Although the sitcom revolved around her character, it was up to Thomas to nudge the male writers and producers toward a more accurate and realistic rendering of a liberated young woman's life.

The idea for this book started clattering around in my brain in the spring of 2015. If you had to pick a triumphant moment for the twenty-first-century surge of revolutionary TV made by and about women, that would be it. More than a dozen new female-centric series created by women premiered in 2015—as many as had emerged in the three previous years combined. At the 2015 Emmys, *Inside Amy Schumer* won Best Variety Show, and Jill Soloway accepted an award for directing the series she'd created, *Transparent*. The same year, at the Golden Globes, four of the five nominated comedies, *Orange Is the New Black*, *Girls*, *Jane the Virgin*, and *Transparent* (which won), were made by women. On the drama front, Shonda Rhimes reigned over ABC's Thursday-night lineup with three hit series, making her one of the most powerful producers in Hollywood.

For most of TV history, broadcast networks had focused on series that could deliver a mass audience to advertisers, with particular emphasis on eighteen-to-thirty-four-year-old guys. Entertainment executives, who were mostly men, seemed to believe viewers wouldn't put up with complex female leads, even as audiences lapped up series about cranky or difficult men. Women couldn't be chubby, dark-skinned, or too far north of thirty, either. In the early years of the twenty-first century, though, those tightly held beliefs began to loosen. The TV industry was in crisis, threatened by an onslaught of cable and digital outlets. Where once ABC, CBS, and NBC divided up the entire American viewing populace among themselves, now they had to fend off an ever-multiplying number of rivals. The crisis became a moment of opportunity; cable and digital executives grew more receptive to programming that appealed to niche populations, and anxious broadcast networks took a few more risks in response. As a result, women began to enter through the ever-widening cracks in the system.

This is a tale of the extraordinary women responsible for an upheaval in pop culture, the reverberations of which continue to shake up the television landscape today. They've filled our screens with a throng of unruly female characters and stretched the format farther than we ever imagined it could go. So many aspects of women's lives (as momentous as female friendship, as mundane as period pain) had never been depicted with any depth on a small screen because network executives believed that these things were inherently dull or off-putting. Nowadays, we take it for granted that we'll be seeing female experiences depicted provocatively and hilariously on our screens—courtesy of a bevy of irreverent female writers, producers, directors, and performers.

Shonda, Jenji, Mindy, Lena, Tina—all those loud, visible female showrunners have made television feel like an equal-opportunity dream factory. Most of the young female TV writers I've interviewed came of age watching series such as *Gilmore Girls*, *My So-Called Life*, and *Grey's Anatomy*, and took for granted that Hollywood would make space for them. However, despite the recent spate of high-profile, Zeitgeist-defining shows conceived, written, and starring women, television remains a male-dominated industry. Anecdotal evidence suggests that female showrunners earn less than their male counterparts, and there are still far fewer women in those positions of power. According to a report by the Center for the Study of Women in Television and Film, out of all the series on the air in the 2016/17 season, only one in five broadcast TV creators was female. It's only slightly better at the supposedly more adventurous cable and streaming outlets, where 26 percent of creators are female. The report notes something else, though: shows with at least one female creator hired far more women writers and cast more women in major roles. It's an ever-expanding circle in which powerful female showrunners can enable others to create cultural images and narratives that inspire the next generation of powerful women.

This book celebrates the modern era of female-driven and female-focused television, which I trace back to the twin disruptions of *Roseanne* and *Murphy Brown*. After all, when you're living through what seems like a golden age, it's important not to take it for granted, to remember that things weren't always so golden, that it took decades of struggle and perseverance in the face of preconceived ideas and outright exclusion to get here.

The founding mother of the American TV sitcom, Gertrude Berg, is almost completely forgotten nowadays. In the 1920s, she created the radio sensation *The Rise of the Goldbergs*, a serial about a Jewish family (broadcast at a time when Nazism was emerging in Europe), and then retooled it as *The Goldbergs* for the early days of television. Writing, starring in, and producing the comedy series from 1949 to 1955, she retained creative control while playing a matriarch with a shtetl accent. *The Goldbergs* became one of CBS's top ten shows in postwar America. A cross-promotional dynamo, Berg spun out of this franchise live shows, books, a line of housedresses, and a movie.

A former chorus girl and movie actress who spotted the possibilities of television as her ingenue options waned, Lucille Ball negotiated with CBS executives about creating her own comedy series. They were hesitant to cast her Cuban husband, Desi Arnaz, as her costar, so the couple convinced them by forming a production company and taking a live prototype of *I Love Lucy* on the road. The ensuing series about a zany, enterprising redhead and her exasperated bandleader husband was the number one show in America for most of its six years on the air. Ball ignored the prevailing norm of having an all-male writing staff and hired Madelyn Pugh, who remained with her for the entire run of the series. That women's point of view showed itself in Lucy, a willful figure who constantly rebelled against her husband's orders. Ball and Arnaz made the canny decision to produce *I Love Lucy* themselves, and to shoot it on film. (In those days, TV shows were generally performed and broadcast live and not preserved on tape.) Such innovation later allowed them to syndicate the series, keeping *Lucy* on television screens for decades and making Ball a role model for generations of funny ladies—not to mention a wealthy woman.

Although the Pill had hit the market in 1960, and Betty Friedan's million-selling *The Feminine Mystique* helped kindle second-wave feminism upon its 1963 publication, liberated women were rarely glimpsed on TV. This all changed when *That Girl* premiered on ABC in 1966. Rising starlet Marlo

Thomas had proposed a series based partly around her experience as a young actress living in Manhattan on her own. She wanted to call it *Miss Independence* but lost the battle. Thomas formed her own production company, Daisy Productions, and sought out female writers, but as a sign of how constrained things were for women, she was never credited on-screen as producer. "I ran the show, I signed the checks," she later said, "but I chose to play down my power, so as not to be too threatening" and risk scaring off the "best and brightest men in comedy."

Despite its breezy tone, *That Girl* was groundbreaking in its depiction of a young single woman focused on her career and her desires, rather than on reeling in a husband. "You did not have to be the wife or the daughter *of* somebody, or the secretary *of* somebody . . . you could *be* the somebody," Thomas has said. Although the network heads worried that audiences would be turned off by all that female independence, the show was an instant hit, a sign perhaps of changes in society that TV had ignored. As Thomas recalled in her memoir, *Growing Up Laughing*, "[T]his girl, who seemed like a revolutionary figure to the men in suits who did the research, was not a revolutionary figure at all. . . . There were *millions* of 'That Girls' in homes across America." As the show wound up its five-year run in 1971, the network, still resolutely misunderstanding *That Girl*'s appeal, proposed the traditional "happy ending": a wedding. Rejecting this conventional closure for something truer to the energies roiling the era, Thomas insisted that *That Girl* conclude with the couple en route to a women's lib meeting.

After a successful run as spry housewife Laura Petrie on *The Dick Van Dyke Show*, Mary Tyler Moore, along with husband Grant Tinker, formed MTM Enterprises to produce *The Mary Tyler Moore Show*. Its 1970 launch coincided with *That Girl*'s final season—almost as if the baton were being passed from one TV icon of single working womanhood to another. But unlike Thomas, Moore didn't feel the need to tiptoe around male hang-ups about empowered women: her authority was never in question, on-screen or behind the scenes. Her character, Mary, called her boss "Mr. Grant" and sometimes hesitated nervously to ask for what she deserved, but that didn't stop her from forging ahead. It didn't stop Moore, either, her power and ownership emblazoned in the very title of the series. "You never forgot for a second that she was in charge," director Alan Rafkin once wrote. The show's producers hired an unprecedented number of women—at one point, a third of the writers' room was female. Scribes such as Treva Silverman and Susan Silver delighted in pouring their own experiences with dating, double standards, and workplace wrangles into the mouths of Mary and Rhoda, Mary's equally single best friend.

During a conference on Women in Public Life held at the University of Texas in November 1975, Gloria Steinem imagined what aliens from outer space might make of American women if all they had to go on was TV and movies, as Jennifer Keishin Armstrong relayed in her book *Mary and Lou and Rhoda and Ted*. "First of all, they would be convinced that there were twice as many American men as there were American women. It would be quite clear that we slept in false eyelashes and full makeup. Some of us would be taken to be a servant class of some sort. If we lived alone, we would almost have to be widows, at least until recently." This absurdly out-of-date picture, Steinem pointed out, was being challenged and changed by *The Mary Tyler Moore Show*, along with Norman Lear's new series, *Maude*.

Although ideas from the women's movement permeated mainstream America throughout the seventies, their impact on prime time remained minimal: there were Mary and Rhoda, there was Maude, and there was the working-mom sitcom *One Day at a Time* (co-created by actress Whitney Blake), but that was about it. Behind the scenes, things were equally unequal. A 1974 Writers Guild of America report revealed a shocking statistic: only 6.5 percent of prime-time shows that season had hired even a single woman writer.

It wasn't until the early eighties that women really started to write and run more shows. That's when writing partners Barbara Corday and Barbara Avedon finally got *Cagney & Lacey* on the air. They had been trying to pitch a buddy movie about two female police detectives since the mid-seventies.

Corday's producer boyfriend Barney Rosenzweig had originally suggested the idea, inspired by a book she'd given him: Molly Haskell's feminist film critique *From Reverence to Rape: The Treatment of Women in the Movies*. After multiple false starts and cast changes, *Cagney & Lacey* landed on the air in 1982 and became a hit for CBS, winning not just a huge audience worldwide but also a run of Emmy Awards.

Corday argues that people were excited by Christine Cagney and Mary Beth Lacey not because they were fighting crime but because viewers wanted to see wise older women muddling through their complicated lives. Cagney was a hard-drinking and sharp-edged single chick; the more nurturing Lacey was a working woman with a supportive husband. "What people wrote letters about most were the bathroom scenes, where two women actually sat and talked about everything in their lives," Corday says. "Eavesdropping on those conversations—it sounds silly, but it was very groundbreaking for women. There was nothing else like that on television." The show followed through on its feminism behind the scenes, too, hiring dozens of female writers and episode directors. Among those writers was Ronnie Wenker-Konner, mother of Jennifer Konner, the future co-showrunner of *Girls*, which would ultimately push intimate women's bathroom conversations farther than Cagney or Lacey could have imagined.

Many of the women who pioneered prime time did so in partnership with men, usually their husbands. Y chromosomes just seemed to make male network execs feel more comfortable. That was true for Lucille Ball, Mary Tyler Moore, Barbara Corday, Whitney Blake, *Golden Girls* creator Susan Harris, and Linda Bloodworth-Thomason. Bloodworth-Thomason honed her skills writing for *M*A*S*H*, *Rhoda*, and *One Day at a Time* before launching a production company with husband Harry Thomason to create sitcoms such as *Designing Women*, a southern hothouse of female workplace repartee. Corday suggests that a lot of women writers back then clung to the creative side: "They didn't see themselves as businesspeople, and their husbands did." Even so, she says, "Barney and I were very aware that whenever we would go to a meeting, the executive would talk directly to him. The two of us would be sitting on a couch, but the whole conversation was directed to one person."

One of the first to ditch the male-partner trend and step out on her own was Anne Beatts, a comedy writer who parlayed her Emmy-winning stint on the original incarnation of *SNL* into a TV deal. *Square Pegs*, her sitcom about two nerdy girls (one of whom was played by a young Sarah Jessica Parker), premiered on CBS in 1982. A cult classic, *Square Pegs* unsuccessfully pushed for an all-female writers' room. Says Beatts, "I only wanted to hire women because it was about the experience of young girls in high school, but the network made me hire a token male writer." (That token male, Andy Borowitz, would go on to create *The Fresh Prince of Bel-Air* and to found *The Borowitz Report*.)

Much more common was for series to hire a token female writer, as if too many women might turn the room into a kaffeeklatsch. "When I started, the networks and studios were run by men, and they tended to gravitate toward male material, toward male writers and showrunners," says Jenny Bicks, who launched her career in the early nineties, eventually ending up as a writer on *Sex and the City* and then as showrunner for *Men in Trees*, *The Big C*, and *Divorce*. Being "the only woman in a room of, like, twelve or thirteen men" was the norm, something that Bicks experienced time and time again. And if trying to carve a path through prime time has been challenging for white women, the difficulty was multiplied for trailblazing women of color such as Yvette Lee Bowser (*Living Single*, *Half & Half*) and Mara Brock Akil (*Girlfriends*, *Being Mary Jane*).

Female TV writers grew accustomed to thinking of other women as their competition for the tiny number of slots available—*because they were*.

———————

Chances are you have only a vague idea of what a showrunner does. The word came into common usage in the late eighties and nineties. Before that, the person in charge of a TV series was called the executive producer, and he (almost invariably a he) was typically a business-minded type who managed the production and commissioned writers to churn out scripts. Slowly but steadily, though, decision-making power slipped into the hands of TV writers. You started out as a staff writer and worked your way up to executive producer, with the result that, on any given show, there could be a horde of people with various "producer" titles running around. The person who had overall control of the set came to be called the showrunner—and increasingly, writers assumed that powerful role. Writing tends to attract socially awkward introverts with shoddy math skills, but suddenly the nerds were managing multimillion-dollar productions.

Today *showrunner* is an elastic term that can encompass varying degrees of creative and managerial control over a TV series. That might mean developing the original concept, overseeing a cast and crew, shepherding a writers' room, consulting with directors, editing episodes, maintaining a budget, and negotiating with studios and networks. The showrunner is the visionary in chief, operations manager, and financial officer all rolled into one.

"Being a showrunner is a terrible job," declares Jane Espenson, who wrote for *Buffy the Vampire Slayer*, *Gilmore Girls*, and other series before graduating to the role of showrunner on *Caprica* and *Husbands*. "Suppose you are a writer who is happy at your keyboard and you've risen through the ranks because you write really good scripts. Now you are running the show. You may not feel like schmoozing the actors and keeping the network happy. It requires so many different skills, and most of them are not the ones that got you that job."

By the first years of the new millennium, thanks in large part to the rise of the Internet, it had become increasingly common for viewers to follow TV with the auteur-focused intensity of a French cinephile rifling through *Cahiers du Cinéma* in the sixties. Television fans rabidly dissected and debated their favorite shows on online bulletin boards and blogs, with a forensic attention to plot and character that would birth a new and distinctively twenty-first-century form of critical discourse: the recap. I first experienced this kind of TV nerd frenzy through the cult of *Buffy* creator Joss Whedon.

It had never occurred to me to scour a show's credits until I stumbled onto *Buffy* boards and encountered fans who could instantly distinguish between an episode written by David Fury and one written by Marti Noxon. That same degree of narrative close analysis became a hallmark of fan fervor over shows created by HBO's flock of Davids: *The Sopranos* showrunner David Chase, *The Wire*'s David Simon, and *Deadwood*'s David Milch.

Showrunners were now treated as visionary world-builders. The hungry maw of the Internet demanded a constant diet of insider information, and showrunners became celebs in their own right, doling out teasers and tidbits. What better spokesperson for a series than the person who created it? Talk to anyone who works in TV, however, and you'll discover that television production is immensely collaborative. Even the most multitalented genius can't do it alone. There's often some sort of showrunning partnership, such as the one forged by Shonda Rhimes with Betsy Beers, or Tina Fey with Robert Carlock. Beyond that, each episode depends on the work of a hundred or more people: casting, lighting, sound, costumes, set design, shooting, editing.

Nearly all series also rely on writers' rooms. This refers to a collection of people who usually sit in an office brainstorming plot points and dialogue, and then go off to write full episodes individually. Some showrunners spend most of their time in the room with the writers; others (particularly those who also star in their series or juggle multiple shows) assign head writers to manage the process. On some sets, the procedure is organic and communal; on others, the showrunner (or sometimes the head writer) takes the raw material generated in the room and rewrites it to give the scripts a uniform voice. Some rooms glide smoothly through the seasons, while others are fueled by panic, anguish, and ego. As Tolstoy might have said had he lived long enough to visit a television set, "Every unhappy writers' room is unhappy in its own way."

The gonzo workplace behavior of some critically acclaimed male showrunners mirrored that of the macho antiheroes in their dramas, as if the set were a stage for them to play out their own psychodramas. "It's almost like a war situation," writer Terence Winter said of working on David Chase's *The Sopranos*. Director Tim Van Patten echoed this savage sentiment: "If David finds your Achilles' heel, he will go for it, at war or play." *Deadwood* and *Luck* creator David Milch has been described as a brilliant, generous, and addictive personality driven to create a chaotic environment. Even after Milch was known to have lost many millions of dollars to gambling, HBO continued to work with him and publicly sing his praises.

Tina Fey once generalized that while men tend to go into comedy to misbehave, "the women I know in comedy are all dutiful daughters, good citizens, mild-mannered college graduates. Maybe we women gravitate toward comedy because it is a socially acceptable way to break rules." Lena Dunham, Mindy Kaling, and *Broad City*'s Abbi Jacobson and Ilana Glazer may impersonate women behaving badly, but behind the scenes they are hardworking perfectionists. There's less room for reckless behavior when an entire gender is being judged on the basis of how one performs, as Roseanne Barr discovered.

"The history of women in television is: if women are 'difficult,' they don't work again," says Norma Safford Vela, who wrote for *Roseanne* and other hit shows. Conversely, men who perpetrate foul workplace behavior rarely get their comeuppance (though that began to change in the fall of 2017, when a wave of sexual harassment revelations forced a number of powerful men to resign, in Hollywood and beyond). Safford Vela recalls having footballs thrown at her head on one set; in another writers' room that she describes as "a frat boy world," a producer pinned her to the floor and taunted, "Violence against women!"

Showrunning requires the commanding style of a general leading an army into battle. "You have to be really good at making decisions," says Ayanna Floyd, who wrote for *Private Practice* and *Empire* before developing series of her own. "You might literally make ten decisions in a matter of minutes and if you're not good at that . . . it can kill a show."

But what happens when female assertiveness is mistaken for aggression or bitchiness? Before they created the hit series *The Middle*, DeAnn

Heline and Eileen Heisler ran a show they heard might be canceled. So Heline called the network president to clarify. Heisler, who overheard the conversation, recalls, "She couldn't have been more straightforward and professional, but later we were told that DeAnn was being *uppity*." Actors and executives began telling the duo they'd acquired a "difficult" reputation when "all we did was passionately fight for what we believed as any showrunner worth their salt would." Heisler says that the out-of-control or hostile behavior of the gonzo male showrunner simply isn't an option for women: most successful female showrunners "run a pretty tight ship, and they get their scripts in on time because, if you're a woman, you have to be reliable."

Many of the women I interviewed for this book are very thoughtful about the kind of atmosphere they cultivate behind the scenes. *Transparent* creator Jill Soloway, who lost out on jobs after being tagged as "difficult," leans toward a kind of soft power that relies on communal creativity: "Gathering the crew and saying, 'I just want to let everybody know that nobody is going to get in trouble today, nobody is going to get called out for making a bad choice. I don't know what's going to work, but let's see what happens.'" After working on toxic sets for many years, *Weeds* and *Orange Is the New Black* showrunner Jenji Kohan says her goal is simply to "run a healthy show, where everyone is good at what they do and kind to one another. And when they're done, they go home."

In this book, I've chosen to chronicle a handful of women who've risen to prominence by bringing unique female characters to the small screen, but this shouldn't diminish the accomplishments of the many others not mentioned here who fought their way through the industry. Nor do I mean to suggest that only women can evoke powerful female characters; *Buffy the Vampire Slayer* mastermind Joss Whedon staked that fallacy in the heart. Another major TV landmark, *Sex and the City*, is absent from this book because, although largely written by women, it was created and run by guys: Darren Star and Michael Patrick King. It is worth noting that King's first real TV break was writing for *Murphy Brown*, and Whedon got his start on *Roseanne*.

When I embarked on this book, there were more women running shows than ever before. This rise of twenty-first-century female-centric television coincided with an unexpected resurrection of feminism.

Not so long ago, young women had distanced themselves from that F-word, the term seemingly a sour relic from a long-ago liberation movement. But by 2015, describing yourself as a feminist was not just legit but also trendy: You could pledge allegiance to lady blogs such as *Jezebel*, *Feministing*, and *The Hairpin*, which served up politics, pop culture, and confessional essays. You could commodify your dissent by purchasing THIS IS WHAT A FEMINIST LOOKS LIKE T-shirts and SMASH THE PATRIARCHY tote bags. You could find icons such as Beyoncé performing at an awards show in front of giant letters spelling out FEMINIST, and *Harry Potter* star Emma Watson speechifying about gender equality at the United Nations.

This mainstreaming of feminism dovetailed perfectly with the new wave of woman-powered television, shows that offered varied representations of female life and often engaged with serious issues such as abortion, equal pay, and violence against women. This period also overlapped with Barack Obama's progressive two-term presidency.

The Obama White House advanced LGBTQ and women's rights. An avowed feminist, the president appointed two women to the Supreme Court and created a White House Council on Women and Girls to make sure all policy treated women fairly. Michelle Obama traded First Lady primness for stirring eloquence, using her pulpit to support girls' education. ("Compete with the boys," she told young women at one public event. "*Beat* the boys.") And Hillary Clinton dusted off her suit jacket after the bruising 2008 presidential primary and became a hard-driving secretary of state, one of the most potent and respected figures in world politics. At every level of American society and culture, women were more visible, and more visibly empowered, than at any other time in our history.

"Small advances spark resistance, resistance that in turn provokes propellant bursts of reactive fury," Rebecca Traister wrote in *Big Girls Don't Cry*, her account of the 2008 campaign. And so it was in 2016, when Donald Trump took the presidency. Fueled in part by the reactive fury of misogyny—who will ever forget the venomous way he spat "such a *nasty* woman" during the final moments of the final presidential debate on October 19, 2016, as if closing his deal with the American electorate?—Trump's election was intended as a blow to the cause of women (as well as people of color and sexual minorities of every kind). The accumulation of small but significant cultural gains during the 2000s—gains that were not just mirrored but arguably amplified on television shows such as the ones celebrated in this book—triggered a thousand-ton backlash.

Whether it was Shonda Rhimes's "color-blind" approach to casting her hugely popular dramas or the gender-fluid complexities explored in Jill Soloway's *Transparent*, television was transmitting a vision of an America that was racially vibrant and sexually progressive, a vision that turned out to be too far ahead of the actual reality of much of America, which was still attached to traditional values and traditional inequities of power. Not only were these series creating female characters living realities that Trump would undoubtedly consider *nasty* but some of the showrunners were actually on the campaign trail in 2016 stumping for Hillary.

Excavating the culture wars era of the late eighties when researching the parts of this book that deal with *Murphy Brown* and *Roseanne*, I felt almost dizzy as I realized we'd come full circle: all the way back to "the Backlash," as Susan Faludi dubbed it at the time. The drive to roll back women's reproductive rights, negate affirmative action, and defund the National Endowment for the Arts and PBS, and the attempt to insert Christianity into the classroom—it appears that the Moral Majority is back, with a fresh coat of white paint.

Just as *Murphy Brown* and *Roseanne* were prime targets for the religious right's venom in the early nineties, now the alt-right has fixated on Lena Dunham and Amy Schumer as the poster girls of "cancerous" feminism. These women represent so much that is horrifying to Trumpites: they not only loudly support causes such as gun control and trans rights but also exude confidence in their intelligence and a comfort with their bodies, apparently unconcerned with male approval. An enclave of Trump supporters clustered at a subreddit called "the_donald" encouraged haters to flood Amazon with one-star reviews of Schumer's memoir (and, later, did the same with Netflix and Schumer's comedy special). *Breitbart* covered Lena Dunham's every move with obsessive attention because, as then-*Breitbart* editor Milo Yiannopoulos explained to Bill Maher, "The Democrats are the party of Lena Dunham. These people are mental, hideous people."

From single mom Murphy Brown to *Girls*'s single mom Hannah Horvath—these are the antiheroines of the middle American imagination, the women whom deplorables love to deplore and who make Red-staters see red.

Events overtook me during the writing of this book: what looked like the forward march of progress turned out to be one of history's grand zigzags. When I started, the golden age of female TV seemed like a permanent advance; now it feels significantly more precarious and embattled. Most likely, this period will prove to be another chapter in the long saga of cultural combat to decide what kind of country America will be. In a way, it makes the creative force waged by these women all the more crucial.

CHAPTER 1

Look Back in Anchor:

Diane English's *Murphy Brown* and the Culture Wars

Diane English and Candice Bergen embrace while
shooting the final episode of *Murphy Brown*. May 1998.

Eighties America was in the throes of a culture war. Ronald Reagan and the religious right were hacking away at the social advances of the sixties and seventies. Before he was first elected president, Reagan had ripped the Equal Rights Amendment out of the Republican platform while backing an amendment to outlaw abortion along with certain forms of birth control. Once in office, he slashed funding for the Equal Employment Opportunity Commission and demonized poor black "welfare queens." Meanwhile, Senator Jesse Helms and Reverend Jerry Falwell targeted artists for "indecency." Assaults on abortion clinics mounted.

Despite all these attempts to unravel the gains of feminism, shoulder-padded women charged into the workplace throughout the eighties. Madonna and Janet Jackson ran roughshod over the *Billboard* charts with pop-feminist singles such as "Express Yourself" and "Nasty." Geraldine

Ferraro became the first female candidate from a major party to run for vice president. More and more women were choosing to delay marriage, or stay single altogether. A 1985 Virginia Slims poll revealed that 70 percent of female respondents felt they could have fulfilled lives without marriage, and a *Woman's Day* survey found that only half of married women said they would marry if they could choose again.

Yet a stream of sociological studies trickled into the media that seemingly undermined this surge of female independence. They warned that working women were lonely and unappealing to men, their biological clocks ticking as loudly as time bombs; that there was a "man shortage"; that divorce was imperiling the American family. *Newsweek*, in its 1986 cover story about the "Marriage Crunch," sounded the alarm that a forty-year-old single woman was "more likely to be killed by a terrorist" than to tie the knot. Conservative columnist Mona Charen wrote in the *National Review* that feminism "has effectively robbed us of one thing upon which the happiness of most women rests—men." Hollywood's version of the emotionally destitute career woman arrived with the 1987 blockbuster thriller *Fatal Attraction*, starring Glenn Close as high-powered Manhattan book editor Alex Forrest. Seemingly independent and sexually dynamic, Alex morphs into a needy psychopath when her married lover tries to end their affair: "I'm thirty-six years old; it may be my last chance to have a child!" She is eventually put out of her single lady misery by her lover's virtuous homemaking wife, who (spoiler alert!) guns Alex down.

According to Susan Faludi in her landmark book *Backlash: The Undeclared War Against Women*, the 1987/88 television season represented the "high-water mark" of the antifeminist wave in pop culture. The professional organization American Women in Radio and Television decided not to present its annual award for ads that featured women positively because none qualified for the category that season. On prime-time television, only two out of the twenty-two new dramas featured adult female leads. In a *New York Times* article entitled "TV Turns to the Hard-Boiled Male," about the rise of macho characters in prime time, *Cheers* creator Glen Charles offered up his show's puckish hero, Sam Malone, as "a spokesman for a large group of people who thought [the women's movement] was a bunch of bull and look with disdain upon people who don't think it was." That season, TV networks bet on the machismo renaissance, greenlighting shows such as *Houston Knights* (rugged cops), *The Oldest Rookie* (older rugged cops), *The Highwayman* (rugged cop of the future), and *High Mountain Rangers* (rugged wilderness cops). All of them flopped.

Then, in the fall of 1988, two of the most brazenly feminist sitcoms ever to grace prime time premiered just weeks apart: *Murphy Brown* and *Roseanne* would rule American remotes for the next decade, redefining our ideas of "family values" and inciting unprecedented controversy.

Murphy Brown was a career-focused single woman, an abrasive forty-year-old broadcast journalist "living like a man and making no apologies for it whatsoever," as series creator Diane English noted. The character's name was deliberately masculine, like *Fatal Attraction*'s Alex Forrest. English liked to describe Murphy as "Mike Wallace in a dress." Wearing chic, loosely constructed suits like prêt-à-porter armor, Murphy had little time for polite small talk, let alone flirting or love affairs; she channeled all her energy into exposing corporate criminals and government scandals. Murphy, in other words, epitomized the kind of career woman who sent the religious right into convulsions. Immensely popular and wildly provocative, she was a heroine you either admired or abhorred.

Over its ten-year run, *Murphy Brown* inspired countless trend pieces, newspaper editorials, and college dissertations about its feminist spirit. English and her staff were hesitant to embrace the label, however. "[I]f feminism means that my female characters or my friends or myself are respected, in all walks of life, then I'm a feminist. But I don't get involved in the politics of it very often," English insisted back in 1989. She further suggested that her character disliked the label: "You don't hear feminist polemic coming out of her mouth. She is what she is."

———————

Diane English didn't grow up with dreams of being a big Hollywood writer. Born into a blue-collar Catholic family in Buffalo, New York, she faced limited options. Her father worked at the local power plant; her mother was a housewife. In school, English wrote stories and plays to drown out the complications of her life, including her father's struggles with alcoholism. "I was part of a group that was sort of the outcast group in school," she told the *Los Angeles Times* in 1992. "You know, we were the ganglies and the overweights and the ones with the thick glasses and the braces. . . . And we used to get together on the weekends at each other's house and listen to old Elaine May and Mike Nichols records and then do our own sketches on tape. We would write little songs and plays and perform them." At Buffalo State College, she found a mentor in Warren Enters, a cofounder of the Cherry Lane Theatre in New York City, who was helping to build the college's drama department and who encouraged English to become a playwright. In 1971, she sold her red Volkswagen Beetle for five hundred dollars and swapped her hardscrabble Buffalo existence for a hardscrabble Manhattan existence.

"I was going to be the female Neil Simon," English recalls now, sitting in her Sherman Oaks office wearing a crisp pinstripe blouse and dirty-blond bob. "But I didn't know anybody in New York, and I had no money at all." By then, she had developed an idea of who she wanted to be: the kind of person who lives on the wealthy Upper East Side rather than the cheap and bohemian downtown. "I didn't have a phone for the first nine months of living in New York because I couldn't afford it," she says, laughing. "But I had this Upper East Side taste."

English took a job at the public television station WNET to pay the bills; instead, it changed her life. It was there that she met Joel Shukovsky, a young graphic designer from Long Island who caught her attention with his distinctive duds: bright-yellow corduroy pants, big aviator glasses, and black patent-leather clogs. He quickly became her partner in love and work.

When asked to make suggestions on a script for PBS's adaptation of the

Ursula K. Le Guin novel *The Lathe of Heaven*, English took the initiative and substantially rewrote it. The resulting movie got great ratings, rave reviews, and a Writers Guild Award nomination. "Once *Lathe* hit the airwaves, I had agents calling and saying, 'You have to move to Los Angeles; this is where the work is.'" Although she was hesitant to leave Manhattan, English says Shukovsky had taken some production classes at the New School and "had this crazy idea we were going to go to Los Angeles and start a production company and start making television shows. Nobody believed that we would do it, and we were too dumb to know we couldn't do it. So we did it," she says with a wry smile. English calls Shukovsky the big-picture architect and herself "the sweat equity."

English wrote nine TV movies in three years, most of which never made it to the screen. This was followed by an offer to develop a new sitcom for CBS about the New York District Attorney's office. She fancied herself a more serious writer, but Shukovsky saw the series as the first step to a Hollywood empire. The script for *Foley Square* was greenlit immediately, with Margaret Colin starring as Alex—there's that gender-neutral name again—a young, ambitious assistant district attorney trying to impress her grizzled male boss. Since English was a sitcom novice, she, like her show's heroine, was overseen by veterans. Showrunners Bernie Orenstein and Saul Turteltaub knew the drill with the single-woman sitcom, having worked on *That Girl* decades before. The network hoped to draw young independent female viewers by running the show after *Mary*, Mary Tyler Moore's 1985 return to a prime-time sitcom years after the finale of *The Mary Tyler Moore Show*. "The awful thing was everybody kept pointing at Margaret Colin and saying, 'She is the *new* Mary Tyler Moore,'" says English. Neither show survived to the next season, but English was quickly granted her first solo showrunner gig. CBS brought her in to salvage *My Sister Sam*, a short-lived star vehicle for *Mork and Mindy*'s Pam Dawber.

Shukovsky patiently waited in the wings for the moment when he could try out his mogul skills on an original show of their own devising. He knew that English "wanted to do something about a woman who broke the rules and had some parts of her own personality, for better or worse." The idea for *Murphy Brown* "just literally fell into my head perfectly formed" while driving to work, English remembers. "I knew all the characters, I knew what the first season was."

In 1987, CBS was third in network ratings—out of three. The channel once known as the "Tiffany Network" for its quality programming had little to keep it afloat in prime time beyond *Designing Women* and *Newhart*. Standing in a daunting wood-paneled room before a throng of executives, English presented her idea for a sitcom about a single, middle-aged female broadcast journalist returning to the job after a stint in rehab.

The executives were intrigued. They just had a few changes.

"The request was: could she be coming back from a spa because she had been so stressed out by her job, instead of the Betty Ford Clinic?" English recalls, her voice tinged with sarcasm. "Oh, and could she be *thirty* instead of forty?" English refused, insisting, "'Why don't you let me write the script the way I see it, and if, after it is done, you feel like she is not somebody that anyone can relate to . . .'" Her voice trails off.

"That was their concern: that nobody could relate to this woman. The word *unlikable* came up all the time. All . . . the . . . time," she says irritably, waving her hand as if to swat away a bug. "They would apply those terms to female characters often, but men don't have to be *likable*."

———————————

English wrote the pilot script exactly the way she'd imagined it. She finished it on a Sunday night, and the next morning, March 7, 1988, the Writers Guild announced it was on strike. That meant English's original script could not be revised. CBS execs were up against a wall: they could either go with the "middle-aged woman after rehab" version of Murphy or drop the series. There was concern that the strike could go on for a long time—it lasted five months—so they chose to film the script almost exactly as drafted. Nearly all network television shows are products of heavy compromise, with jagged edges sanded off by crews of note-giving executives. The writers' strike allowed English's vision to make it to air with edges, and rehab backstory, intact.

The role had been written with *Big Chill* star JoBeth Williams in mind, but the actress had a new baby and didn't want to tie herself down to a weekly TV show. The network then pushed for twenty-something *Dynasty* bombshell Heather Locklear. But English became convinced that Candice Bergen was the perfect Murphy. A child of old Hollywood, forty-two-year-old Bergen was a movie star with highbrow cred, married as she was to French film director Louis Malle. She exuded a kind of glacial, WASPy self-possession in movies such as *The Group* (as a sophisticated lesbian at a women's college) and *A Night Full of Rain*, a Lina Wertmüller film in which she starred as a feminist photographer. But that didn't mean she didn't know how to be funny: she'd been nominated for an Oscar for playing Burt Reynolds's ex-wife in the 1979 comedy *Starting Over* and had been *Saturday Night Live*'s first female host.

Bergen saw *Murphy Brown* as a chance to tap into her "bawdiest self." After reading the pilot script on a plane, she was drawn to the role as if to a dare, and immediately called her agent. When English met Bergen in New York, a deep connection instantly sparked between actress and showrunner, over the script but also on a personal level. The two women were born nine days apart, and as English has said, "We've played out a lot of the same emotional beats in our lives." They quickly discovered that they wore the same lipstick and perfume. Bergen describes English in her memoir, *A Fine Romance*, as "very Anglo-Saxon, alert, confident"—details just as easily applied to her.

Convinced she'd found her Murphy, English brought Bergen to LA to meet with the execs. It should have been a shoo-in—gorgeous movie star deigns to take role on lowly small screen—but CBS boss Kim LeMasters did not trust English's judgment. He demanded that the actress audition for him. Barnet Kellman, the distinguished theater and TV director who would help forge the look and feel of *Murphy Brown*, says he quickly rehearsed scenes with Bergen, now gripped by anxiety—which only worsened when they arrived at the studio: LeMasters kept them all waiting for forty-five minutes. "Bad things happen when you start thinking too much," English says, recalling Bergen's increasing panic.

LeMasters finally ushered them into his office, making a grand gesture of closing the room's curtains with a remote control. For Bergen, it felt like "an interrogation room." In her nervousness, she blew the audition, and the imperious network president made it clear he was dismissing her from consideration.

At this point, English did something she deems "either fearless or stupid": she demanded that LeMasters reconsider. Says Kellman, "I have never seen a producer not immediately go silent when the network president spoke. But Diane just said, 'We are going to talk about this *right now*. Not when you're ready—you are going to deal with me now, with Candice Bergen waiting in the hall.' That was wild. That's an internal strength. She knew what she wanted; she felt she knew what she was worth. She believed in the work."

Much to everyone's surprise, LeMasters agreed to trust English's instincts. He then marched into the hallway so he could be the one to bestow the good news on Bergen. Afterward, the newly anointed Murphy Brown repaired to a nearby restaurant with English and ordered a round of stiff drinks. "I could see the look on her face," English says. "It was like, *What have I done?*"

Bergen relaxed when she met the rest of the cast, at a welcome dinner at English and Shukovsky's Malibu home. The actors who would play Murphy's colleagues on the fictional news magazine *FYI* were mostly unknowns. Former model Faith Ford was almost as much of a neophyte as her character Corky Sherwood, a former Miss America who was meant to be representative of the dumbing down of TV news then taking hold. Bergen was charmed by Ford's southern naïveté: "I called her the Swamp Queen," Bergen writes in her memoir. "She'd come in with stories about her momma and daddy and their huntin' camp in the bayou, shootin' gators. You just looked at her agape; how could such a person exist in Burbank?"

Grant Shaud was a twenty-seven-year-old with few credits who flew in from New York to audition just a week before shooting on the pilot began. When he snagged the role of upstart *FYI* producer Miles Silverberg, Shaud had to race out to buy clothing, as he had arrived with no luggage. Robert Pastorelli, accustomed to playing rough characters onstage and on-screen, landed the part of Eldin Bernecky, Murphy's eccentric housepainter, unofficial life coach, and (eventual) babysitter. The roles of empathetic journalist Frank Fontana and veteran newsman Jim Dial went to more seasoned players: Joe Regalbuto of prime-time soap *Knots Landing* and theater actor Charles Kimbrough, star of several Sondheim productions on Broadway.

Thanks to the writers' strike, preproduction had to be crammed into three weeks rather than the usual five months. "It's going to be murder," Shukovsky told a reporter back then. "Our decision is that quality will not suffer—our private lives will suffer; we will have none."

TV scripts are usually rewritten multiple times, sometimes up until the last second. The strike removed that option, but Barnet Kellman, primarily a theater director, saw this as an opportunity rather than a problem. "I said to the cast, 'The way I want to approach rehearsals is that this is Shakespeare. It's a dead playwright, and the onus is on us to find out what makes this work. We are detectives solving this riddle.'" Kellman injected the scripts with breakneck energy, wanting to evoke the knife-edge chaos of a live newsroom.

"We needed people who could talk and [who] loved language," says Kellman. "It was a fast show. Especially for then." Both he and English were inspired by Ben Hecht's play *The Front Page* and by the movie *Broadcast News*, which conveyed "the fanaticism of getting the show to the air."

Then there was *FYI*, the news show at the heart of *Murphy Brown*. "I wanted [that] to be very real," he says, sitting in his home office, where he keeps an embroidered *FYI* pillow, the one memento he took from the show's set. Bergen credits Kellman with creating the illusion of looming deadlines and frantic activity. The series was shot in front of a live audience at the

Warner Bros. studio, on the same soundstage where *Mildred Pierce* and *My Fair Lady* once filmed.

English expected actors to follow the wordy script verbatim: no improv allowed. Sometimes Bergen ended up in tears trying to memorize huge chunks of dialogue; she once hid some of her lines inside a mug as a cheat—and then forgot and poured coffee over them.

English describes her approach to running *Murphy Brown* in terms of her being a "catastrophizer," by which she means someone able to anticipate, and avert, disasters. "I look ahead, I see what's going to happen, I get to it before it does. I am a Virgo rising," she offers with a hint of a smile. "All my neuroses came together in a positive way in this job."

Although this was English's first time as the sole executive producer, former colleagues say she was a natural. Korby Siamis, who had worked on *Foley Square* and *My Sister Sam* before becoming English's second in command on *Murphy*, goes so far as to say that the Diane English working method could be *the* exemplar for a well-run TV show: "You are organized, you have a clear vision, and you fight for it. You appear democratic so that everybody really feels they are contributing. But the truth is, it comes down to that singular vision."

As an example of that in practice, Siamis recalls an early meeting at which English pitched story lines to a roomful of CBS execs. One episode revealed that Murphy had previously been married for only six days. The president of the network wanted them to change it so that Murphy had been married at least six months or a year. "We came back to the office, and Diane was like, 'Yeah, it's six days,'" Siamis says with a chuckle. "It never came up again."

As tough as English could be when protecting her vision against interference from above, no one recalls her ever losing her temper on set—which is not to say there weren't problems, such as the time Robert Pastorelli (who later died of a heroin overdose) came to a table read intoxicated. "Bobby brought demons with him," says Kellman sadly. "He respected the hell out of Diane, but around the third episode, he came to the table read and it was clear there was something wrong. We are all looking at each other and tip-toeing around the obvious, which was that there were substances involved." After the table read, Kellman says English took Pastorelli aside and told him if he ever came in drunk again, she would fire him. "She loved this guy . . . but she had no doubt, she had no fear, and she didn't raise her voice. She just did the thing that everybody else was afraid to do."

It's easy to imagine Murphy as a version of her creator writ large: avidly ambitious, effortlessly elegant. Yet where English worked smoothly and quietly to get what she needed, Murphy was obnoxious and noisy. It was funnier that way—and it was also something that hadn't been seen on tele-vision before. Back in the seventies, the blunt honesty of Maude and the plucky femininity of Mary Richards had felt fresh. Then there was the south-ern feminist drollery of *Designing Women*, a comedy paired with *Murphy* on CBS's schedule to compete with ABC's *Monday Night Football*. Murphy's character took it a step further, though. She was a human tempest, a ruthless dervish whirling through prime time.

Threaded through the series are passing references to affairs with fa-mous men and wild drinking sprees in Murphy's pre-rehab days. She has been banned from the White House and jailed for refusing to reveal a source. Murphy fires a new secretary every episode because no can satisfy her standards. She regularly taunts the religious right and dresses down mi-sogynists (such as the comedian character in one episode based on Andrew Dice Clay). Murphy wants to work, and play, as hard as the men around her—or harder. In the early episode "Soul Man," she hears that uptight old-school anchorman Jim Dial is taking male colleagues to a formal event at his all-men's club. "I don't get to go for one reason and one reason only," she fumes. "A pathetic little . . ." she pauses, holding her fingers an inch apart, ". . . Y chromosome." Seething, she eventually schemes her way in by digging up scandalous secrets on the club's board members. Next thing you know, she is striding into the inner sanctum wearing a houndstooth jacket, a brown silk tie, and a sly grin.

Murphy looked like a feminist and acted like a feminist, but the writing team responsible for "Soul Man," Tom Seeley and Norman Gunzenhauser, insisted at the time that the episode wasn't meant to convey a political point. "We didn't write that to make a statement. Here is this headstrong broad who wants to get into this all-men's club, and that's a great situation."

The scenario resonated with plenty of viewers who enjoyed seeing a fearless woman negotiate the minefield of daily indignities and compromises of the typical sexist eighties workplace. "I think I was writing about women I knew, I was writing about myself, I was writing about Candice," English says now, sitting at her desk. "I didn't see Murphy as radical, but I saw her as definitely filling a need. That character did not exist on television then, especially in comedy. Murphy was living her life without any regrets, without any guilt, without any man in her life helping her out of tough situations. This was a woman that we all wanted to be."

Candice Bergen began to identify so strongly with her character that even her husband, director Louis Malle, noticed changes, such as the daredevil way she behaved behind the steering wheel. "It's the first time I've ever seen my husband hold on to the handle and put his foot on the floor [bracing himself] when I've been driving," she told the *Washington Post* in 1989. "I insist I've always driven that way, but he said, 'What's happened to you? You're driving like a commando. This character is really taking you over.'"

Although *Murphy Brown* wasn't an instant hit—it lurked somewhere around number thirty-six on the list of top shows that first season—the critics adored it. Howard Rosenberg of the *Los Angeles Times* declared Bergen's character "tyrannical-but-vulnerable too." In contrast, *Rolling Stone*'s Bill Zehme emphasized Murphy's invincibility, calling her "a zesty ballbuster who stomps through doors, rattling hinges loose, trailing a wake of high-octane wisecracks." Reviews and features often noted what a long way we'd come from *The Mary Tyler Moore Show.*

Yet Murphy wasn't actually that far removed from Mary Richards generationally—in the show's backstory, Murphy arrived at *FYI* the same year Mary left WJM: 1977. English's staff had been deeply influenced by that series; in fact, Korby Siamis taught herself to write scripts by watching and analyzing *Mary Tyler Moore* episodes. The *Murphy Brown* writers' room even had the words THEY DID THAT ON MARY posted on the wall, a reminder not to recycle the beloved show's single-working-woman-in-the-media story lines.

English saw Murphy as part of a continuum: "There was a chain that started with Marlo Thomas on *That Girl*, which then begat *The Mary Tyler Moore Show*, and then we were the next link." Each show nudged independent womanhood as far as it could within the constraints of mainstream entertainment, something parodied in *Murphy*'s season-two episode "TV or Not TV." Its opening sequence features a goofy, pratfalling Murphy capering to a sugary *That Girl*-ish theme song that asks "Who's that girl? You think you know her, she's a real live wire . . . It's Murphy, Murphy, Murphy Brown!" (The parody would be echoed seventeen years later in the opening minutes of *30 Rock*'s pilot, a fake-out sequence where we meet Liz Lemon capering through the streets of Manhattan accompanied by a chipper theme song cooing, "That's her, that's her!")

As for English herself, Kellman says, "She kind of merged with Murphy, and Murphy kind of merged with her over the course of the first few years. Diane was inside that Murphy character. All the problems, all the issues were things that Diane deeply cared about." He notes that English adored men ("She was certainly heteronormative, as my daughter at Vassar would call it") while also maintaining a feminist mind-set. "I think she felt that there was a job to be done for herself and for women, but she never gave a sense that men were actively keeping her down. It was the way of the world, and it needed to be changed." But, Kellman points out, "Diane didn't want to deprive Murphy of certain vulnerabilities that are specific to women. That was what the [town house] was about. That was the place where Murphy didn't have it all. She had the fine furniture and all that, but . . . clearly the problem was there was no guy at home," he says with a grin. "That was the thing; it was hard to have it all."

"Having it all" slid into American women's vocabulary circa 1982, thanks to that guru of swinging singletons Helen Gurley Brown and her aspirational self-help book *Having It All: Love, Success, Sex, Money—Even If You're Starting with Nothing*. A phrase that initially sounded utopian soon became a truncheon used to clobber women who couldn't perfectly balance work and family life (especially with no help from men). Whether you were a single working woman, a stay-at-home mom, or a working parent, you were doing it wrong. As former National Organization for Women president Patricia Ireland once put it, having it all had "come to carry with it a sense of being overwhelmed, as you see on the T-shirt in the NOW store that says: I AM WOMAN. I AM INVINCIBLE. I AM EXHAUSTED."

Articles, books, and real TV news magazines much like *FYI* relentlessly picked over the idea that ambition for women came at a devastating cost. This anxiety hovered over Murphy, who at the start of the series struggles to find equilibrium without alcohol. The pilot episode, "Respect" (which won Diane English an Emmy), opens with that Aretha Franklin song playing as the camera pans over framed magazine covers hanging in Murphy's office. "Move Over, Mike Wallace!" screams *Time*. *Newsweek* boasts an image of Murphy and Ronald Reagan under the headline "Head to Head with the President," while *Esquire*, as if voicing the subliminal fear inspired by powerful women everywhere, features a sexy image of Bergen accompanied by the words "Who Is Man Enough for This Woman?"

In the episode, returning to work after a month in rehab, Murphy flings herself back into the fray via a live interview with Bobby Powell, a handsome young man who allegedly had an affair with a married woman running for vice president of the United States—an inverted riff on the then-recent Gary Hart–Donna Rice scandal. After work, Murphy heads back to her empty, luxurious Georgetown home, where she kicks off her heels and belts out an off-key rendition of another Aretha Franklin song to bookend the episode: "Natural Woman." In the world of *Murphy Brown*, there is no reason that a demand for respect can't coexist with the desire to be a natural woman.

That song returned as a coda two seasons later, in one of the series' most infamous episodes: the one where Murphy gives birth.

The specter of motherhood so often looms over TV's single career women, inducing in characters such as Murphy Brown (and, later, in *30 Rock*'s Liz Lemon and *Girls*'s Hannah Horvath) a mixture of longing, panic, and shame. As a narrative device, it makes perfect sense: like real women who have the financial resources to make choices about their lives, female characters of childbearing age are faced with choices about whether to devote themselves to working, parenting, or both. They're forced to consider the scope of their ambition and the compromises required. Contemplating motherhood also taps into a rich vein of anxiety over their ability to nurture and of ambivalent memories of their own moms (in Murphy's case, an aloof, patrician figure played by Colleen Dewhurst).

Murphy Brown started flirting with the idea of motherhood shockingly early. In the sixth episode, "Baby Love," a pregnant friend urges Murphy to join the club: "Do not miss this experience or you'll regret it til the day you die." By the end of the episode, Murphy is swathed in a scarf and dark glasses while paying a research visit to a sperm bank and asking best friend and colleague Frank if he'd consider donating some of his swimmers. (Frank has his own existential panic when he finds out he has low-motility sperm.)

Like the 1987 movie *Baby Boom*, in which Diane Keaton plays a high-powered lady executive who suddenly inherits a baby, *Murphy Brown* coaxed laughs from the fish-out-of-water scenario. In "Brown Like Me," Murphy is left alone with her father's infant son. As the baby wails inconsolably, Murphy, clad in black velvet for an awards ceremony where she will be honored, lectures him, "I know your type! You think you can just snap your fingers and we come running? Let me tell you something, buster, those days are over. Ever heard of Gloria Steinem? Does the name Betty Friedan ring a bell?" Of course, within minutes she is rocking him like . . . a natural.

The idea of Murphy getting knocked up had been percolating since the earliest days of the show. Bergen adored being a mother to her young daughter, Chloe, and she told the *Los Angeles Times*, "I thought it would be too tragic if Murphy didn't have a child . . . Going into her late 40s in a career in which she was an aging success, with no friends, no relationship, and no child, I thought there was not too much funny stuff to be gotten out of that." English herself did not have kids, but she thought an unwieldy new challenge would be good for Murphy. Some of the show's writers worried that it would be a show killer, but English fended them off. "I always thought that there was a way for her to have this baby and be a very irreverent mother."

English recalls visiting the New York office of a magazine editor friend who had just had a baby. "She opened a drawer, and she had put bunting in the drawer, and she put the baby in the drawer," English says. "I thought: *That is something Murphy would do. That would be so great! Bringing the baby to work when women weren't supposed to do that.*"

By this point, *Murphy Brown* had a couple of successful seasons under its belt and seven Emmys, including for Best Comedy Series and Best Actress. (The show would ultimately rake in eighteen Emmy statues and sixty-two nominations.) Although network execs had sought to defang Murphy at the start, now the top brass pretty much left the series to its own devices. *Cagney & Lacey* creator Barbara Corday, who had become a CBS executive by this time, says, "I would call Diane every week on the morning after the show was on and say, 'Great show, thank you!' I never gave her a single note, that I recall." So there was little to no pushback on Murphy's pregnancy.

"It never occurred to me in one million years that a woman who was forty-two and had a one-night stand with her ex-husband and got pregnant and decided to go forward with the pregnancy—that *that* would somehow become controversial," English says emphatically.

CBS's standards had loosened substantially since the *Mary Tyler Moore Show* era, when the network insisted that viewers would not accept a divorcee as their heroine. And there were recent precedents: the female leads in *Moonlighting* and *The Days and Nights of Molly Dodd* had gotten pregnant out of wedlock. Besides, 1.2 million babies were born to unmarried American women in 1990 alone. Even so, the writers took some precautions: they decided that the baby would be the product of a one-night stand with Murphy's ex-husband, during a brief reconciliation, and the couple even had blood tests to make sure neither of them had AIDS, which was very much in the news then.

So it was, during the season-three finale, that a disheveled Murphy walks into her bathroom and gazes with horror at a plastic stick that has turned blue.

The May 1991 episode was the number one show of its week, and newspapers reported that "there wasn't even a ripple" of controversy. Ratings remained high during summer reruns of the season, and fans speculated: would she opt for motherhood or an abortion? "It's not an easy choice for her," English told a reporter at the time. "Serious consideration is given to both sides, the right to life and the pro-choice. This is not something you can sidestep. And we're prepared for whatever flak we get."

The true gravity of her situation cushioned by humor, Murphy tries to imagine squeezing a baby into the life of a journalist. "What am I going to say: 'Excuse me, Mister President, could you speak a little louder, I can't hear you over my *breast pump*'?" she howls anxiously. Meanwhile, her boss Miles worries that he'll be jumped in a dark alley by religious culture warrior Reverend Donald Wildmon. "How many unmarried pregnant role models have you ever seen on prime time?" he squeals. "*None! Zero!*" The fictional head of the news division is even more nervous. "Brownie," he says gruffly, "I'm responsible for a multimillion-dollar operation that does not thrive on taking risks. I don't see that I have any choice but to take you off the air." (He eventually changes his mind.)

That scene had been inspired by a real-world kerfuffle in which *60 Minutes* executive producer Don Hewitt, who served as a consultant to *Murphy Brown*, refused to accommodate correspondent Meredith Vieira's desire to work part-time after she had had two babies in quick succession. The question of how a newswoman could juggle an all-consuming job and family life was increasingly topical: the year before, Connie Chung, one of the first female network anchors, announced she was quitting her newsmagazine to focus on getting pregnant.

By the time *Murphy Brown* returned in the fall, viewers were on tenterhooks waiting to see what she would do. CBS acknowledged that the network had lost some advertisers, and there was pushback from the religious right. In its newsletter, the conservative Media Research Center protested the season opener's "pro-choice rhetoric—[Murphy] and her co-workers made over 15 references to the 'choice' or 'decision' she had to make. Throughout the show, all arguments regarding the decision centered on the impact a baby would have on Murphy's career and the quality of the child's life, ignoring the child's right to life."

Fans had other worries: they wrote and called the producers expressing concern that their favorite warrior would be domesticated. Murphy worried right alongside them. In the baby-shower episode—guest-starring real-world newscasters such as Katie Couric and written by young screenwriter Michael Patrick King, later known for *Sex and the City*—Murphy recoils at her colleagues' tales of changing diapers in airplane bathrooms and accidentally lapsing into baby talk with workmates. NBC anchor Mary Alice Williams quips, "I once asked [newsman] Garrick Utley if he had to make a boom boom."

Approximately two-thirds of American network TV viewers, a massive proportion even by 1992 standards, watched Murphy Brown's water break at the end of season four. One minute she's grilling a tobacco company shill about liability lawsuits, the next she's in a hospital with a tiny infant, terrified by her animal nature. "My body is making *milk*," she exclaims, part horrified and part awestruck. "It's like one day you find out you can get bacon out of your elbow!" Korby Siamis, then a relatively new mother, cowrote the episode (called "Birth 101") with English. "I could never have written that line if I hadn't lived it," she says. The episode concludes with Murphy awkwardly trying to bond with her baby boy by cooing an off-key rendition of "Natural Woman," a blissful callback to the final moment of the series' pilot.

Bergen has said that singing to the baby was her idea: "I wanted to sing [the song] again but mean it." The idea that only childbirth made Murphy a "natural woman" inevitably offended some feminists. Siamis recalls being surprised to hear from women who were disappointed, or who felt the show cast judgment on those who didn't have babies. "I never wrote thinking, *Now I'm for* this *segment of the population*. It was one character. We were not trying to change the world."

But independent women pissed off by Murphy's maternal instincts turned out to be the least of the show's problems.

On May 18, 1992, English was celebrating her forty-fourth birthday with an afternoon of horseback riding. *Murphy Brown* had just aired its fourth-season finale; it was to be English's last episode running the show. She and Joel had decided to leave the series in the hands of the show's writers to work on other projects and build their television empire.

"I went for a ride thinking about how amazing the last four years were," she says.

The next day, her office was plunged into chaos. Vice President Dan Quayle, campaigning on the West Coast on behalf of George H. W. Bush's reelection, made a speech aimed at shoring up the conservative Republican base. In the aftermath of the LA riots following the beating of Rodney King, Quayle attributed the violence to a collapse of "family values" in inner cities. Along with the impoverished black unwed mothers whom he accused of breeding this "lawless anarchy," Quayle blamed unwed mother Murphy Brown for "mocking the importance of fathers by bearing a child alone and calling it just another lifestyle choice."

Suddenly, Murphy Brown was more than a popular TV character; she was at the center of both the presidential campaign and the culture wars.

As the story gripped the American media and public alike, English rejected requests to be interviewed by Dan Rather on the *CBS Evening News* and to debate Quayle on *60 Minutes*. The *New York Daily News* headlined its front-page story "Quayle to Murphy Brown: You Tramp!" A retiring Johnny Carson quipped in his *Tonight Show* monologue that he had finally decided on his next career move: "I am going to join the cast of *Murphy Brown* and become a surrogate father to that kid." The *New York Times* front page featuring a photo of Murphy and baby still has pride of place on English's office wall.

In its initial news report on the kerfuffle, the *Los Angeles Times* noted, "Told of Quayle's comments, a senior Bush campaign official replied only, 'Oh, dear.'" Governor Bill Clinton's camp moved quickly to take advantage of the incident, with press secretary Dee Dee Myers declaring that "the world is a much more complicated place than Dan Quayle wants to believe. He should watch a few episodes before he decides to pop off."

Although English must have known the series was making a striking statement at a time of cultural retrenchment, she recalls being stunned by the massive public response to Murphy's private (not to mention completely fictional) decision. "Seeing Dan Quayle doing a tour of the aftermath of the LA riots and basically blaming it on me, saying, 'That show, that character—*that's* why we are up in flames!' I remember sitting in front of the television watching that, thinking, *I'm just trying to make a show*."

CBS News president Howard Stringer advised English to make a single statement. It was a powerful one: "If the vice president thinks it's disgraceful for an unmarried woman to bear a child and if he believes that a woman cannot adequately raise a child without a father, then he'd better make sure abortion remains safe and legal." At that very moment, the Supreme Court was deciding *Planned Parenthood v. Casey*, a pivotal case that upheld the core of *Roe v. Wade* but also opened the door for states to pass new restrictions on abortion.

Instead of letting the *Murphy Brown* controversy subside, Quayle decided to crank it up. At a visit to a junior high school in postriot South Central LA later that week, Quayle lectured one hundred Latino and black students about having children out of wedlock. "What would you prefer," a fourteen-year-old girl in attendance asked a reporter, "a single mom, or a dad who gets drunk and beats your mom?" After the event, Quayle elaborated on his issues with *Murphy Brown*, dragging the whole entertainment industry into the battle: "My complaint is that Hollywood thinks it's cute to glamorize illegitimacy," he said. "Hollywood just doesn't get it."

Hollywood fired back. Linda Bloodworth-Thomason, creator of *Designing Women* (as well as a dear friend of Bill and Hillary Clinton), bristled at Quayle's suggestion that "people who are in charge of these television shows aren't really American," with its echoes of Senator Joseph McCarthy's un-American witch hunt. "It's sort of to be expected he'd comment on this fantasy character as a way of solving a real problem. . . . Next [the Bush administration] will be blaming [TV doctor] Doogie Howser, M.D., for the lack of a health care program in this country."

During the presidential-election summer of 1992, the term *cultural elite* spread through America's public conversation like wildfire. It was a vague but evocative phrase for the kind of liberalism propagated by Hollywood and the mainstream media and on college campuses on the coasts, a set of permissive and relativistic attitudes that conservatives feared was eroding the traditional values of the heartland. As Quayle's approval ratings spiraled downward, he dug a deeper trench in June, when he made a speech at the Southern Baptist Convention in Indianapolis's Hoosier Dome. In between denunciations of abortion, sex education, and homosexuality, he positioned the presidential contest as a moral battle between the cultural elite and family values. Cultural elitists lurked in "newsrooms, sitcom studios, and faculty lounges," Quayle claimed. "I wear their scorn as a badge of honor."

That same month, Quayle used the "cultural elites" trope to energize the antiabortion movement, telling the members of the National Right to Life Committee, "I know it can be discouraging playing David to the Goliath of the dominant cultural elite. In Hollywood and elsewhere, your opponents have a lot of money, a lot of glamour, a lot of influence. But we have the power of ideas, the power of our convictions, the power of our beliefs."

Young people in the hall carried posters with the words: MURPHY BROWN DOES NOT SPEAK FOR US . . . BUT DAN QUAYLE DOES.

The media happily amped up the war of words with articles such as "Is Hollywood Ruining America?" *Time* featured Candice Bergen on its "Hollywood & Politics" cover, with the headline "Murphy Brown for President." Meanwhile, *Newsweek* created an issue devoted to "The Cultural Elite," formulating a Top 100 list that included Oprah, Madonna, and . . . Dan Quayle.

Looking back, English now admits it was a "very, very scary" time. Photographers were camped outside her house, and a steady stream of threats came through to her office. "I had constant anonymous phone calls on our office answering machine saying, 'We want to kill you.'" Metal detectors had to be installed to protect the live audience for *Murphy Brown*, and Bergen was given a full-time security detail. The American Family Association's Reverend Donald Wildmon called for a boycott of the series and its sponsors by "Americans who are tired of having their values ridiculed." There was even speculation that Bergen might lose her lucrative contract as spokeswoman for the Sprint telephone network. In the end, the boycott never happened, and Bergen stayed on Sprint's books for another six years.

———

Three months after the childbirth episode aired, *Murphy Brown* triumphantly picked up three Emmy Awards—for Best Comedy Series, Best Actress, and Best Direction. In Bergen's acceptance speech, she thanked the vice president and the show's writers "for their words and for spelling them correctly"—a barb slung at Quayle for his embarrassing misspelling of the word *potato* at a kids' spelling bee. (Not only did he add a superfluous *e* at the end but he also corrected a child who'd spelled it right.) Picking up the Best Comedy Series award, English paid homage to the show's brave sponsors before thanking "all the single parents out there who, either by choice or by necessity, are raising their kids alone. Don't let anybody tell you you're not a family."

The return of *Murphy Brown* was almost as eagerly awaited as the answer to *Dallas*'s infamous "Who killed J.R.?" story line. Would Murphy keep her baby? Would she be a good mother? Would these fictional characters respond to the insults flung at them by real-world politicians? The answer to this last question was an across-the-board, emphatic *yes*.

In order to keep the details under wraps, the producers limited access to scripts and shot several versions of a few scenes. English, who had handed the show over to producers Gary Dontzig and Steven Peterman after moving on to other projects, says even she didn't know how they would handle Murphy's rebuttal. In "You Say Potatoe, I Say Potato," Murphy returns to the office in a double-breasted suit, looking as sophisticated and unruffled as ever and bragging about having nailed a mob boss. Then her secretary starts wailing, like a baby, and Murphy wakes up to her real nightmare—that is, life as a single mother coping with an inconsolable infant, Avery, named after her recently deceased mother. When she visits the office briefly to cry on her colleagues' shoulders, Murphy gets little sympathy. Ever the stiff-upper-lip type, Jim Dial tells her to look on the bright side: "In the old days, a woman bearing a child out of wedlock would've been stoned to death!" It is her dear friend Frank, always a model of soft modern masculinity and the product of a large family, who teaches Murphy how to comfort her own baby.

Murphy is just getting the hang of rocking baby Avery to sleep when the nightly newscaster announces that Dan Quayle has called out Murphy Brown for her "poverty of values" and shows a real news clip. At the *FYI* offices, her colleagues swap copies of actual newspapers touting "Murphygate." An enraged Murphy complains to Frank, "I agonized over this decision!" He reminds her that Quayle is a national joke, saying, "Tomorrow he's probably going to get his head stuck in his golf bag, and you'll be old news." The final nail in the Quayle coffin comes when Murphy herself addresses the issue from her pulpit at *FYI*. Flanked by single-parent families, she somberly intones that, in these difficult times, we could hold Congress responsible, or an administration that's been in power for twelve years . . . "or we could blame *me*." She chides Quayle for his narrow definition of family values and calls on him to realize that "families come in all shapes and sizes." The episode ends with an ever-mischievous Murphy dumping a truckload of potatoes on the vice president's lawn.

Two and a half decades later, sitting in her cozy Pacific Palisades living room, Siamis has her own theory about the furor. Going back through old scripts from early seasons, she realized something, she says: "We did a Dan Quayle joke every week. We didn't set out to do that, but we were commenting on what was going on in the world, and he would just tee them up. They were always smart jokes . . . but we were relentless!" She shakes her head. "He had his feelings hurt."

Bush and Quayle lost the election to Clinton that fall. English sent the new commander in chief a congratulatory telegram, telling him, "You're not really president until *Murphy Brown* does its first Bill Clinton joke." She recalls that he responded by inviting her to the inauguration, saying, "All your fans helped get me elected." And, of course, the Quayle controversy helped the series: *Advertising Age* estimated that ad prices went up more than 100 percent from the previous season, and the ratings soared. The birth episode lured seventy million viewers, and *Murphy* finished the season as the third-most-watched show of the year.

Murphy Brown was English's brainchild, but she was eager to move on. Since season two, she and Joel Shukovsky had been trying to negotiate a better deal with the studio. "We had even approved a press release that CBS was going to put out in April saying we would not be coming back to the show," English told a reporter in 1990. "Without us, there was no *Murphy Brown*. And we saw the network coming out way ahead of us."

Shukovsky "had a very big vision," says Barnet Kellman, who remains in close contact with most of the original *Murphy Brown* team. "Joel recognized how few people have a second big hit. Even though he felt Diane was a towering talent—and he was right—he thought there was a time limit, the clock was ticking."

In the tradition of husband-and-wife TV empires like Lucille Ball and Desi Arnaz's Desilu and Mary Tyler Moore and Grant Tinker's MTM, the couple wanted their own production company, Shukovsky English Entertainment, to create shows for which they controlled the rights and would reap the rewards of syndication (where the real TV money lies). Looking back, English says that Joel was eager to "break out of the Warner Bros. crib" because many of the production duties he wanted to perform were taken care of by their studio. He got to be in casting sessions and read scripts, she says, "but, really, *Murphy* was my deal. I was really running the whole thing, and he was just being patient and waiting for the next one."

The next one was *Love & War*, a rom-com starring Susan Dey (of *Partridge Family* and *L.A. Law*) and Jay Thomas (a *Murphy Brown* regular) as an odd-ball couple who bore some resemblance to English and Shukovsky. "I was in a solid relationship where the balance of power was constantly shifting and required attention," English told the *New York Times* before the show premiered, "and it seemed like a lot of women were trying to figure out how to take everything we had gained in the last decade and maintain that in a relationship."

Love & War was part of a four-series, two-movie contract that was said to be worth forty million dollars, with Shukovsky English finally in control of production. Shukovsky's attitude seemed to rub some in the industry the wrong way, however. When Shukovsky English replaced staffers on the *Love & War* pilot with a nonunion crew, a media tempest ensued. An unapologetic Shukovsky protested, "You don't need four guys to run a camera. You can do it with one person with the right equipment—and do you know how much coffee and paper cups you can save that way?" *Love & War* was canceled after three seasons. Several subsequent Shukovsky English comedies faltered, including *Double Rush*, starring Robert Pastorelli; the Louie Anderson vehicle *The Louie Show*; and *Living in Captivity*, a multiracial comedy about a gated community, whose writers' room included a young Matthew Weiner and several staffers who would go on to write for Weiner's show *Mad Men*, among them Lisa Albert and Janet

Leahy. A regime change at Fox knocked it off the network schedule part-way through its first season.

Shukovsky's fantasy of a Diane English sitcom empire never did come to pass, although their partnership continued for years afterward. (They divorced in 2012.) English spent fourteen years pursuing her dream project: a remake of the all-female classic *The Women*, the Clare Boothe Luce play previously made into a George Cukor movie. She worked on the script as directors came and went and studios passed on the project. "There was a tremendous fear that an all-female cast, not bolstered by Tom Hanks or Will Smith, would never be able to make any money at the box office," she told a reporter at the time. English eventually raised the money, wrote the screenplay, and directed the film herself, with Meg Ryan, Annette Bening, Eva Mendes, Jada Pinkett Smith, Candice Bergen, and Carrie Fisher in the ensemble. Finally released in 2008, the movie was panned by many critics but did decently at the box office. English continued to write screenplays (including a film designed around the perspective of the first female president's husband) and television pilots for the likes of HBO.

Murphy Brown carried on in its creator's absence, but as ratings started to droop, English was invited back a few seasons later to consult. "I think they were really feeling the burden of trying to figure out how this baby thing worked," she recalls. "Women loved Murphy because she wasn't a mom and she wasn't a wife and she wasn't all those traditional things. The trick was to keep her Murphy while she was being a mom. But the writers were all young parents just having babies themselves, and I think some of the scenes with Murphy and her baby became a different kind of Murphy, and people sensed that . . ." English pauses. "People loved her for what she started out as. They didn't want her to change."

Yet over the show's run, Murphy did change, facing one of her most daunting transformations in season ten. English had agreed to come back as showrunner for the final year, and found her creation had mutated into something she almost didn't recognize. "The comedy had gotten so broad that I wanted to bring it back to its roots a little bit, so we came up with: well, what if she got breast cancer?" English and the writing staff spoke to a lot of cancer survivors, listening out for the funny details amid the heartbreak. The show's infamous marijuana episode, in which straitlaced Jim procures pot for Murphy in a Washington, DC, park and the whole *FYI* team tokes up, remains for English "a perfect example of how you could take such a serious subject and find humor and social commentary in it."

At the end of the show's run, Bergen called her time as Murphy "a great liberation for me—in the way it liberated people watching it. I loved playing a woman who didn't take [crap] from anybody. All of us hate the part of ourselves that forces us to do that. And even when we don't take it, our retorts are never the quality of Murphy's. We don't have an A-level team of writer-producers writing our rejoinders."

Just as Murphy became a polarizing symbolic figure in the culture wars, her creator became something of an icon in her own right, even appearing in a Hanes panty hose ad campaign featuring career women in the early nineties. TV showrunners and writers rarely achieved household recognition status back then, let alone female showrunners. Yet it would turn out that Murphy Brown and Diane English were just the beginning of a twin-threat transformation of the television status quo: a foretaste of a future in which unabashedly bold women took the lead on-screen and powerful women called the shots behind the scenes.

CHAPTER 2

From Rage to Riches:
Roseanne Barr and *Roseanne*

Roseanne's working-class heroines Roseanne Barr and
Laurie Metcalf on set during the filming of season one.

A family sits around a cluttered kitchen table, arguing and roughhousing.
Finally, the man at the table leans over to smooch his wife. She cheerfully
wipes off the kiss, letting loose a peal of bawdy laughter.

That was how America met the Conner family on October 18, 1988. In
its minute-long opening sequence, *Roseanne* conveys a concrete sense of this
rambunctious working-class household. There are bills on the table that are
probably overdue, and kids interrupting as their parents shrug them off.
There are dowdy clothes and bad hair and faded wallpaper. But most of all,
there is that glorious laugh of Roseanne's hanging in the air, a perfect chord
of raucousness and affection. It signals a family life bound by love but not
muddied by sentimentality.

Roseanne was an instant hit: watched by more than twenty-one million
viewers, the debut episode beat the World Series game it was up against (LA

Dodgers versus Oakland A's) to win the night's ratings. By the end of the season, it had become the country's number two prime-time series, topped only by another family sitcom, *The Cosby Show*.

Although there was a small but well-loved lineage of classic comedies set in ordinary American homes, from *The Honeymooners* to *All in the Family*, *Roseanne* depicted a family more real than any seen on television before. Sunk deep in middle American mundanity, the show emphasized the "working" in working class. Roseanne and hubby Dan toil at jobs that are often menial, yet hard to keep. He cobbles together a living with drywall jobs; she works in a plastics factory. A summons from her kids' school means Roseanne has to leave work early and lose money; an unexpectedly small paycheck might result in disaster. If they are lucky, they'll scrape together enough cash to keep the lights on this month. Everything in the Conners' life is a compromise: there will be no matching living room furniture, no top-tier education for their kids, no time for Roseanne to work on the novel she dreams of writing.

The show's originality resided above all in the character of Roseanne herself. No television sitcom had ever revolved around such a fierce, sharp-tongued virago before. Take the scene in the first episode in which five women sit around a table during their break from the assembly line at the plastics factory, talking trash about men. One of the workers picks up a chocolate donut and quips, "A guy is a lump, like this donut. Okay. So, first, you gotta get rid of all this stuff his mom did to him." She flicks toppings off the donut's surface. "Then you gotta get rid of all that macho crap that they pick up from the beer commercials. And then, there's my personal favorite, the male ego," she says, devouring a chunk of the donut with a mischievous wrinkle of her nose.

That donut crusher? It's Roseanne. There is power not just in what her on-screen character says but also in the harsh quality of Barr's voice itself. Rarely had such a caustic tone been heard in prime time, one that regularly expressed such brazen resentment toward her duties as homemaker and mother. "I put in eight hours a day at the factory and then I come home and put in another eight hours . . . And you don't do *nothin'*!" she rails at Dan in the debut episode. *Roseanne* was already spelling out the feminist concept of women's "second shift," even while making it wonderfully obvious that this on-screen marriage was grounded in deep wells of mutual respect.

And then there was Roseanne's physical appearance: had such a large, unglamorous woman ever been the star of a prime-time show before? Lucille Ball frumped herself up for her deliriously loony jobs, such as her brief stint in the chocolate factory—but even working the assembly line, she never took off her lipstick and pearls. Ball had been a showgirl and movie star before creating this platform for herself; the mismatch between her conventional cuteness and her wacky facial expressions and hijinks was a big part of what made *I Love Lucy* so funny.

Barr was an altogether different beast, one whose own journey to Hollywood had included stints in a mental hospital, a commune, and a feminist bookstore, and as a stay-at-home suburban mother. Her very presence on TV as a plus-size woman who was confidently sexual and comfortable in her own skin was a rebuke to the body-obsessed, aerobics-addled eighties culture.

Murphy Brown, a show about a wealthy WASP propelled by an unshakeable sense of her own cultural power, became a critical darling and standard-bearer of feminism over at CBS. *Roseanne*, meanwhile, spoke to a frustrated majority struggling in Reagan-era America, where the minimum wage stayed frozen at $3.35 an hour for nearly a decade and where the income gap between rich and poor grew ever wider. The Conners weren't a saccharine brood like the families of *Full House* or *Growing Pains*; their crowded, shabby home wasn't the role model household of *The Cosby Show* or *Family Ties*. But neither was *Roseanne* a cartoonish parody like *Married . . . with Children*. You laughed *with* the Conners, not *at* them, and the laughter was often accompanied by twinges of empathetic pain.

Barr never made any bones about her roots in the women's movement, and steadfastly refused to soften her edges. She saw herself as a disruptor, in twenty-first-century-speak, a woman who proudly called radical feminist philosopher Mary Daly her mentor and began her stand-up comedy career telling jokes in a lesbian bookstore. Although *Roseanne* never pounded its viewers with political statements, it was steeped in a sort of ambient critique of class and gender inequality. Over its nine-year run, the series wove in story lines about domestic violence, unemployment, birth control, and gay marriage while off-screen, out in the real world, a culturally divided America fought over the Gulf War, the Republicans' Contract with America, the vilification of Hillary Rodham Clinton, the Anita Hill testimony at the Clarence Thomas hearings, and the Monica Lewinsky scandal.

Life as a cultural bellwether exacted a price, though. Behind the scenes, there was chaos from beginning to end—a nonstop stream of talented writers and producers coming and going, a titanic struggle for control, and a star coming into her own power and being devoured by it. Trying to piece together the story of the show's creation feels a bit like decoding *Rashomon*: there are so many different people with conflicting or contradictory tales.

Depending on whom you listen to, Barr either was responsible for the show's greatness or rode its coattails; her marriage to Tom Arnold either destroyed her career or extended it; she was either a feminist heroine or a cautionary tale. Or maybe it's a case of *all the above*.

"A fat, loud, dark Jewish girl with no ass or waist"—that's how Roseanne Barr describes her young self to me. She grew up poor in the Mormon enclave of Salt Lake City, under the sway of her Lithuanian-Jewish grandmother. Bobbe Mary ran an apartment building full of people who had fled the Nazis. "I would go out to the backyard—there was a big shed with trunks of everything they had shipped over, and they had numbers on their arms. I never thought this was a very happy world."

Barr tells me this while ensconced in the front room of her production studio. Old *TV Guides* with her face on the covers decorate the walls, along with a large painting of a goddess under a full moon. Her son Jake, who runs the studio, works in a back room. Every time a door opens in the building, a mechanical voice announces the activity, as if we're in a high-security environment. The studio hides in plain sight on the main street of LA beach town El Segundo, but even if someone peeked in, they might not recognize Barr. I almost don't—her deep brown hair is gone, replaced by a short shock of whitish blond that stands straight up when she rumples it. She arrives wearing absurdly large sunglasses, looking thin and a bit spaced out, as if all the air has been squeezed out of her. Sometimes she loses the thread of her thoughts, stopping midsyllable, laughter replacing the missing words. She was recently diagnosed with macular degeneration and glaucoma, which will eventually leave her blind, and says pot helps ease the pain.

Many different versions of "the Roseanne Barr story" have been re-counted in the media, including in a trashy made-for-TV movie and in her own memoirs (all three of them). She is an entertainingly unreliable narrator, the details of her self-portrait constantly shifting over time. There are accu-sations of sexual abuse in the family, depictions of multiple personalities, war stories from marriages gone epically awry. But the accounts overlap enough to establish her story's landmark events. And with a larger-than-life life like Barr's, the big picture is what counts.

As a baby, Barr says, she wore away the skin of her nose with her little fist and was put in a restraining jacket. She offers up this raw image in her first memoir, 1989's *My Life as a Woman*, in which she also remembers want-ing to be a writer from a tender age. "Even when very young, I knew that I would be the one person in a long ravaged line of storytellers . . . that would make it out of poverty and resignation, to be a writer." Earning the family nickname Sarah Bernhardt, after the famous stage actress of yesteryear, she writes, "I entertained like mad, because I was afraid if I didn't everyone would start to talk about the Holocaust."

Jealous of her mother—"she was the beautiful girl of our Jewish com-munity and I was her fat daughter who chewed on my own hair"—Barr funneled her resentment into sharp humor. Nibbling the frosting off the top of a coffee cake, she tells me, "The first time I told a joke, it was like a punch in the face, and I loved it. My big fat uncle Sherman was eating my grandma's soup. He called her a wetback or something because she was an immigrant, and he would say, 'You use too much chicken fat in this soup. In this country, they don't cook with chicken fat.' So, I go, 'If you don't like it, why are you eating three bowls of it, fat ass?'" She starts to giggle just saying those words again. "Everyone laughed, and he would get mad. But it was like, I was going to speak truth to power right in his face. And then I would hide behind my grandma."

At the age of sixteen, Barr got hit by a car, an accident that seemingly triggered a descent into mental illness that culminated in a stay at a Utah state mental hospital. "I was out of that world called Normal for a very long time," she writes in *My Life as a Woman*, suggesting that it permanently altered her perspective. During a 1989 Barbara Walters interview special, Barr spoke about her time in the institution: "I'm trying to think about how to talk about it . . . Some parts of it are unspeakable. It was a very horrifying place." Trying not to succumb to Walters's maneuvering to make her cry on camera, Barr continued, "It was Dante's Inferno, you know? It was a place where you come out of it and you become something else. Or else you die. And I came out of it."

After emerging from the hospital, Barr got pregnant. An unwed eighteen-year-old living on welfare, she decided to give up the baby girl for adoption. She then lived in a Colorado commune, married hotel night clerk Bill Pentland, and had three children with him—all before the age of twenty-five. As a frustrated young mother in Denver, Barr found a kind of salvation in the Woman to Woman bookstore, a feminist collective where she says she and her sister Geraldine educated themselves in the politics of female liberation.

"It was a lesbian feminist bookstore," Barr says, "and the first thing they said to me was, 'We would prefer if you would say "lover" rather than "husband."' I was like, 'I'm not going to lie about my life, and you're not going to tell me what to say.' So I was always at odds." Although this period of consciousness-raising profoundly influenced her, Barr says she ultimately rejected the academic jargon of eighties feminism as elitist.

While working as a cocktail waitress at a local Bennigan's, she became convinced that some of her bitchy comebacks could be turned into an act. Her father had always adored stand-up comedy, and she bonded with him as a kid over comedy records and *The Ed Sullivan Show*. Barr saw stand-up as a safe, nonthreatening public forum for a Jew in the mid-twentieth century. Yet she also knew that comedy could have an incredible subversive power: It was "somehow about language and also somehow about politics, and somehow about rebellion, and resistance and anarchy." She once compared it to poetry, an art form that could "change the way you hear and feel and see."

Her husband created a mock mic stand for her out of a broomstick and screwdriver, so she could practice at home. She began telling jokes in the parking lot of the feminist bookstore, for a mostly supportive audience. But Barr felt frustrated by the narrow-mindedness of the radical sisterhood. In a letter to a lesbian comedian from that time, she wrote, "I'm going all over this town with stories about what my life experience as a woman has been. I performed at a lesbian coffeehouse and received the stunned oxen look from all the women/womyn/chicks there . . . I have a place and reason for being in this movement. Deal with me."

Soon, she'd found a female stand-up partner and was plying her act at a local comedy club to even more startled patrons. Years before Sarah Silverman and Amy Schumer, Barr loved shocking her audiences with loutish language: "I don't know why lesbians hate men," she would offer. "They don't have to fuck them." She ended her set by announcing, "People say to me, 'You're not very feminine.' Well, *they can suck my dick*." The fact that she was a chubby woman with a voice piercing enough to bore a hole through your cranium—well, that just added to the sneak attack.

There was no cultural cred in being a married housewife with three kids—not in feminist activist circles and definitely not in the testosterone-drenched stand-up comedy world. Yet Barr built her uncool reality into the core of her act. It coalesced around the persona of a "domestic goddess," a travesty of housewifery inspired, she says, by Helen Andelin's *Fascinating Womanhood*, a book her mother admired, designed to show readers how to get what they want out of men. The act took off, and after traveling the comedy circuit, she ended up at LA's famed Comedy Store. Mitzi Shore, the club's legendary owner (and the mother of actor and comic Pauly Shore), watched Barr's ten-minute audition and immediately put her on the main stage. "I never did that before. I never did it since. She was instant," Shore has said. That swiftly led to a gig on *The Tonight Show*, a successful national concert tour, and a 1987 HBO special. Pentland quit his job, the family moved to LA, and Barr began meeting with producers about how to turn her domestic goddess shtick into a sitcom.

———————————

While Barr was sniffing out Hollywood partnerships, a powerhouse television production company was independently developing a comedy series about blue-collar women. Marcy Carsey and Tom Werner, responsible for the massively successful *Cosby Show*, had teamed up with *Cosby Show* writer Matt Williams, the son of an Indiana assembly-line worker. "The idea originally was to take one married woman with kids, one divorced woman with a child, and another woman who is single, put them in a factory in Indiana—because that's my background—and explore all the things they confront and how they survive, in almost every case because of their terrific sense of humor," Williams told the *Los Angeles Times* in January 1989.

Carsey-Werner spotted the affinity between what Barr hoped to create and Williams's work-in-progress. Soon they'd managed to combine the two projects, yet seemingly left both Barr and Williams under the impression that each was the driving force. "I was told that *Roseanne* was *my* show and that Matt was *my* head writer," Barr has written. "Marcy and Tom told Matt that it was *his* show and that I was *his* star. Naturally, we both thought we were sitting on top of the world when it was just a one-seater." Williams spent time observing Barr and her family, and acknowledged that the comedian had "a lot of input," saying at the time, "I lay no claim to her character. That is the character she developed in her stand-up routines, and I wanted everything I could get from her about it . . . [W]hat Roseanne brought to the mix that I didn't was the strong feminist point of view." He noted that she also changed the show's focus from three women to one family with three children, just like her own: "We all wanted the show to have a realistic mom. But it was going to be more Roseanne's responsibility than mine to decide how much of an edge to keep on the character."

After months of meetings between the two, Williams turned in a draft of the pilot—and Barr says she was aghast. The show was called *Life and Stuff*, rather than *Roseanne*. And the sister character (who would eventually be played by Laurie Metcalf) had become central to the script, with Roseanne shoved to the margins. "My character was totally passive, like just about every other woman on TV . . ." she writes in *My Lives*. "My character spent most of her time sitting in the corner like a stump, saying 'And then what happened? And then what happened?' June Cleaver was Patty Hearst compared to this character." In Barr's account, when she asked what had happened to her character, Williams replied, "I just didn't think people would like you as the main character." Carsey urged the two to work together, but this only further enraged Barr, who complained that Williams "couldn't understand that the female character could *drive* scenes, that the family functioned *because* of her, not in spite of her. I gave him books on feminist theory, talked into tape recorders for hours, lectured him on motherhood and matriarchy for hours and hours, but he just never caught on."

This was not an ideal partnership by any stretch of the imagination, but somehow a script materialized that each could live with while the producers began searching for actors who would complement Barr. According to casting director Risa Bramon Garcia, Barr advocated for her stand-up comedian friend Tom Arnold to play the role of husband Dan, but the producers wanted to surround her with pros: "Their belief was she could act well among strong actors—and that was true." Garcia had just seen John Goodman in a play, and they summoned him to a fluorescent-lit conference room for a taped audition. According to Williams, "We brought him in the room, he looked at Roseanne, and said, 'Scoot over.' She said,

'Shut up,' he plopped down, and it was like they had been married for sixteen years."

Barr tells me that the bonds among the actors who played her fictional family felt like a chemical reaction: "You're giving off a pheromone that is real, and you can sense it is real. The fact that me and John and Laurie, we all love to make each other laugh, and the kids, too—we had a blast making each other laugh."

Behind the scenes, though, there was less hilarity. In fact, the set became an intensely hostile workplace, with Barr storming off repeatedly. Enraged to discover that the show's "created by" credit was going to Williams, Barr protested to the producers and the Writers Guild, to no avail. She also demanded that Carsey and network executives be banned from the set.

Barr claims Williams had his assistant producer keep a tally of how often Roseanne belched and farted while entertaining the audience in between tapings, to prove how unmanageable she was. Things got so bad that Goodman and Metcalf were asked if they would do the show without Barr; they refused. Goodman told a reporter years later that "there would have been no show as far as I was concerned . . . Because she was, in her own beautiful way, she was always right, you know?"

During the filming of the fourth episode, Barr had a meltdown after a confrontation with the show's wardrobe master over her character's clothing. "I wanted vintage plaid shirts, T-shirts, and jeans, not purple stretch pants with green-and-blue smocks," she wrote in *New York* magazine years later, but was told that one of Williams's producers had asked the wardrobe master to ignore Roseanne's requests. "I grabbed a pair of wardrobe scissors and ran up to the big house to confront the producer . . . I walked into this woman's office, held the scissors up to show her I meant business, and said, 'Bitch, do you want me to cut you?'"

Not one to keep her fury bottled up, Barr also posted a declaration of war on her dressing room door. It read in part: THESE ARE THE PEOPLE WHO ARE GOING TO BE FIRED IF THEY'RE NOT NICE TO ME. PEOPLE WHO I AM THE BOSS OF—EVERYBODY . . . ALL PRODUCERS, ALL WRITERS, ALL SUBJECT TO

CHANGE. Among the names that followed was the president of ABC. She would regularly update her shit list, keeping track of anyone who opposed her until the series was a hit and she had free rein.

Then there was Barr's infamous bed-in. Unlike John Lennon and Yoko Ono's publicity stunt, this was not a politically idealistic spectacle of love and peace but a declaration of war. Upset by a line in a script that she believed undermined her character—she was supposed to tell Dan, "Well, you're my equal in bed, but that's it"—Barr sat in the Conners' bed and refused to say the words. She insisted it was not something Roseanne Conner would utter: she might rib him for not doing housework, but she would never outright demean him. Although Barr sometimes rewrote dialogue, this time Williams was adamant that she say the line as written.

Lawyers were brought in to try to compel her, but still she refused. Barr says she spent the next day in her trailer, until finally the script was changed. As then-husband Pentland once observed, "It was like the Cuban missile crisis, when Dean Rusk said, 'The other guy blinked.' From that moment on, she had control of the show and made it into a much better product."

The series premiered on ABC in October 1988, to blockbuster ratings. It would finish its debut season as the second-most-watched show in America, rising to number one by season two, just as Barr had predicted.

Roseanne appeared at a time of economic uncertainty, as the stock market crash of October 1987 curtailed the greedy, *Dynasty*-style excesses of the Reagan era. Over the course of the entire series, Roseanne Conner was laid off from a parade of low-paying jobs, and Dan opened and then lost a small business selling motorcycles. Rarely had the American working class had such poignantly authentic representatives on TV. But the series made viewers laugh more often than cry with its stinging one-liners. "Mother . . . our school's having a food drive for poor people," daughter Becky tells Roseanne. "Tell 'em to drive some of that food over here," she snaps back. When young son DJ finds an unemployed Roseanne trying to sell magazine subscriptions by phone, he asks what she's working on. She doesn't miss a beat: "I'm ordering new children."

———————

In the fall of 1988, Roseanne Barr became a TV icon. Yet she still felt undermined on her own set, so she threatened to quit. By the end of December, executive producer Matt Williams was sent packing. Jeff Harris, a writer who'd worked on the sitcom *Diff'rent Strokes*, replaced him, but things didn't exactly settle down. Another figure had arrived to convulse the set: Tom Arnold.

Barr had met Arnold at a comedy club in Minneapolis in 1983. In *My Lives*, she writes that they did coke together; then she watched him do an act in which he killed fish and set them on fire. Arnold "had this undercurrent of uncomfortableness . . . like a guy who wants to behave but just can't seem to help himself," she recalls, "a guy who's learned to live with always being sorry for something." The two became best friends, and he started writing jokes for her. Sometimes they even dressed like twins.

Instead of being cast as Dan, Arnold ended up playing Dan's sidekick, Arnie. Now Barr was leaving her husband for Arnold and insisting that the comedian also be hired to the writing staff, which had been decimated in a wave of firings, just as Barr had threatened. Norma Safford Vela, a writer on season two, says a producer gave her a rough assignment: "Go teach Tom Arnold to write."

Although Barr had a great deal of input into *Roseanne* scripts and story lines and, over the years, performed many of a showrunner's tasks, she did not spend a lot of time in the writers' room as episodes were being hammered out. She believed that Arnold understood her working-class characters and would be a good ambassador for her in the process—but the show's writers gave him the runaround. "We all thought he was one hundred percent talent-free," Safford Vela explains. Barr, she continues, "was very upset because she thought we didn't respect her choices, and it's like, well, no, we just don't respect *this* choice. You have one billion good ideas, but this one is shit. He is destructive and he is bad."

Safford Vela says Barr "was great with the rest of the cast; the crew loved her. It was really just fighting for power and the voice of the show. . . . That season got ugly. But the show still got to number one." The level of back-stabbing intrigue resembled the royal court of Henry VIII. Writer Barbara Klaus once described a script meeting in which Arnold and Barr belliger-ently provoked their haters: "She straddled him in a chair, looked into his eyes, and emitted a belch that echoed through the soundstages." According to Barr, when Jeff Harris attempted to fire Arnold, he shouted, "*I'm not fired! You're fired, fucker!*" Arnold then marched over to Barr and urged her to stand up to Harris and show him who was boss. "This is not a fucking democracy. It's a Queendom," he said.

Barr and Arnold married in January 1990. Two months later, Harris offi-cially departed, announcing in a full-page ad in *Daily Variety*, "I have chosen not to return to the show next season. Instead, my wife and I have decided to share a vacation in the relative peace and quiet of Beirut."

"It was a little tough to talk to Roseanne at that point because she was mostly under Tom's influence and just really struggling with her own mental health," recalls Safford Vela. "And who wouldn't be, with that much change in her life? She had everything she had worked for suddenly handed to her, and it was not the way she had imagined." She not only had a hit show but she was also shooting a major motion pic-ture (*She-Devil*, an adaptation of Fay Weldon's wickedly funny feminist novel, in which she costarred with Meryl Streep). Meanwhile, Barr was embroiled in that *amour fou* with Arnold, who, adding to the chaos, had a major drug problem. Also, her kids, plunked down in the middle of a Hollywood tabloid nightmare, were acting out.

"When you have a huge success, there are aftershocks of it in the real world and in your family," Roseanne tells me now. "I remember I was film-ing one of the first episodes and I got a call saying, 'Your daughter has run away.' On *tape day*. They were always fucking with me on tape day! And I'm in every scene," she says, screwing up her face at the memory. "Having indiscriminate sex . . . it was a lot for my family to take." By the spring of the show's first season, daughter Jessica was in rehab, and the *National Enquirer* had inadvertently reunited Barr with Brandi, the child she had given up for adoption as a teenager.

One fledgling writer who found opportunity amid the rubble of the *Roseanne* set was Joss Whedon. Whedon showed up on his first day well aware of the backstage drama, expecting some kind of pep talk from Barr to instill loyalty. Instead, she told the writers that if she found anyone talking to the tabloids they'd all be fired.

Despite this discouraging atmosphere, Whedon kept his head down and wrangled credits for six scripts on season two, a great haul for a novice TV writer. He has said that Tom Arnold championed his work, showing it to Barr. She took Whedon to lunch and asked him how a twenty-five-year-old guy understood the character of a midwestern mom so well. Among his scripts was "Chicken Hearts," in which Roseanne has to suck up to a patronizing teenage boss because she needs the job, and "The Little Sister," an episode that Whedon says originally addressed abortion. The initial idea was that Jackie would drunkenly reveal to niece Darlene that she'd had a termination—a bold move in 1989, the year the Supreme Court ruling on *Webster v. Reproductive Health Services* upheld a Missouri state ban on the use of public employees and facilities for performing abortions. A woman's right to choose was a topic that the avowedly feminist Whedon could sink his teeth into. Days later, network pushback transformed Jackie's abortion into a miscarriage; the final version of the script bore no trace of that radical plotline. Instead, Jackie drunkenly confronts Roseanne because she doesn't support her sister's desire to become a police officer. "Welcome to my dream and my first heartbreak," Whedon has said.

Whedon had a little more fun with "Brain-Dead Poets Society," in which tomboy Darlene is forced to read her own poem aloud at school culture night, and Roseanne shares with Darlene her own youthful desire to be a writer (and her love of Sylvia Plath). When Darlene finally gets onstage in a peach dress, looking pale and awkward, she transforms before our eyes from smart-ass kid to the melancholy nonconformist she will become in future seasons: "To whom it concerns / I just turned thirteen / too short to be quarterback / too plain to be queen." As she watches from the audience, Roseanne's eyes fill with tears; a moment later, she leaps up to snap a photo of her mortified daughter.

Although he was getting a chance to hone his skills, Whedon nevertheless felt frustrated when his poetry episode was revamped, as was par for the course in television. "He couldn't believe we would rewrite that script because, you know, he had done a really good job," recalls Safford Vela. "I said, 'Look, this is television, and this is what will happen on every show until you run the show. In the meantime, go write your own stuff. Do you have an idea for anything?'" He mentioned an idea for a vampire movie. Safford Vela told him, "Focus on that and don't worry about this show." Whedon spent the rest of his contract working on a draft of the screenplay that would become *Buffy the Vampire Slayer*.

Now firmly in command of the series, Arnold and Barr were on a high. It was to be short-lived. *Roseanne* producer Tom Werner, who owned the San Diego Padres baseball team, invited his star to sing the national anthem at Working Women's Night. Her screeched rendition of "The Star-Spangled Banner" sounded "like a yodeler singing through a tubal ligation," Barr would snark years later. She ended the botched song by grabbing her crotch and spitting—a cheeky but misjudged attempt to satirize macho ballplayers.

A deafening roar of disgust filled the San Diego stadium; within hours it had spread to the rest of the country. Radio talk show listeners called for a boycott of her show, the *New York Daily News* renamed her "Roseanne Barr-f," and President George H. W. Bush deemed it all "disgraceful." An entrepreneur even tried to capitalize on the backlash with the Roseanne Hate Club, advertising BAN ROSEANNE T-shirts in *Rolling Stone*.

The media uproar didn't dent the show's ratings, though. Barr's chutzpah played well with her audience. The entertainment industry wasn't so impressed, however, and the series continued to be snubbed by the Emmy Awards. While *Murphy Brown* racked up the statuettes, *Roseanne* didn't win any of the awards for which it was nominated. Barr herself would win the lead-actress Emmy only a single time (in 1993), whereas Candice Bergen won so many for *Murphy* (five) that she eventually withdrew her name from consideration.

Yet *Roseanne* just got sharper and funnier as the show moved into its third season. A whole new squad of writers was hired, among them a very young Amy Sherman-Palladino (then still Amy Sherman). "They were starting fresh, and they needed chicks," says Sherman-Palladino, especially chicks who could write for the daughter characters Becky and Darlene, both growing into teenage complexity. Sherman and her writing partner Jennifer Heath were inexperienced and cheap, a winning combo. Their first introduction to the Arnolds was at a gathering at the couple's beach house on the day after the "Star-Spangled" debacle. "They had taped every single newscast about it," Sherman-Palladino has said. "So we just sat there and watched, like, four hours of people saying how Roseanne was a horrible person for singing the national anthem."

Bob Myer had taken over as the head writer, and Sherman-Palladino says she learned a great deal from him. "That's where I learned to make the small big and make the big small," she says—like dedicating an entire episode to the tiny trauma of Darlene's getting her first period. Becky and Darlene—as played by Alicia "Lecy" Goranson and Sara Gilbert, respectively—really came to the fore during this era of *Roseanne*, with story lines that went far beyond the standard TV kid tropes. Darlene plunged into adolescent depression, while Becky sought birth control and later got pregnant. Contraception and teen pregnancy were very thorny topics in the eighties and nineties, when the religious right and Republicans (via laws such as the 1981 Adolescent Family Life Act, popularly known as the Chastity Act) successfully pushed to fund abstinence-only education rather than Sex Ed. Sherman-Palladino and Heath's Emmy-nominated episode "A Bitter Pill to Swallow" has Becky enlisting Aunt Jackie to help her ask Roseanne for contraception. The look that passes between the adult sisters is astounding, cycling from shock through horror to fear and finally to acceptance. At the gynecologist's office, Roseanne worries that her little girl no longer needs her. "Of course she needs you," Jackie counters. "She needs you to pay for the pills!"

The series often played up the shtick of Roseanne Conner as a "bad mom"—a persona Barr helped propagate and that would pick up speed in pop culture decades later, in books such as Ayelet Waldman's 2009 memoir *Bad Mother* and the 2016 movie *Bad Moms*, with women coolly wearing the term as a badge of honor. A refusal of the whole "having it all" con, it became a way of pushing back against the guilt and unrealistic expectations of perfect motherhood. Why pretend you'd rather change a baby's diaper than kick back with a margarita? As Waldman wrote, "We shrug at the orange Cheetos dust smeared across our children's mouths . . . happy to confess our sins because we are confident that those who come closest, and with the most sanctimony, to emulating the self-effacing, self-sacrificing, soft-spoken, cheerful, infinitely patient Good Mother are the *real* Bad Mothers."

Roseanne offered a rare public admission—in the midst of the religious right's family-values crusade—that parenthood could be a rotten, soul-sapping affair, especially when you throw a low-wage job or two into the mix. Roseanne is often sarcastic and dismissive to her kids. (When DJ asks why she's so mean, she replies, "Because I hate kids . . . and I'm not your real mom!") In the third season, she gets into a pissing match with new next-door neighbor Kathy, an upwardly mobile helicopter mom who ticks off Roseanne for not knowing where DJ went with her son. "I have three kids and a job, so I can't be everywhere," Roseanne snaps back. "I gotta trust my kids, and they're still alive, so I have obviously done something right."

Despite this bluster, Roseanne never actually neglects her kids (although, there is one episode where the family forgets DJ is playing hide-and-seek and finds him hours later, asleep in a kitchen cupboard). She doesn't spend a heap of time cleaning the house, and nightly dinners lean more toward hot dogs and beans than lovingly prepared pot roasts. Yet we see her character struggling every week to figure out how to be a decent mom while making a living and not entirely letting go of her sense of self.

"I had three kids, and that's how I lived," Barr tells me earnestly. "I wanted to be a different kind of mother in my real life and on TV. I was kind of obsessed with it because, as a kid, Donna Reed—well, all the mothers on TV—were not like what I knew." Those classic TV mothers were horrible, she says, "because they were always making the husband look like a dolt. What do they call it? The fist in the velvet glove." Whereas the Roseanne character "was kind of like my grandma. She was a real Jewish matriarch, and she ruled with a wooden spoon. You did not want to get hit on the upper thigh with that thing."

Of course, Roseanne Conner was not written as a Jewish woman; that would have made her family seem too exotic and outsiderish, at least from a network perspective. The history of television is one in which generations of Jewish writers put their words in WASPy characters' mouths. Before *Roseanne* had even aired, Barr vented to the *New York Times* that she was struggling with Hollywood's tendency to whitewash reality. "We're raising our kids as Jews/anarchists, so that's kind of what I'd like to have my TV family be. But, yeah, this is TV."

Roseanne nevertheless threaded cultural politics through the series in relatively seamless ways. There was the season three Halloween episode in which DJ wants to dress as a witch; a horrified Dan tries to persuade his son to trade his gender-bending costume for an ax-murderer outfit. Meanwhile, Roseanne, clad as a bearded dude, ends up at a bar where the local guys mistake her for a real man. "It was awesome!" she trills to Jackie. "It reminds me of that movie where the lady hangs out with these gorillas and they accept her as one of their own!" But Roseanne can't help herself and ends up instigating a fight with the guys in the bar; Dan arrives just in time to save her from getting clobbered. "Leave him alone—he's my husband!" Dan shouts, mocking his own gender rigidity.

Two of Barr's siblings are gay, and in later seasons, the show would introduce several major gay characters, including Roseanne's friend Nancy (played by Sandra Bernhard). The infamous "Don't Ask Don't Tell" episode, cowritten by gay staff writers Stan Zimmerman and James Berg, nonchalantly challenged homophobia, even as antigay ballot initiatives were circulating in almost a dozen states (and three years before Ellen DeGeneres's infamous coming-out episode aired on the same network). ABC considered shelving or censoring an episode in which Roseanne visits a gay bar and is kissed by a lesbian (played by Mariel Hemingway). Barr and Arnold threatened to take the show to another network, and ABC ultimately ran the episode with a parental warning. The night before it aired, Barr mocked the idea that her own network thought it "shocking to see a woman kiss another woman but not shocking to see a woman raped, mutilated, and shot every two seconds" on television. ABC officials said that of the one hundred calls they received in response to the episode, 75 percent of them were positive.

During the presidential campaign of 1992, while the world was waiting for Murphy Brown to sucker punch Dan Quayle, Barr bragged to the *Los Angeles Times* that she found that kind of overt engagement in politics tedious. "We're not going to talk about who the Conners are going to vote for. I think people would turn us off real quick," she said, noting that her television family didn't trust the left or right wing. "They're somewhere in the middle of it all, not knowing what anything stands for anymore. So really what they do is go to work and come home to be with their family, and try to make do." Added Tom Arnold, "We don't do jokes about Dan Quayle. He won't watch our show because it would be too painful, because it's reality."

The Conners' reality encompassed domestic abuse: Roseanne's sister, Jackie, a former cop, confesses that her seemingly nice boyfriend Fisher is beating her. "I remember going to write that and thinking, 'Oh shit, how do we make that funny?'" says DeAnn Heline, who began writing for *Roseanne* with her partner Eileen Heisler in season five. "That was the great thing about *Roseanne*—you could tackle any topic and go to dark places. And those actors were so good. I remember we had written a scene where Dan is in jail because he beat up Jackie's boyfriend, and Darlene comes to post bail. Darlene just goes, 'Well well well well well.' That got a three-minute laugh, just from her saying that. That is when writing is most satisfying, is when you can do something real."

Soon after the domestic-abuse plotline aired, Barr would publicly accuse her own father of molesting her. (Her parents denied it, and she later partly retracted the claim.) This trauma echoed through "Wait Till Your Father Gets Home," an episode written by Sherman-Palladino later that season about the death of Roseanne and Jackie's father. Although she feels toxic with rage at his memory, Roseanne ends the episode by venting her grievances over his casket, in a speech Barr says she wrote herself. "Thank you for your humor," she mutters in conclusion. "I loveyougoodbye."

Sherman-Palladino basks in the quality of scripts from that era. "Roseanne had banned the studio and the network [executives] from the show, so we never saw them; they weren't at table reads. I think they were allowed to come to the shows, but they had to stay in the greenroom; they just sat there. You didn't have the bullshit interference and the stupid buzzwords of *stakes* and *story engine* and these idiotic words that they latch on to that make them feel like they're giving you a note," she sputters. "It was a *pure* experience." (And one that would set Sherman-Palladino up for disappointment and confrontations with studio suits for decades to come.)

Barr says now that her main wish was to "break through as many things as I could. And I really had the writers who could do it, too." But while they were finessing the scripts, she says she was the one called to account. "I would have to be the one who would stand there in front of the network censor." His name was Neil Conrad and, says Barr, "He was extremely conservative. But if I could make him laugh, he'd say okay. It was kind of like my family—if you could make them laugh, you could say anything." Conrad proved his sense of humor in a cameo, appearing as himself at the end of an episode about DJ's erections. Roseanne impishly tries to find an expression acceptable to him: "What about 'pitching a trouser tent'? 'Bootin' up the hard drive'? 'Popping a wheelie'?" Conrad's feigned outrage delights her.

In this virtually executive-free bubble, Barr "gave notes if she felt like it, or she and Tom just went off in their electric wheelchairs and zoomed around while we went back to the writers' room and worked," Sherman-Palladino recalls, referring to the couple's penchant for using motorized wheelchairs to get around the set. She says it was a remarkably functional work environment while it lasted: "I don't know what he was like as a husband, but the thing about Tom was he wanted that show to keep going."

———

"They kept saying women ain't funny. All through my career, some Bozo would say, 'I gotta give it to you, most women aren't funny, but *you* . . .'" At age sixty-three, Barr shakes her head as if she still can't believe it. "It was that token thing. Then you'd hear them say the same thing to the next woman." Although she made an effort to hire female writers for her series, Barr treated many of them much the way she did male scribes—which is to say, brutally. At one point, she decided to make the writers wear numbers around their necks rather than address them by name. Sherman-Palladino was number two. Stan Zimmerman and James Berg were twelve and thirteen, respectively.

Eileen Heisler (who had left before numbers were assigned) described the *Roseanne* writers' room as "a crowded car ride on a vacation. You were stuck in this small space for hours and hours and hours . . . but everyone could speak their mind and it was a messy, real, passionate discussion. And if Roseanne didn't like the script, you had to rewrite the script." Barr was also prone to irrational edicts. "She would meet Joan Collins at a party, and she would come in on Monday and say, 'I want Joan Collins in the episode next week,'" says DeAnn Heline. "So it was that kind of thing. She's not in the writers' room, so you are just there late hoping that this is what she wants."

Barr insists she was just pushing to achieve the smartest show possible. "I was the big boss bitch. I'm not your mother. You're getting paid ten grand a week, you owe somebody *something*." She continues: "I worked with some writers that, no matter how hard you beat them down—and it was fun to try—no matter how much you beat them down, they kept coming up with better and better shit, because they would be like, 'We might get fired if we don't get off this couch and deliver laughs!'"

Heisler, who along with Heline went on to work for *Murphy Brown* (and later to co-create the sharp working-class family sitcom *The Middle*), recalls that "table reads on *Murphy* were like great sex. The cast would look at you like, 'Which one of you guys made this funny joke?' They really appreciated it." Whereas, on *Roseanne*, she says, "It was kind of an atmosphere of fear."

By the midpoint of the series, Barr was living the surreal existence of a superstar—dogged by tabloids, divorced from everyday reality. Says Heline, "She occasionally would want to wear some outfit on the show that Roseanne Conner would not have worn, and Tom would say, 'Rosie, you can't wear that. That is not for a woman from the Midwest. You've gotta go change.' And she would listen to him. He got what the show was, and so, in that season at least, he was a force for good."

Not content with steering Barr's ship, Arnold commandeered a show of his own: *The Jackie Thomas Show* featured him as an obnoxious sitcom star with a backstory much like Arnold's. The reviews for the 1992 ABC series were mixed (Tom Shales of the *Washington Post* called Jackie Thomas "a character smaller than life"), and Barr responded by faxing some reviewers nasty letters. Ever the diplomat, she took a similarly aggressive approach with her own network. Outraged that ABC didn't immediately renew *Jackie Thomas* (because it wasn't getting the blockbuster ratings they'd expected in the time slot after *Roseanne*), she went on talk shows threatening to move her own series to another network. A pissed-off ABC proceeded to ax *Jackie Thomas*. However, not wanting to lose Barr, who, uncontrollable as she was, had the number-two show in America, ABC committed to developing new programs with the Arnolds' production company.

One of the ideas developed was a sitcom based around the all-female R&B quartet En Vogue. Sherman-Palladino remembers being asked to write the pilot and meet the group. "None of them could talk, and I thought, *That's it. It's over!*" she recalls. But the Arnolds liked the script, so the decision was made to cast proper actresses, including a young Salma Hayek.

"The night we shot the pilot, Roseanne kicked Tom out and had Tom's bags delivered to the stage while we were shooting. So, we're sitting there, and Tom is in a state of shock, and guys with bags are coming in . . ." Sherman-Palladino shrugs. "That was the end of *that*."

Barr filed for divorce in April 1994, the climax of a string of wild spectacles dubbed "Roseanne & Tom's Traveling Media Circus" by *People*. Those publicity maneuvers included the announcement of a three-way marriage among Roseanne, Tom, and his twenty-four-year-old assistant, Kim Silva, who was rumored to be the catalyst for the divorce. Barr then accused her husband of physical abuse, recanting the accusation later but ultimately following through with the divorce.

The traits that made Barr such a supernova—her fuck-everyone-and-say-anything attitude, her compulsion to go too far and push too hard—were the same ones that would inevitably trip her up. Her power came from being an outsider, and eventually she would provoke the establishment into casting her out again.

"It was when she and Tom broke up—that's when things went completely haywire," says Sherman-Palladino. "That's when things started happening like *the lottery*." In the show's final season, Roseanne Conner wins $108 million in the state lottery, triggering a series of episodes that bear no resemblance to anything that had come before. Jackie dates a prince, and she and Roseanne fly to New York City, where they hobnob with the jet-set crowd. The sisters mingle with a magazine editor played by Marlo Thomas and a perfume magnate played by Arianna Huffington.

Absolutely Fabulous characters Patsy and Edina (Joanna Lumley and Jennifer Saunders) also pop up out of nowhere in that episode. At the time, Barr was working with Saunders to adapt the politically incorrect portrait of two shameless, booze-soaked British fashionistas for American television; she recognized Patsy and Edina as fellow travelers in the sisterhood of unruly women. It soon became clear that American networks would require *Ab Fab* to strip away its most loutish elements, however. Roseanne could get away with being a loudmouthed woman because she was grounded by her ordinary family; two single older women doing drugs, sleeping with younger men, and genuinely thumbing their noses at motherhood couldn't find a place on American network television in the nineties. The American *Ab Fab* project was dropped.

Even in its last three seasons, *Roseanne* continued to cycle through executive producers and writers, including Eric Gilliland, Cynthia Mort, and Daniel Palladino. (The last would meet and marry Amy Sherman after both had left the series.) Janet Leahy, who wrote for *Roseanne* toward the end of its run, says some of the "ludicrous" story lines resulted from Barr eventually taking on too much control. "It is one thing to have editorial power and another to have creative power, and I think that crossed over in the end, and that was part of the problem." She recalls that one of the writers had pitched an alternative twist to the lottery plot: "[The Conners] had a lottery ticket on their fridge and they had won the lottery, but they never knew it because they never checked the ticket. That, to me, is brilliant and real. And then the show wouldn't have gone off in that weird direction," she says with a laugh.

Barr never discussed her rationale for the lottery plotline much, but she did tell *Spin* magazine that it was her way of returning the show to its roots (the saga of her real life) and to communicate "how dreams come true. You know, the American dream and how these incredible things happened to *me*, who used to be this housewife with all these kids." She said she'd always planned to end season eight with Roseanne Conner doing stand-up comedy: "I was always showing these poor people, who were working really hard but never getting ahead. I realized I came here literally out of a trailer because I *didn't* believe that. And I have to correct that because I can't leave these characters in a place where their hard work never pays off." And yet, in the May 1997 series finale, the lottery is revealed to be a fantasy—a fictional tale written by Roseanne Conner to console herself in the wake of Dan's death from a heart attack.

After nearly a decade of cultural dominance and personal chaos, Barr left the prime-time airwaves. She was exhausted but immensely powerful—

or so it seemed. A 1995 *New Yorker* profile referenced a deal for her company Full Moon and High Tide to produce four more series. Barr estimated she'd be worth a billion dollars by the end of the twentieth century. In the following years, though, she seemed unable to build on her show's massive success. There was talk of doing a spin-off focused around son DJ that never materialized. A plan to do an ABC talk show special in which she'd interview Mike Tyson fell apart. Roseanne turned her back on her longtime network and proceeded to shoot the talk show for syndicator King World (Oprah's distributor) instead. "I figured I would be making Oprah money, so I told ABC to F—off—another of my genius moves!" she wrote in her book *Roseannearchy*. Later, there would be several reality shows featuring her extended family and failed attempts at sitcoms (such as *Downwardly Mobile*, a 2012 comedy pilot that reunited Barr and John Goodman) before, in 2017, ABC announced a reboot of *Roseanne*.

There was also a run for president as the 2012 Green Party candidate. "I do like making trouble on behalf of the public," Barr says now, her brassy voice tempered a bit by age. But she gets impatient at ordinary folks' penchant for self-deception. "Like George Carlin says, the owners of this country are in a club, and you ain't in it. Don't lie to yourself!" Asked if she thinks she extended Carlin's legacy of populist comedy, she pauses. "I think I did my part when it was my time to do something. And I sure had fun doing it, too." She lets loose a sudden hoot. "Christ, it was fun!"

Of course, not *all* of it was fun. "I got caught in the middle of something, and it was so huge and so unstoppable it was like a speeding train," she told a reporter at the end of *Roseanne*'s run. "I've seen it happen to other people when they start to get famous or they have great success. I think a lot of people just spin so far out of control that they die."

Sherman-Palladino feels great sympathy for her former boss. "We were the number one sitcom, and you got thirty million viewers every week. . . . But [Roseanne] was never a really happy woman. She had so much power, and I don't know that she got to enjoy any of what she did. She was really a target, and she never got the respect in the town she should have."

Judd Apatow first met Barr as a twenty-two-year-old, when he was hired to write material for her stand-up act. He, too, remains in awe of her creative chutzpah. "A lot of people painted it as out-of-control behavior, but really, it was someone taking control of her world as best she could, being the person she was. She made landmark television for a really long time, and it was done in a unique, eccentric way," Apatow says. He pauses, then adds, "Okay, at times it was probably really unhealthy. But what she left behind is so groundbreaking. We had Maude and Rhoda and Mary Tyler Moore, and then Roseanne took it to a whole other level."

Roseanne Barr is now a Ghost of Television Past, so strange and contradictory that it's hard to believe she was once one of America's biggest TV stars. From her prime-time pedestal, she brought all kinds of progressive notions about gender and class to the homes of a nation convulsed by a culture war. She found a way to turn the insult of being poor and a woman inside out: Although Roseanne Conner sometimes pretended to be lazy and a lousy mom, she was neither. Always finding a way to keep the family afloat, she supported her kids through elopements, pregnancy, and disappointments, and she bolstered her husband through job loss, depression, and illness.

Murphy Brown and *Roseanne* launched and ended around the same time, and many commentators saw the shows as two sides of the same coin. At a moment when a retrogressive notion of "family values" loomed over the culture, both shows provided a realistic and contemporary conception of what a family could be—fluid, imperfect—and in the process paved the way for future shows such as *Modern Family*, *Fresh Off the Boat*, and *Transparent*. While Murphy represented the upscale end of left-wing America, Roseanne shouted out to the neglected underbelly of the eighties—the poor, the overweight, the silent and frustrated white working class.

Together, they were a feminist superhero team. Yet Diane English and Roseanne Barr say they never met in all that time. English admired her competitor greatly, but Barr felt alienated by the kind of middle-class liberal feminism Murphy Brown represented.

Eileen Heisler, who wrote for both shows, felt strongly back then just how different Murphy and Roseanne were from the standard TV heroines. "They were sarcastic, flawed, messy, naughty, not always nice. Murphy— that was one of the most fun characters to write ever because she knew what she wanted and she'd step all over people to get it and then be surprised it wasn't what she wanted." But it was *Roseanne* that ultimately played a part in inspiring *The Middle*, the sitcom Heisler and Heline created two decades later about a working-class Indiana family struggling to pay bills and do right by their scrappy, eccentric kids. "*The Middle*'s roots are *Roseanne* for sure," she says. "We loved the marriage of Dan and Roseanne and the dignity of people *trying hard*."

There was no doubt that Barr was *Roseanne*'s heart and its conscience, goading everyone around her to be faithful to that vision. "She knew the truth and she could smell it when something wasn't true or real," notes Janet Leahy. "There were so many writers, but there was an absolute voice that ran through that show: hers."

CHAPTER 3

Walking and Talking as Fast as They Can:
Amy Sherman-Palladino's *Gilmore Girls*

Amy Sherman-Palladino and Lauren Graham celebrate
Gilmore Girls's one-hundredth episode, December 2004.

Strolling across the Warner Bros. backlot on a sunny spring day, I search for the landmarks of Stars Hollow. That's the small-town idyll at the heart of *Gilmore Girls*, where oddballs roam free, members of Sonic Youth and Yo La Tengo compete to be town troubadour, and civic pride wafts through every shabby-chic street.

First, I spot Miss Patty's dance studio, where Stars Hollow's town meetings take place. I peek through the window hoping to see tiny ballerinas doing pliés inside, but the barn is empty. Around the sun-soaked square are the familiar outlines of the town's main drag, including Luke's Diner, site of the slow-simmering flirtation between gruff owner Luke Danes and single mom Lorelai Gilmore. But the retro signage has been stripped off, and other hints of change are all around: there's a trendy boutique called Diva Dish and even a cupcake store. It's not the spoils of gentrification to blame, though; it's the relentless pace of a working TV backlot, where they've already begun clearing the sets of the *Gilmore Girls* reboot to make way for a new season of *Pretty Little Liars*.

A few blocks over, though, the *Gilmore Girls* crew has taken up residence on a generically urban street. Netflix has briefly revived the series as *Gilmore Girls: A Year in the Life*, nine years after its original incarnation ended. Extras in gowns and tuxes mill aimlessly up and down the street, waiting to be called. I am directed through the front door of a building, where I find myself plunged into a disconcerting scene: a smoky tango club surrounded by decadently dressed dancers. Everyone seems to be frozen in impossibly angular poses. Realizing I have walked into a rehearsal, I dart through the tightly packed bodies.

Midway through the room, I nearly crash into a small woman dressed in a black tunic and purple fedora. It's *Gilmore Girls*'s creator Amy Sherman-Palladino, who is conducting the dancers with a beatific smile on her face. I keep moving, and tumble through the looking glass to the other side—the dark, cluttered backstage area known as Video Village, where the directors, writers, wardrobe people, and everyone else not needed on set are crammed into or behind director's chairs.

Sherman-Palladino plops down in her seat next to her husband and writing partner, Daniel Palladino, boyish-looking in a tan blazer worn over a hoodie. The two stare at a monitor, which shows a Baz Luhrmannesque fantasia unfolding in the next room. Thirty-four-year-old actress Alexis Bledel, who was just nineteen when she first played Lorelai's daughter, Rory, glides through the club's beaded curtain with ex-boyfriend Logan (Matt Czuchry), who's clad in a steampunk top hat and suit. Ten seconds into the take, Sherman-Palladino yells, "Cut!" and rushes out to confer and lay hands on dancers. Shooting proceeds in this staccato way. Bledel heads back to Video Village between takes to sit silently in the corner, pale and luminous as she swigs water and looks at her phone. They finally get through a full scene smoothly, but when Logan dips Rory romantically, her arm hangs down limply. "It kind of looks like a flopping fish," Sherman-

Palladino says, wrinkling her nose. She eventually directs the couple to end in a tight romantic clinch instead of a dip, forever banishing Rory's fish arm to the cutting-room floor.

"Can you spot the eighty-three-year-old dancer?" Sherman-Palladino calls out gleefully at one point. An elderly lady with close-cropped red hair wearing a short satin dress glides past the camera. It turns out that this is her mother, Maybin Hewes, a former dancer. Sherman-Palladino points out that she has partnered her mom with a *Dancing with the Stars* pro. "He's treating her like a goddess. It feeds into all my childhood anxieties that everyone loves her and no one understands me!" she quips in her gravelly voice, shrugging mournfully like a borscht-belt comedian.

During a break in the action, Bledel and Hewes both bustle into Video Village. They plant themselves in front of Sherman-Palladino, beseeching her attention. For a moment, sitting there in her purple fedora, the showrunner looks just like Lorelai Gilmore, juggling the needs of her real-life mother and fantasy daughter, orchestrating the intricate machinery of a television production—all while talking incredibly fast.

When *Gilmore Girls* first premiered on October 5, 2000, nothing about the series suggested it would turn out to be one of the decade's most beloved TV portraits of female relationships, or that it would become such a cult hit that it would eventually merit a revival.

Originally airing on the WB, a fledgling network then known mostly as a ghetto for teen soaps such as *Dawson's Creek* and *Seventh Heaven*, Sherman-Palladino's series was saddled with a name that hinted at a homespun family drama or a sappy chick show. *Gilmore Girls* might as well have marched into the world with a sign around its neck reading DON'T TAKE ME SERIOUSLY. In its seven seasons, it won only a single Emmy Award, for Outstanding Makeup, despite having some of the best writing and acting of its time.

Just a year before *Gilmore Girls* premiered, HBO had catapulted *The*

Sopranos into the pop-culture firmament. Along with *The Wire*, *The Sopranos* set a template for quality TV that equated depth and substance with troubled male characters, roiling masculine energy, internecine power struggles, and regular eruptions of highly realistic violence: think *The Shield*, *Dexter*, *Sons of Anarchy*, *Rescue Me*, *Breaking Bad*. It's no coincidence that this sort of show was invariably run by a male auteur, for whom the turbulent antihero on-screen often seemed to function as a mirror-image surrogate. Women remained secondary figures in these male psychodramas, and female television showrunners longing to create dramas with a less macho tone found themselves stymied.

Almost by definition, then, "serious" television offered minimal scope for women either behind the camera or in front of it. *Gilmore Girls*'s immersion in the emotionally tangled lives of intelligent women meant it had virtually no chance of being seen as an important show. Where were the murderous rage, the brooding moral quandaries to be found in Stars Hollow? Instead, there were small daily compromises, romances, and pleasures. Tony Soprano strangles a man during his daughter Meadow's college tour; Lorelai merely ponders her own thwarted college dreams and knack for self-sabotage during the Gilmores' similar visit to Harvard. *Gilmore Girls*'s blend of quiet emotional drama and chatty screwball comedy stranded it in the category known as "dramedy," a slight (in both senses) term often applied to women-centric series that more or less defined them as lightweight. *The Days and Nights of Molly Dodd* and *Sex and the City* were early recipients of the label, later followed by *Weeds*, *Nurse Jackie*, and *Girls*.

If Sherman-Palladino believed it was possible to create a sharp-edged female-focused series with wide appeal, that's because she began her TV career on just such a show. Writing for *Roseanne* in her early twenties, Sherman-Palladino earned the sitcom its only script Emmy nomination when she wrote (along with partner Jennifer Heath) the episode about Becky and birth control. "Starting on *Roseanne* was the best and worst thing that could've happened," she says now, both because the writing standards were so high and because Barr, at great emotional cost, carved out a kind of network freedom that Sherman-Palladino would struggle to replicate through the rest of her career.

The first time I interviewed Sherman-Palladino—for a 2004 feature in the *Village Voice*, where I was the TV critic—she joked that in Stars Hollow, Al Gore was president. An idealized liberal bubble, this small New England town was the kind of place Hillary Clinton probably had in mind when she said, "It takes a village": quaint yet progressive, cozy but not narrow-minded, accepting of strangers and its own native eccentrics. Above all, it was a place run largely by women, where female autonomy and ability were taken for granted. The town was full of female business owners and bosses (including Lorelai, who ran a local inn in tandem with her obsessive-compulsive perfectionist chef, Sookie). And daughter Rory's role models were icons of female achievement and authority, such as Christiane Amanpour, Gloria Steinem, and Madeleine Albright.

Meanwhile, out in the real world, the one where George W. Bush ended up in the White House instead of Gore, America was increasingly dividing into Red states and Blue states. The Republicans pushed policies that, in an echo of the Reagan-Bush backdrop to *Roseanne* and *Murphy Brown*, slashed family planning funding in favor of antiabortion and abstinence-only programs. Offering a consoling vision of a kinder and more tolerant America, *Gilmore Girls* was one of the things that helped me get through the Dark Ages of the 2000s. How eerie that the show should return on the eve of an even bleaker period of backlash, with the sequel airing only a few weeks after the November 2016 election. Perhaps in the imaginary idyll that is Stars Hollow, Hillary Clinton beat Donald Trump?

———

On a chilly November morning in 2015, I meet Sherman-Palladino at a tiny Brooklyn café just around the corner from the apartment she shares with her husband. She is taking a break from the couple's self-imposed exile as they scramble to draft a script for the Netflix reboot. Using her elbow to nudge aside a stroller blocking her path to the table as if it carries an infectious disease, she yanks off her leopard-print cap and lets a cascade of black curly hair unfurl before tucking it away again. Her phone periodically pings with texts from Dan, who is at home reanimating Stars Hollow.

Sherman-Palladino grew up steeped in old-fashioned show biz in Los Angeles's suburban San Fernando Valley. Her mom was a dancer in Broadway musicals; her dad, Don Sherman, a Catskills comedian turned TV writer/actor, appeared on series such as *The Monkees, Maude,* and *Barney Miller* throughout Amy's childhood. Although she wasn't raised religiously, she marinated in Jewish comedy; Jackie Mason and Shecky Greene were regular visitors to the Sherman house. Discovering her father's beat-up copy of the record *2000 Years with Carl Reiner & Mel Brooks* was a life-changing experience, introducing young Amy to Brooks's Two-Thousand-Year-Old Man character. A comic voice that was "fast and furious and human and exhausted and hilarious," Brooks made her want to be part of the Jewish cultural continuum. As she once recalled, "I instantly adopted a New York accent. I became Van Nuys via Brooklyn (well, Brooklyn in the forties)."

After training as a dancer, Sherman-Palladino took some classes with LA improv troupe the Groundlings in her early twenties. There she befriended Jennifer Heath, who suggested they try writing spec scripts ("spec" being code for the sample episodes of existing TV shows you'd have to write to apply for a staff job). Sherman-Palladino signed up for a sitcom-writing course at UCLA, which led to a gig for the duo on *City,* a star vehicle for *Rhoda* actress Valerie Harper. Although *City* didn't last long, it got the two women job offers on *Roseanne.* In those days, Sherman-Palladino was still keeping her options open for a dancing career and says she simultaneously got a callback for a role in the touring company of *Cats.* After some deliberation, she chose *Roseanne* over Rumpleteazer.

Roseanne Barr says she had immediate affection for Sherman-Palladino because of her penchant for funny hats and her perfectionism: "She is one of the people who can keep coming back with funny, and funnier. You'd better make me laugh louder or you're getting fired. Some didn't do it. But she did."

It had taken just six months between Sherman-Palladino's first spec script and this job on a hit show. Nothing would ever unfold for her with such fairy-tale ease again. After *Roseanne*, she formed the production company Dorothy Parker Drank Here, in tribute to the legendary Algonquin Round Table wit. Over the next several years, she developed some sitcoms that never made it to the air and one that did, briefly: *Love and Marriage* focused on the Nardinis, a blue-collar Italian American couple struggling to raise their rebellious kids in New York City. Fox fired entertainment chief John Matoian the month *Love and Marriage* premiered; his replacement, Peter Roth, promptly canceled it. A stint followed on *Veronica's Closet*, a late '90s sitcom starring Kirstie Alley as a fashion executive, produced by *Friends* creators Marta Kauffman and David Crane. Sherman-Palladino doesn't mince words about her time on the show, describing it as a "terrible experience." Crane, she says, "is a lovely and very talented man, and it was nice watching him do his thing. But other than that . . ." She raises one eyebrow meaningfully. The writers' room was "toxic with people who all wanted to be on *Friends* and would sit in that room and make one fat joke after another about Kirstie."

On *Veronica's Closet*, Sherman-Palladino says she hit rock bottom. She told her husband, Dan, "'I think I am done with sitcoms, I don't think it's the right place for me anymore.' And he said, 'Just figure out what you really want to do.'"

In the fall of 1999, Sherman-Palladino pitched ideas to several networks. One of them was the WB. A young channel with a tight budget and short track record, it nonetheless had begun to build an audience on two niches underserved by more established networks: African American comedy (*The Jamie Foxx Show*; *Sister, Sister*) and teen drama (*Dawson's Creek*; *Buffy the Vampire Slayer*). Already it had created platforms for the Wayans brothers, Kevin Williamson, and ex-*Roseanne* writer Joss Whedon.

Late in her meeting with the WB, Sherman-Palladino mentioned offhandedly that she'd been toying with a show about a young mom and daughter who are best friends. WB executive Susanne Daniels, already a fan of Sherman-Palladino's writing, was taken with the notion of a brainy teen girl character who wasn't overtly sexy or fixated on boys. She suggested developing it as an hour-long drama. Sherman-Palladino agreed to flesh out the idea but was a little unnerved; not only had she agreed to work on a story that she had barely considered but she was also a half-hour comedy pro with no experience writing hour-long dramas.

A brief trip with Dan to the quaint town of Washington, Connecticut, charmed her: Sherman-Palladino marveled over the pumpkin patch and a diner where patrons served themselves coffee. Stars Hollow quickly populated itself inside her brain, and her show's heroines began to take form: thirty-two-year-old single mother Lorelai Gilmore and her teenage daughter, Rory. Sherman-Palladino fashioned Lorelai as the rebellious only child of a patrician Hartford couple, Emily and Richard Gilmore. She had gotten pregnant at sixteen and run away, choosing to raise her kid in a humbler small-town atmosphere, while also working her way up to become the successful manager of a local inn not unlike the one in which Amy and Dan were staying.

Despite her wealthy upbringing, Lorelai's character owed a great deal to Roseanne Conner. "A lot of Roseanne's point of view went into her," says Sherman-Palladino. "Lorelai had a lot more options than Roseanne Conner, but there was an independence and a 'I'm going to figure this out on my own terms' attitude which came directly from Roseanne."

In fact, *Roseanne* colored Sherman-Palladino's whole approach to *Gilmore Girls*. "I don't know if I thought about it at the time, but the training of my first show was solely about this woman's point of view," she says. "Nothing happened in *Roseanne* that didn't come back to affect her. So if the daughters had a story, it was always about: how will this come back to affect Roseanne? Her point of view permeates everything. She is the alpha in the room, and Lorelai is always the alpha."

Daniels loved the pilot script, which concisely evoked the relationship between mother and daughter against the whimsical backdrop of Stars Hollow. In a meeting at the WB to sketch out plotlines after the network had picked up the show, Sherman-Palladino mentioned an idea for a fight between Lorelai and her socialite mother, Emily, from whom she is estranged. Unable to afford private school for the brilliant Rory, Lorelai accepts tuition money from her parents; in return, her mother exacts a promise that Lorelai and Rory spend every Friday night dining at the family manor. Daniels suggested they instead include this scene in the pilot, perfectly setting up for viewers a central theme of the show: the tangled bonds among these three generations of female Gilmores and the complex matrix of love, money, and familial duty.

Emily Gilmore's sense of self rests on wealth and status, and she delights in lording it over anyone who doesn't live up to her standards, be it her maid (who gets replaced every episode for not satisfying Emily, an echo of Murphy Brown's high turnover of secretaries) or her daughter. Much as Lorelai resents Emily, she has inherited her knack for verbal manipulation. Their relationship is a never-ending battle for the last word. That first family dinner introduces us to *Gilmore Girls*'s trademark mixture of emotional jousting and physical comedy, as the grandparents coo over Rory while belittling Lorelai's career success. This boils over into a confrontation between Lorelai and Emily about the original sin of *Gilmore Girls*: Lorelai's decision to raise her daughter alone.

"You took that girl and completely shut us out of your life," Emily huffs, to which Lorelai replies, "You wanted to control me." She notes that she grew up quickly. "I had to figure out how to live. I found a good job," says Lorelai, pride mingled with petulance. "As a *maid*," Emily jeers. "With all your brains and talent . . ."

After dinner, the camera follows Lorelai and Rory outside the house. "Do I look shorter? I feel shorter," Lorelai deadpans to her daughter. In a later episode, she will note that the day she shattered her parents dreams by telling them she was pregnant "was the only time they ever looked small to me." Lorelai takes empowerment where she can get it.

Finding the right actresses to play the Gilmore women would be key. Alexis Bledel was a New York University student and model with no acting experience; she was struggling with a cold the day she went in to audition, the result of a winter modeling gig in which water was thrown over her shivering body. Bledel's sickly state gave her audition the dose of sleepyheaded realism Sherman-Palladino was looking for in Rory. "We weren't sure she was the right one for the role, but there was just something about her. Those eyes alone!" Sherman-Palladino gasps. "The way she photographed—you hear people saying 'the camera loved her,' but the camera loved Alexis in a bizarro way."

Veteran actress Kelly Bishop struck Sherman-Palladino as the one to play grande dame Emily Gilmore. She had won a Tony Award for her portrayal of the sexy, sarcastic dancer Sheila (partly based on her own life) in *A Chorus Line*, and had appeared in movies such as *An Unmarried Woman* and *Dirty Dancing*. Bishop brought a steely gravitas to the show, especially in combination with the dignified bearing of Edward Herrmann, cast as the bluff but kindly Richard Gilmore. Best known for his turns as President Franklin D. Roosevelt in various made-for-TV movies, Herrmann fell in love with the script—"Here was a girl in public high school who was bored silly with boys and makeup, and wanted to read *Les Misérables*. That, I thought, was charming"—and offered to audition.

Casting Lorelai proved more difficult. A stream of contenders was brought through the WB offices and rejected. "We didn't find Lauren until the *last fucking minute*," Sherman-Palladino says dramatically. Lauren Graham had costarred in a string of unsuccessful sitcoms and was at that moment tied to *M.Y.O.B.*, a struggling comedy that NBC hadn't yet decided whether to cancel. So Sherman-Palladino met the actress knowing she might not be able to have her.

Graham recalls running through the lines with Sherman-Palladino before the audition and being startled by the showrunner's exactitude. "She said, 'Okay, but can you do this *exactly* as written?'" On other comedies, the young actress had been encouraged to improvise. But Graham quickly grasped that Sherman-Palladino's language "needs to be done exactly as written because it's so musical."

They decided to shoot the pilot in Toronto, with Graham in the lead—a decision that Daniels calls "hold-my-breath terrifying." If Graham's other series got renewed, *Gilmore Girls* would have to find money to reshoot with another actress. And money was no trivial matter—as it was, the WB had funded the initial scripts for *Gilmore Girls* in an unusual way: by partnering with the Family Friendly Programming Forum, a consortium of major advertisers hoping to promote wholesome TV. Fortunately, Graham's other series was axed, and the WB picked up *Gilmore Girls* in the spring of 2000. Sherman-Palladino persuaded the network to relocate the set to Warner Bros.' lot in LA, conjuring the faux New England town on the same fictional streets once used for *The Music Man* and *The Waltons*. She also had to replace the two actors who played the key parts of Sookie (Lorelai's best friend as well as the inn's chef) and Dean (who would become Rory's first love).

Sherman-Palladino was sitting in her office in a black miniskirt, combat boots, and a T-shirt that read, I FUCKED YOUR BOYFRIEND LAST NIGHT when casting directors Mara Casey and Jami Rudofsky first went in to meet with her and producer Gavin Polone. Scanning her clothing and quirky, ornate office—a fuchsia velvet-covered creation that one staffer described as "the inside of Jeannie's bottle on *I Dream of Jeannie*"—the casting directors decided Sherman-Palladino might be open to an unorthodox choice for Sookie: Melissa McCarthy, a little-known comedian performing with the Groundlings.

"Melissa came in and read, and I thought I was going to pee my pants," recalls Casey. "I was laughing really hard, and that's not cool!" Sookie was nothing like the characters McCarthy was known for at Groundlings, which were, Casey says, "broad and crazy and fabulous, eating pizza off the floor and falling over. Sookie wasn't a broad character, but Melissa was able to infuse it with her sensibilities and her talent." Sherman-Palladino decided to go to the mat for McCarthy, whose plump figure and zany energy didn't fit the network-television mold, even for a sidekick role. "It was a tricky sell," Sherman-Palladino recalled at the ATX Television Festival in 2015. "She is different, and different is sometimes not the easiest thing to embrace."

Casey soon grasped that there were two ways to go with *Gilmore* characters: "It was either good-looking or the quirkier the better. If [an actor] was going to be making out with Rory, he had to be good-looking." Jared Padalecki came in during a brief visit from Texas and was cast as Rory's first boyfriend, Dean. Scott Patterson—the actor who plays Luke Danes, Lorelai's true love—started out as a recurring character rather than a series regular thanks to a tight budget. That was how the *Gilmore* production team often brought actors on board, slipping them under the radar on an episode-by-episode basis so they didn't need to get network approval. Sean Gunn was a perfect example of that stealthy strategy: the character actor was cast in the first episode as a cable installer. He returned in the next episode as a swan delivery guy. Jami Rudofsky had heard that Sherman-Palladino's dad played a series of different characters wearing different hats on the eighties comedy *Gimme a Break* and suggested they try the same gimmick with Gunn. Eventually the role settled into Kirk, one of the great TV weirdos of all time, who cycles through every job in town, makes amateur movies, and suffers from night terrors that cause him to run naked through Stars Hollow.

Gilmore Girls's teething troubles went beyond casting. Sherman-Palladino had written a very wordy pilot script, and the executives were insistent that it needed to be cut down if it was to have any hope of fitting the allotted time. But because the show's dialogue is delivered at such a lightning clip, after the shooting was done, the episode actually ran fifteen minutes *short*. There was also the Rory problem: most of the series' early story lines revolved around Rory and Lorelai, but Bledel was too much of a technical novice to carry scenes on her own. She was like a doe caught in the klieg lights. "So Lauren and Alexis had to be in every scene together," says Sherman-Palladino. Because the other plotlines and characters were as yet less developed, all the focus was on Lorelai and Rory—and all the work fell on Graham and Bledel. "The two of them—I almost killed them, but I kind of had no choice because I was still figuring out where my other stories were."

Midway through the first season, the exhausted actresses came to the showrunner begging for a reprieve. Sherman-Palladino began to expand other characters: Rory's best friend, Lane, and nemesis, Paris; love interests (Dean and Jess for Rory, Max and Christopher for Lorelai); and of course Emily and Richard Gilmore: "We realized there are two pros sitting there, why not give them more to do?"

Graham recently rewatched the first episode and was struck by how little plot unfurls: "*Nothing* happened for easily twenty minutes, and you don't care because there is something warm and inviting about the language and the people. Here is this person, she likes coffee, and here's her daughter, and here she is at work and . . . Almost halfway through, you get to the fact that she needs money to pay for her kid's school. That would be the first three minutes of the pilot today—with an explosion and a vampire thrown in."

And yet, seemingly contradicting the leisurely narrative, the show's dialogue pacing was breakneck, like a Ramones song transposed to television or a Hepburn-Tracy movie on speed. "It is the way I write; I love banter," Sherman-Palladino told me in 2004. "Woody Allen at his height—it doesn't get better than that. Those people talk over each other. Comedy plays better faster; it just does." Editor Raúl Dávalos even snipped frames so that the dialogue overlapped or characters seemed to move faster. Says Sherman-Palladino, "You take the air out of something and it's immediately more entertaining."

When bringing in actors for auditions, "we would have to constantly tell people, you have to be *on top* of your lines," says Casey. "It wasn't about talking superfast, it was about coming right in as soon as the other person stops talking. It's kind of a rhythm you pick up." A script supervisor would time takes to maintain velocity. In the second season, Sherman-Palladino mocked her own need for speed: Rory's debate partner, Paris, complains that Rory speaks too slowly, at 135 words per minute compared to Paris's 178. When Rory insists that's a normal tempo, Paris taunts, "For the average Willie Nelson roadie, yes, but not for a winning debate team member."

Graham, who studied English at Barnard, idolized Katharine Hepburn, and cut her teeth on Kaufman-Hart plays, says she was born to play hyperverbal Lorelai. She quickly learned to memorize gargantuan blocks of dialogue but found it harder to master the long tracking shots that required marathon sessions of walking and talking while looking perfectly natural. These were tougher still for the inexperienced Bledel, which meant that Graham was constantly manhandling her on-screen daughter in order to steer her into place—something that actually enhanced viewers' sense of the women's intimacy on-screen.

Even veteran actor Edward Herrmann found the rigors of the series frustrating, occasionally rebelling against Sherman-Palladino's perfectionist desire to have the script performed word for word in repeated takes. Sherman-Palladino fondly recalled him shouting, "We're not puppets! We're not puppets!"

When the show premiered, its galloping gait and fixation on walking and talking earned it an immediate comparison to *The West Wing*. Aaron Sorkin's wordy ensemble drama about the White House had launched just the year before, to great acclaim. A fake Associated Press article posted online even claimed that Sorkin "has been unmasked as the primary voice" of *Gilmore Girls* and that "Amy Sherman-Palladino" was "a pseudonym representing a writing collective of Sorkin, fellow *West Wing* scribe Patrick Caddell, and former *Sports Night* scribe Kevin Falls." Sherman-Palladino gamely addressed the hoax at the Television Critics Association conference in July 2001, telling a reporter, "What's funny is that the rumor wasn't even that I was fronting for him. It was, I didn't even *exist*. Like, my whole existence was wiped out."

The idea that Sorkin or any of these guys could've created Lorelai

Gilmore is absurd. After meeting Sherman-Palladino, one can be in no doubt that the character's DNA stems directly from her brainpan. Her conversational style is a wild onrush of wit lightly creased with crankiness. Although she likes to deflect the idea that Lorelai is based directly on her, pointing out that she has no children nor any desire to be a parent, she does admit, "A lot of my points of view, and of course the fact that I have no attention span, come through in Lorelai."

Graham was warned off taking the role by some of her actor friends, who suggested that mother characters are death traps for a young actress. "Before you know it, you go from playing the college student to the mom. [Screen] moms tend to have very similar qualities, and the moms are endlessly folding laundry and stuff," Graham acknowledges. "But being a mom was like *fifth* on the list of what [Lorelai] was. She was dynamic and a career person and irritated with her parents and very close to her daughter. None of that had a stereotypical quality to it."

Ignoring traditional maternal models, the unmarried Lorelai chooses to coparent her daughter with the entire village of Stars Hollow rather than settle on a partner. A horrible cook, Lorelai takes Rory for breakfast at Luke's Diner more often than not, and the fridge is always crammed with take-out containers. Autopsies would likely have shown a high percentage of these women's bodies consisting of coffee and Pop-Tarts. (Chalk up the implausibly perfect figures and flawless alabaster skin to the magic of Stars Hollow and Hollywood.) Lorelai rarely disciplines her child, which works out fine, because Rory is a preternaturally mature girl, craving order in the face of her mother's seat-of-the-pants chaos.

The secret to Lorelai is that she is written as a teenager herself. Having given birth at sixteen, she retains a kind of adolescent ferocity and sass. Early on, though, Sherman-Palladino had a tough time finding writers who understood the slightly unconventional narrative she had in mind. "That first year, I had a roomful of writers who looked at me like I was speaking Chinese," she recalls. "I kept saying: We are not [writing] mother-daughter stories—we are [writing] girlfriend stories. Lorelai is a child herself, you know? There are moments where she has to learn to be a mother." Instead, she says, her writers, a largely inexperienced bunch, gave her a lot of finger-wagging moralism. She heavily rewrote every script.

At the end of the first season, Sherman-Palladino was tired. She begged her husband, Dan, who was working on the Fox comedy *Family Guy*, to join her as an executive producer. "I told him, otherwise you're going to be a widower. So he did. Once he came over, I had at least one other person who knew how to write the show," she chuckles, then adds darkly, "but there was a trail of tears from the writers we fired. We fired playwrights and award winners; we fired the best."

Among those was Jenji Kohan, who went on to create *Weeds* and *Orange Is the New Black*. She wrote the first-season *Gilmore* episode in which Rory and Dean sneak a tender first kiss in the supermarket aisle and she flees holding a box of cornstarch. ("I got kissed—and I shoplifted!" Rory trills afterward.) "It was a situation in which the showrunner didn't want a [writing] staff, and it was being forced on her," Kohan recalls, with no trace of bitterness. "I took the checks, but it was very unpleasant to be in there, because you are fighting an uphill battle with everything. I have a lot of empathy for Amy; she wanted to do it herself with her husband and maybe one or two others, and she did not think that other people could deliver her vision the way she did."

When I ask Sherman-Palladino if she ever posted a list of enemies à la Roseanne Barr, she replies, "I didn't have an enemies list on the wall. Not *officially*." I wait for a sly grin to follow, but instead, she takes a sip of her drink.

Lauren Graham says, "I don't know what went on in the writers' room, but . . . over time, it seemed like Amy and Dan wrote more and more episodes and directed more and more of them. There was an evolution of 'I like this done a certain way, so why don't I just do it?'" Although the couple worked symbiotically, Amy was often tied up with casting, directing, editing, and dealing with executives or production issues, while Dan tended to run the writers' room because, Sherman-Palladino admits, "He was more patient. I would say, 'Let me just rewrite it!' He would say, 'Let me try to get them closer to what you want.' Which is a real art."

Sherman-Palladino's sensibility pulsed at the heart of the show, which meant that every word of each script ultimately went through her hands. That could be frustrating for writers. "Amy understood what made that show, and it was *her voice*," says Jane Espenson, who came to *Gilmore Girls* after writing for *Buffy the Vampire Slayer*. "So, no matter what you turned in, she was going to rewrite it in her voice. It was very hard to get dialogue on the air." Sheila R. Lawrence, who worked on *Gilmore Girls* and later on Sherman-Palladino's series *Bunheads*, notes that writers nevertheless had huge input into the show's structure, plot, and details. "Because we had such a small staff and because it was such a personal show, we all had our handprints on it in a weird way. On every episode of *Gilmore*, there would be a little moment or a story line that came out of one of the writers' personal lives. Dan and Amy were both really great at mining the embarrassing, horrible things that happen in your life and making them happen to Rory, for instance."

Sometimes it seemed that Sherman-Palladino's ambition outstretched her resources. Hours were hellish on *Gilmore Girls,* and the show ran on a shoestring compared to network series on which she'd previously worked. She had definite ideas of how she wanted everything to look and sound, but not always enough experience to know how to achieve perfection: "I quickly learned, you have to *ask* for snow! We were supposed to be set in Connecticut, so you just *assume* that there's going to be snow available. But nope, you have to negotiate for snow."

Then there was the search for directors who weren't "whiny little baby men," in Sherman-Palladino's words. "The misogyny was really bad that first year." Still, she concedes that some of this early conflict may have stemmed from misunderstandings. "I came from sitcoms, and in sitcoms the writer is king. I didn't understand that the director of drama has a say. And there was a lot of tension because I didn't know shit about the camera, but I knew what I wanted." More than a third of the series' original episodes would eventually be directed by women—including fifteen by Sherman-Palladino herself.

She found a directing mentor in Lesli Linka Glatter, who had directed *Twin Peaks*, helmed the *Gilmore Girls* pilot, and later went on to run *Homeland*. "Lesli is the one who taught me about walk and talks," Sherman-Palladino says. "She is a dancer, and she moves that camera so beautifully." Linka Glatter helped to create the show's swift-moving visual style. But to begin with, Sherman-Palladino drove her nuts. "She would yell 'cut' and then run away from me. And then I would run after her. After a while, it got kind of funny, because she would say 'cut,' and we would both run." Sherman-Palladino waves her arms around in a mock sprint. "To me, that's what the creative process is all about: it's supposed to be a rip-roaring 'I hate you! I love you!' When you work with people who want the quality to be as good as you want it, everybody is going to fight to make it the best it can be."

It took a while before Sherman-Palladino felt the set belonged to her. "If you're a woman and you're too aggressive, you are [seen as] a bitch. You might as well own that. I don't know any other way to do it. At the end of the day, if you haven't taken that final cut in the editing room and you haven't placed the music and you haven't been in that sound mix, I don't know how you call it your show."

Scheduled head-to-head on Thursday nights against ratings monster *Friends*, the series almost seemed like a sacrificial lamb. While *Gilmore Girls* pulled in an average of 3.6 million viewers an episode that first season, *Friends* approached 23 million. (A *MADtv* parody of the show titled *Gabmore Girls* later teased, "It's number ninety-two in the ratings, but that's number one for the WB!")

Five years before, *My So-Called Life*, a series about a smart teenage girl, co-created by Winnie Holzman, had also gone up against *Friends*, only to face cancellation after just nineteen episodes. ABC's Stu Bloomberg told the *Los Angeles Times* in 1995 that the problem with *My So-Called Life* was that "it only got teenage girls." Yet within just a few years, that same young female demographic had become a creative and consumer powerhouse, buoying the success of *Sassy* magazine and the Spice Girls. In 1997, Nick Bennett of brand design agency nickandpaul predicted a girl-power gold rush as corporations homed in on this burgeoning market of single eighteen- to thirty-four-year-olds: "You'll start to see loads of products that reflect this new idea of femaleness. That's what everyone's salivating to tap into."

The WB was perfectly poised to serve young female entertainment refugees with *Felicity* and *Buffy*, but it also needed to raise itself from its dregs as the number six broadcast network (out of six). Appealing to some male viewers seemed key. In the prelaunch publicity thrust, Sherman-Palladino assured *Entertainment Weekly*, "It's not just a chick show . . . and I'm adding a couple more guys." Graham joked in the same article that the network hoped male audiences would be interested: "That's why my shorts will be very short." Lorelai did wear some questionable Daisy Dukes in the second episode, in which she takes Rory to her first day at her snobby private school, but this seemed less about sex appeal and more a sign of Lorelai's disorganized and unorthodox mothering style. (She oversleeps on this momentous day, only to realize her more appropriate clothes are at the dry cleaner's.) It was clear, whatever she wore, that Lorelai was a MILF, a slang word that gained currency right around the same time as *Gilmore Girls*'s debut, thanks to the 1999 blockbuster *American Pie*.

"The show is called *Gilmore Girls*; it's about women, and that right there meant you were going to have to *convince* your boyfriend to watch it with you," concedes Graham now. "Maybe some people thought it wasn't for them because it was a girlie show. These are some of the smartest scripts I have ever read, but there was a presumption . . ."—a presumption that relegated a female-driven show to the cultural margins. In many ways, *Gilmore Girls* played up that femme reputation. Gossamer vocals by indie singer-songwriter Sam Phillips washed over every scene. Sherman-Palladino has compared Phillips's "haunted" music to Joan Didion's writing, telling one reporter, "it sounded like it was coming out of the girls' heads. . . . [I]f they had music going in their head during a certain emotional thing in their life, if they were real people, this would be the music that was going on."

There was never much danger of *Gilmore Girls* getting anything but an A on the Bechdel Test. That's the metric invented by cartoonist Alison Bechdel (inspired by comments made by her friend Liz Wallace) for monitoring how often female characters in a fictional world talk together about a subject other than men. Most *Gilmore* scenes bring together two or more women talking among themselves. Lorelai banters with Rory and her mom, Emily, but also with chef Sookie; Rory regularly confides in her best pal, Lane Kim (Keiko Agena), and eventually finds kinship with her former rival, the abrasive Paris Geller (Liza Weil). Stars Hollow is also a utopian hive of female enterprise. Mia, who owns the Independence Inn, took in Lorelai as a teenager and mentored her rise from maid to manager; Miss Patty runs the dance studio and hosts town meetings; Gypsy operates the local auto-repair shop; Lane Kim's mother is the proprietor of an antiques shop; and Sophie Bloom (played by singer-songwriter Carole King) is the music-store owner who enables Lane to play drums.

Lorelai's desire for Rory to focus on ambition over romance runs like a spine through the series. Although Lorelai was derailed by her teenage pregnancy and never made it to college, she projects her youthful fantasy of attending Harvard onto her kid. Rory surprises everyone by picking Yale instead, and then rebels against her mother's aspirations later by (briefly) dropping out of school, choosing instead to organize society parties, live with her grandparents, and get entangled with wealthy playboy Logan (Matt Czuchry). This monied and entitled world is everything Lorelai despises. Ultimately, though, Rory's dream is to become a serious reporter. She knows that her codependent relationship with Lorelai could make that problematic: "It's going to be very hard to be Christiane Amanpour broadcasting live from a foxhole in Tehran with my mommy." Amanpour eventually made a cameo on the show, as did former secretary of state Madeleine Albright—the latter in a dream sequence in which she plays Lorelai snuggling in bed with Rory, telling her the story of her birth.

Gilmore Girls's emphasis on female power remains consistent but complex. In the second season, Paris—after discovering that students find her ultracompetent but unlikable, à la Hillary Clinton—asks Rory to be her running mate in the high school presidential election. "People think *you* are nice," Paris tells Rory, obviously disgusted. The two girls forge a winning *Odd Couple* alliance that continues at college, where both women work at the *Yale Daily News*. Unsurprisingly, Paris's reign as editor in chief is harsh. "The work will be hard," she declares in a speech intended to rally the troops. "It has to be hard. Nothing less than perfect will be tolerated. Please remember that I am your editor, I am not your mother."

That sounds a bit like a speech Sherman-Palladino herself might have delivered. The same perfectionism that made her a demanding boss also made her a prickly employee. "Once a week, I got a call saying, 'We're going to fire you. We are not happy with what you're doing. You're not taking our notes, blah blah blah,'" Sherman-Palladino says, pulling her knees up to her chest. "Finally, I said, 'You can fire me or you cannot ever call me again. Those are your two choices, because it is like talking to my mother once a week. I am sorry you are tragically disappointed, but I am working twenty-four hours a day, seven days a week, and I literally can't work any harder than I am.'"

The WB's platonic ideal of a show was *Dawson's Creek*, and Sherman-Palladino says they didn't understand her less-plot-driven style of storytelling: "Their stuff was very soapy; it was very angsty . . . lots of hugs and tears. They were used to shows with very short scenes. My pace freaked them out, and my style of shooting freaked them out because I don't like close-ups, and everything they do is a close-up." Rumors circulated that the studio was considering firing Sherman-Palladino.

By its third season, *Gilmore Girls*'s ratings had improved slightly, and critics began to praise the show as a hidden gem. But Sherman-Palladino's perfectionism was resulting in long hours and much ingenuity on the part of the crew. In 2004, she told me that she had "issues with letting go. Dan and I spend so much time making sure details are perfect." She added that her talented crew was accustomed to rush commands: "We call at midnight saying, 'We need a library tomorrow!' and our set person is like, 'Oh . . . kay.' It's controlled chaos, but it really works."

Even today Lauren Graham sounds a little weary as she admits, "It was *grueling* —which I hate to say, because the show itself had such a buoyant quality. But the language and the length of the scenes and the athleticism that it takes to sustain a sentence that long is unlike most television. It's more like theater. And then, add to that filming a ten-page scene in one take, while walking and talking . . . So, yeah, those hours were insane."

Sherman-Palladino also had a notorious habit of distributing scripts at the last minute. "We would get scripts late, like the morning of," says Graham. "And if you get scripts the morning of, if they have written a scene where an entire replica of the town carved in cheese is sitting on the dinner table—you can't make that in a morning!" Several staffers pinpointed the late delivery of scripts as a wily tactic for ducking network feedback, something that dawned on Graham only retroactively: "Years later, I read an Aaron Sorkin interview where he said, 'I turn my script in late because then, what are they going to do about it?' "

A number of *Gilmore* staffers acknowledge that Sherman-Palladino had a reputation for being "difficult" or "volatile." After working with her on both *Gilmore* and *Bunheads*, however, writer Sheila R. Lawrence marvels at "the things she pulls off. Not just in terms of her creative vision, but I saw her with the people on set, navigating disagreements between the [director of photography] and the set designer or whatever. She was really good at mediating and somehow making everyone feel good and heard and getting things done. People can't keep fighting if she is making them laugh."

Further tensions flared over a possible spin-off featuring Rory's roguish boyfriend Jess, played by heartthrob Milo Ventimiglia. *Windward Circle*, as the series was named, never made it to air, except for the pilot, which ran as a regular *Gilmore Girls* episode in season three. But when Sherman-Palladino had pointed to the importance of male characters in the initial publicity push for *Gilmore Girls*, she wasn't being disingenuous. Female characters were the foundation of the series, in quite a revolutionary way for television, but they did not dwell in an estrogen-only universe. Luke, Jess, Dean, Richard Gilmore—all played nuanced supporting roles in the show over its seven seasons, along with Rory's dad, Christopher; inn colleague Michel; Rory's college beau, Logan; and even Paris's boyfriend, Doyle (played by Danny Strong, who went on to write the movies *Game Change* and *The Butler*, as well as co-create the TV blockbuster *Empire*).

In fact, when Netflix announced a reboot that would pick up in the present day, much of the Internet chatter surrounded the Gilmores' guys. The series had ended abruptly with Luke and Lorelai in turmoil, and with Rory rejecting a proposal from Logan to focus on journalism while still harboring feelings for old loves Dean and Jess. So which guy did Rory ultimately choose? During a live cast reunion at Austin's ATX Television Festival, actors Jared Padalecki (Dean) and Matt Czuchry (Logan) both professed to be on Team Jess. (That was the cool choice: mischievous but literary, Jess once pilfered Rory's copy of Allen Ginsberg's *Howl* from her bedroom and then returned it helpfully annotated for her.)

Romantic plotlines propelled *Gilmore Girls* forward, but they were also one of the most traditional aspects of the show. The sexual tension of the "Will they or won't they?" relationship is a TV staple, whether it's David and Maddie in *Moonlighting*, Sam and Diane in *Cheers*, or Mulder and Scully in *The X-Files*. The first time we see Luke and Lorelai together, she is begging him for a fifth cup of coffee in his diner, and he is lightly negging her: "Junkie!" Later in the first season, he abruptly asks Lorelai to marry him. "What?" she says, taken aback. "Just looking for something to shut you up," he snaps, not unkindly.

Sherman-Palladino took great care in building Luke into a grouchy but chivalrous mensch worthy of Lorelai. He's a flannel-shirted fantasy who can stand up to Lorelai but also give her what she needs: coffee, pie, more coffee, clever repartee, home repairs, emotional support, and space to do her own thing. Luke and Lorelai bumped up against each other for four seasons, their friendship deepening even as other, ill-advised affairs kept them apart. When Lorelai gets engaged to someone else, Luke builds her a chuppah, a Jewish wedding canopy. (None of the characters is Jewish, but Sherman-Palladino practiced a version of the old Hollywood adage "Write Yiddish, cast British." Lorelai's most beloved catchphrase is the Yiddish-inflected "Oy with the poodles already!") The episode ends with the two of them standing under the chuppah in her yard—a heavy hint of things to come, though it takes several more seasons for Lorelai to realize she loves Luke. When she finally does, their awkward courting ends in a deliciously romantic moonlit scene outside Lorelai's newly opened inn. But right in the middle of their first kiss, a bloodcurdling shriek rings out, and a stark-naked Kirk runs past the couple in the grip of one of his night terrors, stripping away any trace of sappiness from the season four finale.

Unlike so many pop-culture stories in which the love-fixated woman chases the commitment-averse man, Lorelai is just as ambivalent as Luke. "These are two people who've been single for a very long time; they've never been married and they're very independent," Sherman-Palladino told me back in 2004, "so commingling isn't necessarily going to be the easiest thing on the face of this earth."

After a ratings dip in season four, Sherman-Palladino says, executives threatened to cancel the show. Rory was packing up to go to Yale, pulling apart the core mother-daughter duo; the two women would have to practice their speed banter by email and telephone henceforth. Sherman-Palladino says she had always planned to take the show through Rory's college years, to depict the young woman stumbling toward independence. The show-runner stood her ground. "If you know where your story is going, and you know it's right, they are paying you a lot of money to disagree with them," she says now with a shrug. "You've got to be willing to be fired."

By 2005, a broader audience was discovering the show's charms, not least because of its dense web of pop-culture references. Characters rattled off obscure bands, literary references, and political trivia as if there might be a quiz at the end of each episode—details that delighted the newly blog-riddled Internet. (Blogger began just a year before *Gilmore Girls* premiered, and Television Without Pity, the site that pioneered TV recapping, emerged out of a *Dawson's Creek* fan blog in 2002.)

While the series was deepening its cultural credibility, *Gilmore Girls*'s cast and crew were growing weary by season six. The ensemble nature of the series had strengthened over the years, as Stars Hollow became a vaguely multicultural utopia with characters of various ages, races, and sizes. That had taken some of the pressure off Graham and Bledel—but not quite enough.

"We were so tired, the three of us, we were ready to kill each other," Sherman-Palladino says with a sigh. The actresses were unhappy enough that Amy and Dan tried to persuade the studio to pay for a second camera unit to shorten work hours; they also pushed for more personnel and a promise of two more seasons—they were working on one-year contracts—but to no avail. Tired of waiting, the showrunners packed up their offices and drove off the lot. On April 20, 2006, a press release announced that Amy Sherman-Palladino and Daniel Palladino had chosen to leave the show.

"It was my intention to come back, and the deals got fucked up, and I think everyone was a little taken by surprise," Sherman-Palladino confesses. Many crew members didn't find out until the hiatus between the sixth and seventh seasons. "We were all devastated," says casting director Mara Casey. "That was just a lack of respect toward Amy and Dan [by the network]. I don't know how long that hurt her."

The series carried on for one more season, under the aegis of David Rosenthal and other writers the Sherman-Palladinos had trained. The trademark patter continued in season seven, Luke and Lorelai fought and made up and fought again, and Rory struggled to regain her self-confidence after a season where she'd wandered off course. Casey says, "We continued to try to build the world as it was presented to us, but it was . . . *odd*." Something was clearly missing: Amy Sherman-Palladino's voice. For viewers at home, it was like watching familiar bodies occupied by foreign spirits.

"I was aware in our final season, as good as the writing was at times, it just wasn't the same," Lauren Graham suggests gently. She demanded a producer credit and began to take a more active role in the show that year, which would help her pursue writing and producing projects of her own down the line. Graham says it was ultimately a combination of "fatigue and the feeling that this wasn't the material we started with" that led her and Bledel to turn down sizable raises to stay on for an eighth season.

"You have to be young and a little bit naïve to have such artistic integrity," she continues. "People were mad [at us], other cast members . . . but I didn't know until later. As you get older in this career, you realize it's not going to kill you probably to stay on the show one more year. But at the time, I just thought that to stay could actually diminish the memory of the show and harm it. I really cared about that."

The *Gilmore Girls* finale aired on May 15, 2007, with the town throwing Rory a farewell party as she graduates from Yale and prepares to go on the road to cover Barack Obama's 2008 presidential campaign for an online magazine. With rain threatening to ruin the event, Luke stays up all night sewing together all the neighbors' tarps to make a giant tent, and Kirk presents Rory with a sash made out of his mother's nightgown. The episode put the "sweet" in bittersweet but left many plot elements hanging.

Sherman-Palladino had long dreamed of how she'd end the show, down to the last four words her characters would utter, and could not bear to watch someone else's conclusion. She fantasized about having another shot at wrapping *Gilmore*, but she knew it was a ridiculous dream and moved on to creating a new show for Fox, *The Return of Jezebel James*.

A traditional multicamera sitcom, it starred indie-cool actresses Parker Posey and Lauren Ambrose as estranged sisters who reunite when one asks the other to carry her baby. Before the show had even aired, Posey was complaining to the *New York Times* about the grind: "I'm like a wet rag that's been totally wrung out, stretched, ironed, creased and crumpled and hung out to dry." The show was canceled after just three episodes. Sherman-Palladino returned to the small screen in 2012 with *Bunheads*, an effervescent dramedy about a Vegas showgirl who winds up in a small town teaching little girls ballet. It starred Broadway actress Sutton Foster as Michelle, an amalgam of Lorelai and Miss Patty, with Kelly Bishop as her WASP-ish mother-in-law and banter companion. Despite adoration from fans and critics alike, ABC Family pulled the plug on *Bunheads* after only eighteen episodes.

Meanwhile, the legend of *Gilmore Girls* extended its reach. ABC Family aired reruns of the series for nearly a decade, snagging new fans who would savor details on fan forums, Tumblr, and podcasts. Sites popped up dedicated to Rory's book choices and the music played on the show. There was even a message-board thread devoted to *Gilmore Girls* food references.

The year 2014 was the big bang for *Gilmore Girls* fandom: that's when Netflix began streaming all seven seasons, introducing Stars Hollow to a new generation of viewers who had been too young to watch the first time around, as well as to those who had previously snubbed it. While the show might have seemed like a nerdy feminist pleasure in 2000, by 2014, nerdiness and feminism had pop culture cachet. Nerd king Stephen Colbert even tweeted the news in September 2014: "Obama brought back the Iraq War AND Gilmore Girls is coming to Netflix!?! It's a #ThrowBackThursday miracle!"

The show proved to be immensely binge-able. Stars Hollow had always been an escapist fantasy of a gentler, smarter, leftier America, but now it had period charm, too. The clock was stopped at a moment just before smartphones and nonstop connectivity. And its dense but meandering style differentiated it from contemporary plot twist–dependent TV.

"*Gilmore Girls* breaks a lot of the rules of drama, but it worked because it felt like real life," *Gilmore* writer Jane Espenson suggests. "Real life isn't structured like drama. It really woke me up to how many rules you can break and still be entertaining."

Fast-forward to 2016, and all those years of Internet rumors and fan fantasies and behind-the-scenes negotiations have resulted in a miracle: *Gilmore Girls* returns from the dead. Shot as four ninety-minute episodes to stream on Netflix, *Gilmore Girls: A Year in the Life* falls somewhere between a TV show, a miniseries, and a movie, and was written and directed entirely by Amy Sherman-Palladino and Dan Palladino, with all the major cast members returning (except Edward Herrmann, who died in 2014).

Lauren Graham's career prospered in the post-*Gilmore* years; she starred in the NBC series *Parenthood*, wrote a novel, and developed her own TV projects. Eager as she was to revisit Stars Hollow, she found returning to the nest disorienting—literally. "They had re-created the sets, but apparently no one had exact measurements of what they were, because why would they? Who ever thought we would come back?" she burbles rapidly, à la Lorelai. "So, when they remade it, everything was the same but slightly different, which added to the surreal quality."

Instead of feeling daunted by the long swathes of walky-talky dialogue requiring word-perfect delivery, Graham now craved them. "Before, I sometimes felt the structure was really holding me back, but this time, I was just so invigorated by it." She says that Sherman-Palladino used to joke about giving Lorelai the longest monologue in television history. In the final episode of *A Year in the Life*, Graham says proudly, she has a speech "as long as I have ever spoken on TV."

It comes after Lorelai has left Stars Hollow to go on a wilderness trek inspired by Cheryl Strayed's book *Wild*, hoping to untangle feelings about Luke and grief over the death of her emotionally withholding father. She calls her mother to relate a happy memory of Richard Gilmore from her childhood. Lorelai recalls playing hooky after a boy broke her heart; her dad caught her sitting alone in the mall, crying. "I waited for him to yell at me, to punish me, to ground me forever. To tell me how disappointed he was in me, and nothing came. And finally, I got up enough courage to look up at him, and he was standing there with a pretzel. A giant pretzel covered in mustard." That scene reminds its audience how masterfully *Gilmore Girls* evokes ingrown family traumas—and of course, how integral food is to their relationships.

A Year in the Life packs a full season's worth of Gilmore-ishness into that quartet of episodes. Sherman-Palladino indulges her love of musicals with a show-within-the-show (featuring *Bunheads* star Sutton Foster) and the dance-club scene whose rehearsal I witnessed. There's Kirk screening his independent film and walking his pet pig; Lane's band, Hep Alien, playing a quick set; and a stream of references and cameos that only a pop culture obsessive could digest. Finally, at the end of the reboot, are Sherman-Palladino's long-awaited four final words, which bring the series back to its beginnings in an elegant narrative loop that nevertheless leaves us in a bleaker place.

Graham was relieved that the reboot stayed true to the show's original approach of keeping the women's emotional lives central rather than fixating on romance. "Who the guys were—that was secondary," she insists. "And it's not about 'Can I have it all?,' either. Lorelai has a career, she has relationships, she has her daughter, she has her family. It's progressive without being purposeful about it. It just *is*."

The question of class always lurked in the background of *Gilmore Girls*. Unlike Roseanne Conner, Lorelai Gilmore has a financial safety net if she needs one, but she despises her parents' entitled world and proudly prefers to pay her own way. Whereas Rory has always leaned in the opposite direction: tempted by luxury, her passion for journalism and an independent career seems to be wavering. Once the show's dreamy darling, Rory now teeters on the verge of unlikability—a clever reversal that feels very contemporary.

Casting director Jami Rudofsky, who returned to work on *A Year in the Life*, says that many of the stresses that haunted the original production didn't come into play this time. The whole script was written before shooting started, for instance, so there was no last-second hustle. More important, she says, "Netflix and everyone know it is Amy's vision, and I think they approved every single actor we sent forward. It was like, 'If Amy wants it, great! We know she knows what she is doing.'" And though Sherman-Palladino was managing every element of the production, Rudofsky saw a mellower showrunner. "Amy is coming to it from a different place, of having a second chance."

Graham felt this very profoundly while filming the reboot. "Sometimes you just get *one*. And when you are in the thick of trying to build a career, you might not even realize you are *in the one*." Thinking of how jubilant the Palladinos looked on set watching their characters bolt back to life, I ask Graham if she had noticed a change in their manner. "Oh, they were so happy!" she exclaims, laughing as she recalls a scene in which Sherman-Palladino made Sean Gunn, as Kirk, chase his pig down the street over and over in the middle of the night.

"On the one hand, Amy and Dan are such tough, cynical New Yorkers, and on the other hand, they are watching pigs run down the street and creating this fantasy town where everyone can eat as much junk food as they want. It's nostalgic for . . . for I don't even know what. These characters are hardly ever on their phones, they don't use technology; it's like another time. And thank God. It's her world and we just live in it."

CHAPTER 4

The Vajayjay Monologues:
The Prime-Time Empire of Shonda Rhimes

Shonda Rhimes and Betsy Beers, the masterminds of Shondaland,
seen here in January 2006.

The intersection of Sunset Boulevard and Gower Street was once a power center in Hollywood. Today there's little trace of the studio system's golden age, apart from a shopping plaza decked out in faux Wild West trappings, whose name, Gower Gulch, pays tacky tribute to the former cowboys who congregated at Columbia Pictures hoping to be cast as extras in Westerns. But on the exact spot where Columbia's lot once stood are the premises of a new powerhouse of mass entertainment: Shondaland.

Peek through the front gate of Sunset Gower Studios and you'll spy a row of little buildings on what looks like a quaint small-town street; three floors of offices serve as the base camp for all things Shonda Rhimes. Inside, there's a conference room decorated with a poster from *Crossroads*, the 2002 movie Rhimes wrote for Britney Spears; a spare room filled with detritus such as a *Grey's Anatomy* promotional mailbox; a children's playroom; and the *Scandal* writers' room, inside which several people are splayed on sofas.

Venture into the production office's inner sanctum and you see giant white letters that spell out SHONDALAND hanging on the wall, like the giant *M* in Mary Richards's apartment on *The Mary Tyler Moore Show*. To the right is Shonda Rhimes's light-filled office, at one time occupied by actor / director / producer Warren Beatty. To the left is the workplace of Rhimes's producing partner, Betsy Beers, a wood-paneled den built for Columbia founder Harry Cohn. A fan of despots, Cohn was inspired by Italian dictator Benito Mussolini's office, "so overwhelming that anyone entering it would feel simultaneously awestruck and insignificant," as one of the movie mogul's biographers noted. Cohn notoriously bugged his soundstages and kept people waiting for hours. "We try not to adhere to that here in Shondaland," Beers says with a grin while giving me a tour of the office's most notable features, which include a *Faster, Pussycat! Kill! Kill!* lunch box on display.

Beers points out a secret closet in the bathroom, where you can see the old wooden steps Cohn used to usher out showgirls and starlets he'd persuaded to grant him sexual favors. Rhimes and Beers like to joke about which office saw more sexual activity: Beatty's or Cohn's. They also revel in the symbolism of two women, who together have created some of network television's most successful series of the twenty-first century, taking over this temple of testosterone, this bastion of Hollywood machismo.

"I like to think that ol' Harry is rolling over in his grave because a lady with a white shag rug is sitting in his office. There's a little bit of a fuck-you to it that's refreshing."

The story of Shondaland is sprinkled with refreshing fuck-yous. At a time when the number of unconventional female TV characters could be counted on one hand, Rhimes sneaked a whole squadron onto prime time. She feminized medical, political, and legal procedural genres and rehabilitated the much-maligned notion of a "chick show," proving to networks that her "dark and twisty women" (as she likes to call them) could score big. She brought racial diversity and gender politics to mainstream television, but in a way that millions of viewers absorbed as entertainment rather than a civics lesson—something they'd tweet and recap and meme.

Rhimes has carved out a utopian small-screen realm where smart women reign in hospitals, courtrooms, and politics; where glass ceilings don't exist; and where female power is an unremarkable, everyday fact. On a string of hit shows, she has invented characters of all races who can talk as fast as Lorelai, snarl as eloquently as Roseanne, push as hard as Murphy. Shondaland is in some ways as much a wishful-thinking fantasy-reality as *Gilmore Girls*, how the world ought to be rather than is. It is a place where race is not only irrelevant but largely invisible; where women pursue their ambitions without having to sacrifice happiness, while also being allowed to have abortions, marry jobs rather than men, experiment with sexuality, and make mistakes.

Even better, Rhimes and Beers have turned dream-world ideals into reality, creating in Shondaland a multimillion-dollar bubble within the TV industry, an enclave of female writers, female crew, and female showrunners.

A little girl sitting in a kitchen pantry in suburban Chicago conjuring a fantastic kingdom out of canned goods: this is Shonda Rhimes's earliest memory of her childhood. Before she could even write, she dictated her invented tales into a tape recorder. Later, she crammed fabric-covered journals with an onrush of words. Rhimes says these imaginary realms sustained her through a childhood in which she was often the only black girl in her class, not to mention shy and chubby. She scribbled her way through high school and college, emerging from her shell at Dartmouth, where she wrote for the college paper and acted in school plays. In her senior year, she directed a production of *The Colored Museum*, a satirical George C. Wolfe play ransacking African American cultural stereotypes. She graduated with a degree in creative writing.

"I actually thought I was going to be a novelist," Rhimes tells me. "That was my plan. But when I started writing screenplays and scripts, it was like sitting down at a piano and discovering that I already knew how to play," she says slowly. "It felt much more like, 'Oh! *This* is the writing I am supposed to be doing.'"

After Dartmouth, she enrolled in USC film school's graduate screenwriting program, graduating in 1994 with an MFA, a prestigious writing fellowship, and a thesis script, *When Willows Touched*. A gothic drama centered on a dead body rotting in a cornfield and set in the segregated 1930s South, *Willows* beckoned to Will Smith and Jada Pinkett Smith. Will Smith had already served as Rhimes's first patron, commissioning her to direct a short film called *Blossoms and Veils*, with a cast that included Pinkett Smith and Jeffrey Wright. Miramax floated a three-picture deal, starting with plans for Rhimes to write and direct *Willows*. Demi Moore was linked to another Rhimes property, the interracial romantic comedy *Human Seeking Same*, and Miramax had Rhimes working on a screenplay based on the life of writer Hettie Jones, a white denizen of the Beat movement married to poet LeRoi Jones before he remade himself into black nationalist Amiri Baraka. But as so often happens in Hollywood, these prospects vanished into the ether.

Five years after graduating from USC, Rhimes had no movies to show for all her work. Instead, her break came via HBO, when she wrote *Introducing Dorothy Dandridge*, a 1999 biopic starring Halle Berry as the pioneering African American actress. It won five Emmys, and soon Rhimes was brought in to write a sequel to the popular teen flick *The Princess Diaries* and the Britney Spears movie *Crossroads*.

Rhimes's drift from movies to serial television owed something to happenstance—and to the decision, the day after 9/11, to adopt a daughter on her own. (As she told Oprah, the tragedy made her realize that "if the world's going to end tomorrow, there are things I need to do.") She named her baby Harper, after *To Kill a Mockingbird* author Harper Lee. Clueless about the demands of single motherhood, the thirty-two-year-old thought she could work without a nanny. Stuck at home with Harper and a script she had to finish in a month, Rhimes found herself gorging on TV. The year 2001 just happened to be a transformative moment for television: *Buffy the*

Vampire Slayer and *Sex and the City* were in their prime, and *The Sopranos* was just revving up, laying the groundwork for intricate, long-form narratives. Already frustrated by the sluggish pace of the movie industry, Rhimes was inspired by the new possibilities emerging on the small screen.

Her agents made a deal with Touchstone/ABC Studios, which in turn introduced her to Mark Gordon and Betsy Beers, film producers who also saw TV creatively flourishing. In the movie world, says Beers, who is a former actress and improv comedian, "I would work for six or seven years on something and never know if it was going to get made—and if it did, after working for six or seven years, it would open in a weekend and it might tank. Six to seven years *just gone*." But in the TV world, the interval between conception and realization was way shorter. The two women bonded over a similar taste in movies and a simpatico vision, and they set to work on developing a new drama.

Rhimes doesn't remember her first network pitch meeting, because she says there were so many false starts. "My first go-round with doing a show, I pitched every kind of idea you could imagine. I came up with a million different things because I didn't know how any of it worked." She ended up writing a script about four female war correspondents who reported, drank, and sexed their way through conflict zones.

"Both of us came from movies, and neither of us had any concept of budget, so we had very large action sequences that probably would have broken the bank," Beers recalls with a snicker. But the studio had qualms beyond the financial: a war with Iraq was looming, and a series about hard-partying journalists skirted bad taste. The project was dropped, but exec Suzanne Patmore Gibbs encouraged Rhimes to try again.

"The second time around, I was much more targeted," Rhimes says, "because I didn't just want to write a script [that didn't get filmed]. I wanted to make a pilot." So she asked the studio what ABC head honcho Robert Iger wanted, and was told he was interested in that old network TV staple, the medical drama. Rhimes had worked as a candy striper in high school, and she and her sister were addicted to watching real-life medical procedures on the Discovery Channel. "It was perfect because I was a medical junkie, and so it was very simple to do for me. I just said, 'If Bob wants a medical show, I am going to write a medical show.'"

In the spring of 2003, ABC was trapped in third place among the major networks, frantically struggling to improve ratings by dishing out bargain-basement reality fare such as *Extreme Makeover* and *Are You Hot? The Search for America's Sexiest People*. Execs knew they were doomed unless they overhauled their lackluster scripted programming list. Entertainment division chief Susan Lyne had been searching for a "girls' show" for a while, something sexy and character-oriented that could fill the cultural gap left by *Sex and the City*, which had just ended its six-year run on HBO. Although network prime time traditionally attracted more female than male viewers, shows revolving around female characters often seemed to hit a snag.

ABC turned to a script that had been lurking around the studio: *Desperate Housewives*. If done properly, it could merge *Sex and the City* edginess and *Melrose Place* soapiness. Execs hustled to get it ready in time for fall 2004, along with an expensive desert-island science-fiction blockbuster called *Lost*. While ABC fussed over these two flashy Hail Marys, Rhimes and Beers quietly developed their medical drama. One of the working titles for the series was *Surgeons*, but the duo knew what they wanted to call it: *Grey's Anatomy*.

"Nobody was paying attention to us," Rhimes says. "They were making *Lost*, they were making *Desperate Housewives*." When I laugh, she protests using one of *Grey's*'s popular catchphrases. "*Seriously!* We had no pressure whatsoever. Nobody cared. They had the biggest guy show they could think of and the biggest female-skewed show they could think of, and they were perfectly happy. So we were sort of left to do what we wanted to do." Lyne nicknamed their show "My So-Called Surgical Residency," a nod to the brilliant but canceled teen series *My So-Called Life*, and possibly a hint of the network's low expectations for it.

For Beers, the script's appeal hinged on Rhimes's ability to capture the complexities of women's lives within the straitjacket of a prime-time network format. "There was not a lot on TV at that time that reflected who I was, both in terms of the way women were portrayed and the way people in the workplace were portrayed." Beers was thrilled to find a world depicted in which "you could be good at your job, you could be competitive, you could be dark and interesting and still have incredibly good friends. [*Grey's Anatomy*] was all the things you didn't see on a regular basis on TV, a fully rounded world that was diverse and looks like America."

The show pivoted around young surgical intern Meredith Grey, whose intimate, broody voice-overs would frame each episode. Beers and ABC execs liked the idea of putting novices at the drama's core. "If we can find the point of view of people who don't know what they're doing, the audience can relate and be introduced to the [hospital] and the pressures of the profession." In the pilot episode, one of the interns nearly kills a patient during his first attempt at surgery, earning him the nickname 007, as in "licensed to kill." All the series' characters would regularly screw up.

The pilot kicked off, in fact, with Meredith literally *screwing* up: we see her throwing a hunky one-night stand out of her house before setting off to start her new job, where she discovers that cute stranger is her new boss. This so-called slutty behavior worried some TV execs. Beers recalls attending a meeting where she and Rhimes were surrounded by men: "One gentleman in particular who was not responding positively to the *Grey's Anatomy* pilot mentioned that he couldn't understand a woman who was so irresponsible. What kind of woman would ever, ever do that? I raised my hand and said, 'That would be *me*.'"

Beers shakes her wavy blond hair, grinning. "It is astonishing when the [network's] approach is that women don't do that stuff, because women clearly do. I just wanted to have a show on the air that was something I would watch and identify with."

———

At the dawn of the twenty-first century, female TV characters still faced constricted options. Sure, *Gilmore Girls* was upping the ante with its smart-ladies-on-speed aesthetic, but that version of reality kept things relatively sweet and chaste. And certainly *Sex and the City* had vastly expanded TV's notions of female behavior, with Carrie, Miranda, Samantha, and Charlotte obsessively circling quandaries such as love versus lust, commitment versus independence, heels versus flats. But their idea of independence sometimes seemed to boil down to sex, media status, and consumerism. ("I choose my choice!" Charlotte once wailed, defending her decision to quit her job once she got married.) By the time *Sex and the City* ended, the characters' careers had mostly faded into the background of the romantic story lines.

Rhimes wanted her women to *really* have it all, as Helen Gurley Brown had promised: the rampant sex, the good friends, the important job. *Grey's*'s initial quartet of young female doctors—Meredith Grey, Cristina Yang, Izzie Stevens, and Miranda Bailey—were characters built on a bedrock of ambition and competitiveness. This sometimes nudged them outside the boundary line that delimits traditional feminine likability, but these were qualities their creator understood viscerally. In top Stanford medical school graduate Cristina, she created a drily witty, dragon-slaying alter ego who was "larger than life and sure of her genius." For Rhimes, Cristina was a character she would empower to "do and think and live in ways that voiced my dreams." She also embedded shards of herself in Meredith. "I'm not white or blond or thin, but she went to Dartmouth; I went to Dartmouth. She's competitive; I'm competitive. We both have very formidable mothers," Rhimes told an early interviewer.

The women of *Grey's Anatomy* crave experience, jostling over wounded bodies and competing for the most exotic injuries. "It's like candy! But with blood, which is so much better," Cristina yelps, salivating over the victims of a terrible bike accident. She and Meredith quickly recognize in each other sarcastic soul mates who can dispense with niceties and spur each other to be stronger at work and smarter at love.

Beers knew these "twisted sisters" had to be the core of that first season: "I love everything about the relationship between those two women. These two people who are so different in their approach to things are so united in their devotion and their fierce protection of each other. Shonda figures out ways of articulating the feelings we have that we sometimes don't get to see writ large on the screen."

Although Rhimes has become infamous for her shocking cliff-hangers and gasp-inducing plot twists, the most surprising thing about the *Grey's* pilot may be that the big reveal here was not a suspenseful surgery or a romantic clinch; it was a bleak glimpse of Meredith Grey's emotional baggage, in the shape of her mother. Once a brilliant surgeon who reigned supreme at this very hospital, Dr. Ellis Grey was now being engulfed by dementia. "The crushing responsibility of living up to her mother's legacy while her mother is in a diminished capacity—I found that incredibly moving," Beers remembers. "My mother had Alzheimer's, and that was an aspect of the story, to have something going on that so many of us were dealing with at various points of our lives."

Rhimes turned in her pilot script at the very end of 2003. The last show ABC ordered for the fall season, *Grey's* was almost an afterthought.

Rhimes and Beers were like the blind leading the blind into prime time: neither had ever produced a television show. The pair became "very tightly wound around each other" while making those early episodes, recalls Rhimes. They quickly forged a close friendship, a habit of finishing each other's sentences, and a respect for each other's limits. "We always say that only one of us gets to be crazy at a time. Only one of us gets to be ready to quit at a time."

The best part of not knowing the laws of TV was that Rhimes didn't realize she was breaking them. "Any rules that anybody had or any suggestions never actually sank in," she says. "Mainly because I didn't know that I was supposed to take everybody's notes or be afraid that something wasn't going to get made. I was having a ball, writing television felt very natural to me, and I stuck to my guns because I felt like I knew what I wanted." Since Rhimes had no showrunning experience, she was initially paired with executive producer James D. Parriott, who would help steer the writing staff. The very idea of a writers' room was foreign to Rhimes, who had spent years alone at home penning movie screenplays.

"If you didn't come up getting notes and rewriting and learning a healthy television process, you don't know how to do that system," says Krista Vernoff, who had written for *Charmed* and *Wonderfalls* before joining the first season writing staff of *Grey's*. "Shonda had Jim Parriott and me teaching her how to do television. She was always a genius, but she was coming from movies and didn't want to set foot in the writers' room at first. She would hover in the doorway in a state of terror."

Another consequence of Rhimes's innocence was her decision to practice what the industry calls "color-blind casting"—that is, opening up every role to actors of every ethnicity, which resulted in the celebrated diversity of Shondaland, where doctors, lawyers, and politicians come in every racial and gender flavor. "When Shonda wrote a script, there was no description of how anybody was supposed to be cast," Beers remembers. "We just thought, *We want to see actors of every ethnicity*. Later, we found out it was very unusual," she continues, "but [casting director] Linda Lowy thought it was great because, hey, the entire world of actors is open to us."

Lowy specialized in casting movies, but like Rhimes and Beers, she was growing disillusioned with the film world. "It was a time when things were being dumbed down, people were losing financing right and left." Soon Lowy was hunting for actors to fill the halls of Seattle Grace Hospital.

"Shonda said to me point-blank: I am not giving anybody a last name. I want you to cast it the way you see the world. The only thing that I do insist is that the character of [Dr. Miranda] Bailey is an adorable blond Caucasian actress because I want everybody to think she is the cutest little button and then she ends up being this very scary presence to the interns." Lowy initially proposed blond Broadway star Kristin Chenoweth to play Bailey, a surgeon whose nickname is "the Nazi." Around the same time, though, a videotaped audition came in from Chandra Wilson, an African American theater actress who was then appearing in Tony Kushner's play *Caroline, or Change*. Chenoweth was the bigger name, but Wilson, neither blond nor Caucasian, exuded a quiet power. She got the part.

Key to *Grey's Anatomy* was finding the perfect Meredith and Cristina. Ellen Pompeo didn't have to audition; she was offered Meredith after starring in the movie *Moonlight Mile* with Jake Gyllenhaal and testing for another ABC pilot. On the other hand, casting Cristina turned into a traumatic experience for Rhimes, who didn't feel comfortable with the actress the studio was pushing. The leap from screenwriter to network showrunner was huge, Rhimes realized, requiring endless decisions and the willingness to fight for each one. Should she go into battle on behalf of Sandra Oh, a Korean Canadian actress best known for indie films such as *Double Happiness* and *Sideways*?

Casting Oh was a turning point for the future queen of Shondaland, according to Lowy. "That was the one where Shonda had to stand up as a first-time showrunner and say, 'I want *her*, that's who I want.'"

While Suzanne Patmore Gibbs and others at ABC championed the show, freshly appointed network president Steve McPherson wasn't convinced. "He said really horrible things to me," Rhimes told one reporter. "I literally started keeping a list of how many times he said a certain swear word to me." McPherson's notes included a request to add a macho dude to the cast, which led to the belated creation of Alex Karev, the swaggering working-class intern played by Justin Chambers. (They shot new footage with him and inserted it into the first episode months after it was originally filmed.) Rhimes recalls further network meddling in the second episode, in which Alex and Cristina compete to see how much bad news they can deliver to patients. Executives were not amused by the showrunner's morbid sense of humor. "Doctors joking about a patient dying or hating a patient was taboo, and I would be like, 'It is not about the patients but how the doctors deal with treating the patients!'" she exclaims. "They have an irreverent view of medicine. That's not crazy; that is human."

Flipping through her copy of the original pilot script of *Surgeons*, Krista Vernoff remembers how unusual Rhimes's writing felt at the time, when *Law & Order*–style procedurals reigned supreme. "It was character-driven at a time when character-driven television had been out of style for many years." Her agent had warned her that the show probably wouldn't get picked up because, as Vernoff says, "Shonda was trying to do something that hadn't been done before: take romantic character dramedy and put it in the medical drama format."

The cast and crew worked punishing hours at the start. "We did sixteen- or seventeen-hour days," Chandra Wilson says with a sigh. "We basically lived here creating this show, finding the tone. We even stopped production at one point in season one in order to retool what the tone of the show was going to be."

The grand launch of *Lost* and then *Desperate Housewives* in the fall of 2004 calmed ABC's ratings panic. *Lost* became the network's top-rated debut since 2000, a record beaten a few weeks later by the *Housewives* premiere. (*Housewives* would go on to be the number four most-watched show of the season, while *Lost* hovered at number thirteen.) Neglected stepsister *Grey's Anatomy* was forced to bide its time in the shadows until Easter Sunday 2005. With little fanfare, it was dropped into the 10:00 p.m. slot after *Housewives* as a temporary midseason replacement for another new series, *Boston Legal*.

Initial reviews for *Grey's Anatomy* were underwhelming: Alessandra Stanley of the *New York Times* dubbed it "a Girl Power version of *ER*," while the *Los Angeles Times*'s Paul Brownfield carped that the show "manages to combine *Sex and the City*, *CSI*, *ER* and *The Paper Chase*, wrapped in the kind of alt-rock soundtrack that beckons near the register at Pottery Barn." Worst was *Washington Post*'s Tom Shales, who damned it as "a casserole made of equal parts ham and corn" but condescendingly added that Ellen Pompeo "has one of the sunniest smiles ever seen in a TV medical show."

It's not surprising that critics were puzzled by the series; while *Grey's Anatomy* came dressed as a hospital procedural, Rhimes's intentions were quite different. Woven into graphic medical plot points were snappy dialogue, indie rock by the likes of Rilo Kiley and Tegan and Sara, and small-scale relationship story lines that wouldn't have been out of place on *Gilmore Girls*. Patients' ailments were important mainly for the way they touched on the doctors' turbulent lives.

Grey's's fast-moving slipstream of emotional and physical crises became a form of televisual crack. With more people joining the army of the addicted every episode, the network decided to keep the series on for the rest of the season. This gave the writers more episodes in which to build up the relationships among the interns and crank up the romance between Meredith and her too-good-to-be-true boss, Dr. Derek Shepherd, aka Dr. McDreamy (played by Patrick Dempsey). In the season finale, Rhimes dropped a bomb on Meredith (and viewers) by introducing Dr. Addison Montgomery-Shepherd (Kate Walsh), McDreamy's secret McWife.

By this point, more than twenty-two million people were watching. ABC further stoked the fire with reruns during the summer of 2005, and by the second season that fall, *Grey's Anatomy* had blown up into a pop cultural phenomenon. When ABC gifted *Grey's* with the time slot following the 2006 Super Bowl, Rhimes wrote a two-part nail-biter about a ticking bomb nestled inside a patient's body. That episode pulled in thirty-eight million people—the highest rating for any scripted TV episode since the *Friends* finale a few years before, and an impossibly high number in the more diffuse current landscape.

"By the time we got to season two and then halfway through the Super Bowl episode," Chandra Wilson remembers, "it was like being shot out of a cannon."

Soon, every move the cast made was news, and some surprising moves were made: Isaiah Washington, who played Cristina's love interest Dr. Preston Burke, was accused of using a homophobic slur on set, and after months of bad publicity, ABC announced that he was being cut from the show. Katherine Heigl, who parlayed her role as Izzie into a flourishing movie career, later set off a media firestorm by publicly criticizing the show's writing, suggesting she hadn't put herself forward for an Emmy nomination because the scripts hadn't offered her good enough material to warrant one. *Grey's* had all the hallmarks of a set spinning out of control.

"It's the only time in my career when I've been in the center of a phenomenon like that, where the actors are being chased home by paparazzi and stalked everywhere they go," Vernoff offers, darkly alluding to "mental health issues" among some of the cast. "It was a lot of drama to navigate."

The success of *Grey's* took the industry's prevailing prejudice that audiences wouldn't watch shows centered on women or people of color and crushed it like a bug.

Rhimes reveled in the show's female appeal. When *Los Angeles Times* reporter Mary McNamara visited with *Grey's* writers at the Prospect Studios in the spring of 2005, Rhimes told her, "The guys [on the writing staff] will groan sometimes and say, 'Oh, man, that is such a chick moment.' And I say, 'Those moments are why I watch television. So it stays.'"

With a writing staff comprising more than twice as many women as men, the male perspective was consistently overruled. "We have male characters doing things that we know for a fact no man would ever do," Parriott told the *Los Angeles Times*. McDreamy, for instance, was a pure fantasy figure. He was designed as a succulent morsel for women to feast upon, Rhimes explained to another reporter, "so we can stare at our televisions, turn to our boyfriends, and say, 'Why don't you talk to me like that?'"

Inevitably this led to *Grey's* being derided as the TV version of chick lit: a frothy guilty pleasure. There was plenty of froth, to be sure, along with a soapy stream of tragedies and traumas. Over the years, Meredith removed that live bomb from the Super Bowl patient's body; drowned and was resuscitated; survived a plane crash, a miscarriage, and a C-section; and witnessed a mass shooting in which her husband was injured and her colleagues killed. But Rhimes devised *Grey's* as a kind of Rube Goldbergian pleasure-delivery contraption: a tightly structured, elegantly written drama that delivered sexy thrills at regular intervals for more than a decade while sneaking in ideas about gender, sexuality, and race.

One early battle was over the word *vagina*. Krista Vernoff recalls writing a second-season episode in which ob-gyn Addison explains to a patient how she's going to check her cervical dilation. But the Standards and Practices department at ABC wouldn't let them use the V-word. "I was saying to the woman in broadcast standards, 'This is a doctor! It's anatomy!' I got in a screaming fight with her, and I went to Shonda, ranting," says Vernoff. But instead of going to war over the word, Rhimes told Vernoff that they should gather all the assistants. "We are going to come up with a word that sounds dirtier than *vagina* but that is a nonsense word. If it's a nonsense word, they can't reject it." Staffer Blythe Robe suggested *vajayjay*. Rhimes used it in the episode that aired after the Super Bowl, turning the euphemism into a pop phenomenon. Eventually, they did persuade the network to let them use the actual anatomical term.

"The real cultural phenomenon is that we legitimized and normalized the use of the word *vagina*," Vernoff says. "You could say *penis* in a medical context in TV without anybody raising a flag, but you couldn't say *vagina*. . . . It really truly is the thing in my career I'm most proud of, so that more and more people are raising [daughters] to call their anatomy by its proper name and not thinking of it as a dirty word."

Abortion was a taboo topic that network showrunners nervously avoided (the legendary exception being a 1972 episode of *Maude*, aired just before the passage of *Roe v. Wade*). Rhimes tiptoed around the danger zone at the end of season one when Cristina's secret affair with Dr. Burke results in pregnancy. Convinced there is no room for a child in her life, she decides on an abortion. She cements her friendship with Meredith by designating Grey as her emergency contact for the clinic: "I put your name down," says Cristina. "You're my person."

You're my person—the simple line acknowledged the women's deepening bond with an electricity reminiscent of a romantic couple's first admission of love. It became a catchphrase for single women everywhere.

In the end, however, Cristina didn't need the abortion; she collapsed from an ectopic miscarriage. Rhimes tells me the network didn't exactly forbid abortion: "We hadn't gotten to the 'you can't' stage yet, but . . . " She pauses. "In the early days, everything was a discussion. Everything was a giant ball being pushed uphill because, horrifyingly enough to me, *nothing* had been done before. It was sort of appalling. That the women weren't nice, that the women weren't kind, that the women were competitive—there were so many things that were issues. I decided, *I am not even going to fight for abortion right now. I just can't. The battle will exhaust me too much.*"

Rhimes's retreat was temporary, however. Years later, in season eight, Cristina—now married, but as single-mindedly fixated on work as ever—again gets pregnant, this time with her husband, Dr. Owen Hunt. Owen and Meredith both try to persuade her to embrace motherhood, but she is steadfast. "I need you to get this," she tells them. They do. Meredith, in particular, empathizes that "the guilt of resenting her own kid" would only "eat her alive." And Cristina goes through with the termination. Emotional aftershocks ripple through her marriage, but she is actually allowed to "choose her choice" and live with it.

"We finally reached a point in the show where I felt like, *I am going to tell the story that needs to be told and nobody is going to tell me no,*" Rhimes says crisply. "By that point, nobody said a word. I think it was not just because I had the capital but because the world of television and the world around us had progressed as well."

Rhimes had walked onto the *Grey's* set as an introverted writer, learning to juggle the demands of a network showrunner on the fly. The swarm of tasks and pressures made her miserable in the early years. Beers dropped other projects and became Rhimes's producing partner at Shondaland. "I get to have a purely creative mind and focus on the actors and the writing and talking to the directors and the edit and songs," says Rhimes. "And Betsy runs all of the other pieces."

Almost as soon as they mastered running a single show, the duo began talking about spinning off another. Dr. Addison Montgomery-Shepherd had been intended as a short-lived pot stirrer, but Walsh had rendered her character both funny and sympathetic. A May 2007 episode of *Grey's* served as a "backdoor" pilot for *Private Practice*, a new series with the now-divorced Addison joining a set of older colleagues—sophisticated, sexy, and multiracial doctors, as played by Taye Diggs, Amy Brenneman, Merrin Dungey (soon replaced by Audra McDonald), and Tim Daly—at a Santa Monica clinic. Where *Grey's Anatomy* was focused on "young people who don't have any idea how to do their jobs or how to live their lives," says Beers, the thirty-somethings of *Private Practice* had reached "the next stage of proficiency as people."

Some fans and reviewers negatively compared Rhimes's new slate of *Private* characters to her fierce *Grey's* creations, and there was some internal confusion over what this new show should be. "I think the network was hoping for *Grey's Anatomy: SVU*," Beers admitted a few years later at a public event—in other words, a straight spin-off. "We sort of rushed it into production without having clear ideas as to what we wanted to say. Initially, the show really suffered for it." Even ABC executive Suzanne Patmore Gibbs noted at the time that "we sort of lost sight of Addison as the kick-ass surgeon." But fate interceded in the form of the November 2007 writers' strike, which halted production on the series just nine episodes into what should have been a twenty-five-episode season, allowing them time to correct course. Beers noted that "we took a beat to really examine why we wanted to make it in the first place. And the show about moral and ethical dilemmas that we all face was born." Moving *Private Practice* into the time slot following *Grey's Anatomy* and allowing for some crossover episodes with *Grey's* further shored up the fledgling show's ratings. By the end of season two, Addison and friends had an average of more than nine million viewers.

Grey's and *Private* were filmed in two separate locations across LA—and dashing between them seemed to tax Rhimes's energy. As much as she still thought of herself as an introverted writer, she was now a powerful figure with a sprawling staff and enormous responsibilities.

"Shonda was not in the room very much," says Sheila R. Lawrence, the former *Gilmore Girls* writer who later worked on *Private Practice*. "She would come in a few days a week and hear pitches and tell us how bad they were and then leave again. There is a process on her shows where the very first draft of a script is read aloud with all the writers around the table and then Shonda sits in judgment of it and gives you all of her notes right there on the fly. It was excruciating." Worse, she says, was the intimidation factor: "Maybe she would be surprised by how much fear there was, but when you'd get the word that Shonda was coming to the office, it was like: 'Get that dog out of here; she hates dogs! Move the couch; she doesn't want her back to the window!' People just freaked out."

Vernoff suggests that those who succeed in Shondaland have strong enough personalities to spar with the boss. "Shonda wants you to give her a good fight, but you have to be brave to rise to the occasion of her personality," she says fondly. Rhimes instituted a post-Heigl "no assholes" policy, and those who clicked with her often stayed in Shondaland for many years, making the place feel like an extended family. Writers, actors, and crew members often moved from show to show or developed their own series—for example, Peter Nowalk, who started as an assistant on *Grey's* and went on to create *How to Get Away with Murder*. Actors interested in expanding their skill sets were allowed to direct episodes; Chandra Wilson went on to become one of *Grey's Anatomy's* most prolific directors.

Wilson arrived at Shondaland as much of a TV novice as her bosses, and she watched Rhimes learn to steer a multimillion-dollar business. "She had to figure out 'Oh, I'm a manager? People are looking to me because I am in charge?'" Wilson recalls vividly the day she went to Rhimes to tell her she was pregnant, assuming the show would need to write off her character. "Shonda said, 'What do you think I'm going to do, *fire you*?'" Wilson shrieks incredulously. Instead, the showrunner declared that Dr. Miranda Bailey would also get pregnant. (Of course, being Shondaland, Bailey goes into labor the same day her husband is injured in a terrible car crash.)

Wilson's real pregnancy inspired a plotline that would deepen her character and allow the show to delve into the complications of working motherhood, something Rhimes understood intimately. "Quite a few times, Bailey's crisis has been *How do I manage all these things?*" Wilson says. "*Is it fair that I have ambition when I am a mom and when I am a wife?* Which is all stuff I know Shonda has been faced with, too. She is writing it as she is living it."

Rhimes put her principles to work behind the scenes, creating what Wilson describes as a model for a parent-friendly workplace. Shondaland soon had a thriving on-site playroom. Her attitude, Wilson says, is "It's not about what other shows do; it's about what I believe in—so this is what we are going to do."

———————

While *Grey's* was progressive in its attitudes toward gender and LGBTQ themes—see the lavish wedding of lesbians Callie and Arizona at a moment when gay marriage was in legal dispute—there was one issue the show's characters rarely addressed on-screen: race. Black, Latino, and Asian American doctors thrived (or didn't) on the basis of their brilliance, unimpeded by discrimination or prejudice. Hardly anyone sat around in the break room kibitzing about workplace bias or complications stemming from interracial dating. As Rhimes once told the *New York Times*, she and her friends were "post-civil rights, post-feminist babies, and we take it for granted we live in a diverse world." This was the world her doctor characters would inhabit: a meritocracy where talent triumphs.

The reality of television is that skin color still counts in Hollywood far more than the decades of lip service paid to ideals of diversity would suggest. Most nonwhite actors are consigned to sassy sidekick or one-line token status—if they're lucky. A report by the Ralph J. Bunche Center for African American Studies at UCLA found that white actors nabbed 76 percent of the scripted broadcast TV roles in the 2014/15 season, and 79 percent of cable and 74 percent of digitally streamed roles. Compared to this decidedly uneven playing field, Shondaland looks like the promised land, a world where people of all hues work together and sleep together without comment or conflict.

The first time Chandra Wilson watched the *Grey's* pilot, she says, "I was like, wow, there is something so familiar about the show, but I couldn't figure out what it was. I don't think it even occurred to me when we were shooting that it was me and Isaiah and Sandra all on the same screen, you know what I mean? That shouldn't have been abnormal, but until you saw it on television, you didn't realize how much you missed it."

This was a huge step forward for TV, and a breakthrough for actors accustomed to auditioning only for peripheral roles flagged for stereotypical ethnic "types." Shondaland series created more complex roles for actors of color than pretty much any other network TV shows. Yet some critics worried that its color-blind casting fed into an assimilationist impulse to erase cultural specificity. For instance, African American scholar Kristen J. Warner, in her book *The Cultural Politics of Colorblind TV Casting*, argues that this kind of casting allows the entertainment industry to create the appearance of equal opportunity without the risk of alienating white mainstream viewers with content too far outside their own experience. In other words, color-blind casting fosters diversity in terms of hiring practices, but it goes only so far if the writing doesn't flesh out a truly diverse world in which the protagonists experience reality differently, because factors such as socioeconomics and racial bias restrict opportunity and affect life outcomes.

Although Cristina is played by Sandra Oh, an actress of Korean ethnicity, the character doesn't particularly identify as Asian American. A season-two episode introducing Cristina's mother hinted at the reason for this: she raised her daughter in the Jewish faith of her second husband, a Beverly Hills oral surgeon. It's a fascinating tidbit, but one that never leads to much deeper exploration. Sandra Oh has confessed to finding her character's dearth of cultural specificity frustrating. "It bummed me out because I feel like this could be a great story idea, or even like a joke. But [*Grey's Anatomy's* producers] would not go for it, because it was a show choice," she told the magazine *KoreAm* after leaving the series in 2014. She continued, "The next step for me is not about portraying how we're the same; it's about portraying our differences, exactly who we are."

Rather than starting with the assumption that each character will be white, the Shondaland casting process is open-ended. The initial character description is a placeholder, says Lowy: "Shonda has a definite idea in her mind of how she sees the characters, but she needs me to bring actors into the room so the wheels start turning with that particular person sitting in front of her. Sometimes when we meet actors, Shonda will remain somewhat quiet because she is thinking about how to write for that person, and Betsy and I will be talking like crazy just to keep that person in the room so Shonda can get the idea of how it can work."

It's not that Rhimes, who directed *The Colored Museum* as a college student and launched her TV career with a biopic of African American actress Dorothy Dandridge, lacks interest in the specifics of black identity. Sometimes she even knit black cultural references into *Grey's*, as when she brought in Diahann Carroll (star of 1968's *Julia* and one of TV history's few black TV heroines) and Richard Roundtree (best known as blaxploitation hero Shaft) to play the parents of Isaiah Washington's Dr. Burke.

But Rhimes chooses not to have her characters defined by race and balks at the "black showrunner" label herself, clearly finding the constant media lip service to something that ought to be standard (i.e., "diversity") frustrating. She shrugs off the idea that she and her team are pushing boundaries, assuring me, "I don't think we are going out on any limbs." In her memoir, *Year of Yes*, Rhimes writes eloquently of being "F.O.D." (short for "first, only, different"): "We all have that same weary look in our eyes. The one that wishes people would stop thinking it remarkable that we can be great at what we do while black, while Asian, while a woman, while Latino, while gay, while a paraplegic, while deaf . . ."

She points to the lunacy of being congratulated for writing characters of all stripes and then treating them "as if they were . . . people."

A brilliant black woman holds the most devastating secrets of the American government in her hands, aiding and bedding the white, married Republican president, who is willing to smother a Supreme Court justice to maintain his power. By his side are a gay White House chief of staff, who hires a hitman to wipe out a former intern who had an affair with the president; a female evangelical vice president who whacked her own gay husband; and a scheming First Lady who will eventually run for president herself.

Strip *Scandal* down to this bare-bones description and it sounds like a joke devised by a political studies professor gone AWOL. It's almost as though Rhimes decided to call Hollywood on its wimpy swipes at diversity—and then upped the ante a thousandfold, placing power in the hands of the most marginalized identities and setting them loose upon the American landscape.

The idea for *Scandal* came out of a 2009 meeting with Judy Smith, a former White House press secretary for George H. W. Bush and political-crisis manager who did image cleanup for people like Monica Lewinsky and for DC mayor Marion Barry. By this point, Rhimes and Beers were developing a variety of new series by other TV writers and had a few missteps under their belts, including the short-lived "medical drama goes abroad" series *Off the Map*. Although fascinated by this "fixer," they let the idea of a series inspired by Smith's career percolate for more than a year.

Olivia Pope, the fictionalized alter ego of Judy Smith, eventually emerged from Rhimes's imagination as an enticingly perverse creature: on the one hand, a righteous avenger on behalf of her clients and the public good; on the other, a woman bedeviled by her love for Mr. Wrong, aka President Fitzgerald Grant. Like Judy Smith, Olivia Pope is African American. This was no small decision: *Scandal* would be the first network drama since 1974's *Get Christie Love!* to feature a black female lead. Just as Judy Smith was one of the few black women to penetrate the inner sanctums of Washington, Olivia Pope would be one of only a few black female characters at the highest echelons of television.

Kerry Washington, best known for playing Ray Charles's wife in the movie *Ray*, won the Olivia Pope role. She says she modeled the ultra-dignified Olivia on several omnicompetent women of her acquaintance, including Judy Smith and Rhimes herself: "[Shonda] is very, very close to her characters. It's actually fun for me to witness the things that she is expressing through Olivia."

Yet there was a problem with walking through the political looking glass: Kerry Washington had ties to the real White House. She had passionately campaigned on behalf of Barack Obama and, in 2009, had been appointed to the President's Committee on the Arts and the Humanities. Washington wanted to make sure there was no confusing *Scandal*'s fictional leader with Obama, or besmirching the reputation of America's first black president. For that reason, President Fitzgerald Grant (aka Fitz) had to be white. According to casting director Linda Lowy, her team didn't need to look very far. Actor and director Tony Goldwyn (who first came to public attention in the 1990 movie *Ghost*) was a familiar face around Shondaland from his stints helming *Grey's Anatomy*. Goldwyn was up for a role in another ABC series but didn't get it. The moment she got word that he was free, Lowy ran to Rhimes's office to make the call. They didn't even bother doing a "chemistry read" with Goldwyn and Washington—they just offered him the presidency.

They also skipped steps when casting the role of Quinn Perkins, a young white woman who would join the team of "Gladiators" at Olivia's crisis-management company, Pope and Associates, to serve as a kind of Alice in Viceland, falling down the rabbit hole of political iniquity along with the viewer. Like Goldwyn, actress Katie Lowes had done some time in Shondaland, with small parts in *Grey's* and *Private Practice*. But she recalls being terrified while reading Quinn's role in front of "the most powerful women in Hollywood." Rhimes told her to say the lines faster. "I am a born and raised New Yorker and I have been told to speak slower my whole life," she says without taking a breath, "but Shonda was essentially creating

'*Scandal* pace,'" the breakneck clip that would define the show, much as it had distinguished *Gilmore Girls*. The decision-making process was just as accelerated. Usually the next step would be multiple auditions and screen tests for network and studio execs, but Rhimes summoned Lowes to inform her that she had the part.

Cast and crew sometimes worked all night on the pilot, taking pains to nail the sumptuous but sordid feel of *Scandal*, as well as that speed-freak pace. "Literally, the first line of the first script is that people need to be talking extraordinarily fast," Rhimes explains, "because these people are *busy* and nobody has time for anything else." Lowy says that, in the early days of the series, Rhimes sat on the set with a stopwatch to clock the dialogue speed.

"Olivia doesn't have time to slow down for everybody else's brains," Rhimes quips, adding, "Kerry always says she made Olivia Pope talk as fast as *I* do."

Like Cristina and Meredith and Bailey, Olivia is driven—and though she calls herself a "white hat" (and dresses in a cream-colored palette of designer clothes), her actual day job requires getting her hands dirty cleaning up the messes made by powerful people. She speaks and moves with velocity and precision, as if to outrun the ethical ambiguity of her actions. Olivia is an outsider playing an insider, and Washington quietly inhabits her character's complexity and confusion. After all, much of the real action happens silently *inside* Olivia, an interiority that's rare in a TV heroine, let alone a black one.

Rhimes expects her actors to speak the words in the scripts exactly as written. In fact, she reveals that she actually made a kind of pact with Washington (and all her actors): "It is not her job to judge her character, or to say, 'I don't think my character would do that.' It is only her job to figure out how and why her character does what she does and make it true." That doesn't mean the actress doesn't have feelings about Olivia's machinations. When Washington read the script revealing that her character had helped rig Fitz's presidency, she cried all the way to work. Olivia Pope would not be a perfect role model; she would be as flawed and broken as *The Sopranos*'s Tony Soprano or *Breaking Bad*'s Walter White.

As with Rhimes's previous dramas, *Scandal* premiered to mixed reviews, many along the lines of Matt Roush's *TV Guide* verdict: "This may not be Peabody [Award] material, but if you like a show that's not afraid to go bananas, this might just be your type of low-hanging fruit." (In fact, *Scandal* went on to win a Peabody and several Emmys.) The early ratings were muted, too, but those numbers rose as the show mastered social media, in part thanks to Kerry Washington, who urged Rhimes to have the entire cast live-tweet each episode's broadcast.

By the spring of 2013, *Scandal* inspired more than one hundred thousand frenzied fan tweets per episode; even black pastors were tweeting about the series to try to connect with vulnerable congregants, as writer Stacia L. Brown pointed out in the *Atlantic*. Pastor Tejado Hanchell tweeted during one episode, "#DearSingleSister You can get free from your 'Fitz,' but you can't do it alone. Seek help."

———

It might have been relatively easy to make racial difference seem irrelevant in the closed circuit of a Seattle hospital or a California clinic. How could that work in a show about a black woman having an affair with a white, married, Republican president?

Rhimes says that she intended her version of DC to be a nightmarish alternate-history doppelgänger of the US capital. "In the sci-fi version of *Scandal*, the Oval Office would literally be built over the Hellmouth, you know what I mean?" she says with a chuckle, referring to the portal to the netherworld in *Buffy the Vampire Slayer*. "We talk about the quest for power being sort of an all-consuming thing that really starts to destroy people's psyches as they go forward. And it's juxtaposed against this desperate hope and dream of patriotism that we all want to believe America can be."

Political rights and wrongs seem irrelevant in a show that works on the level of a melodrama propelled by lust—for power, status, glory, sex.

A seemingly heroic figure can be revealed as a villain at any moment. As long as characters' despicable deeds are motivated by believable emotions and carnal voraciousness, viewers keep rooting for them. That is especially true when their actions are accompanied by a sly wink, as when one of Olivia's loyal but bloodthirsty staffers complains with great sincerity, "It's true what they say: If you want someone killed right you have to kill them yourselves."

Even in the first few seasons, however, tiny race-related bombs began to drop. Olivia's relationship with Fitz hinges on a power imbalance, and in one flashback to the early days of their affair, she lashes out. "I'm feeling a little, I don't know, Sally Hemings/Thomas Jefferson about all this," Olivia snaps, referring to our founding father and the slave who bore his children. Standing in the Rose Garden, a moping Fitz accuses her of "playing the race card" and insists that she misunderstands the dynamic. "You own me! You control me. . . . There's no Sally or Thomas here. You're nobody's victim, Liv. I belong to *you*." Rhimes says she had written and then erased the Hemings/Jefferson line from previous scripts; it felt too blatant without deeper context.

At the end of season two, racial consciousness finally asserted itself in *Scandal*. Just as Meredith's mother was used as an emotional reveal in the *Grey's* pilot ("Mom?"), Olivia's father was the twist in the season-two finale ("Dad?"), unmasked as the commander of an all-powerful CIA cabal.

"Olivia Pope had been living a very specific kind of life as a woman of color, and had been dating this white man," Rhimes tells me thoughtfully. "When her father shows up, *blackness* shows up in the show in a very real way—a very seventies old-fashioned, Black Power where-is-the-girl-that-I-raised consciousness shows up." Olivia lives in a largely white world, believing that she has transcended race, or perhaps evaded it. Rhimes intended Olivia's father, Eli Pope (masterfully played by Joe Morton), to serve as a catalyst, she says, forcing Olivia "to stand in the middle of modern black America and figure out who she is."

Dressed in a sleek white jacket, the usually formidable Olivia can barely look at her father when he reappears in her life in season two. "Did I not raise you for better? How many times have I told you, you have to be . . . what? Twice . . ." Looking down, she hoarsely whispers, "Twice as good." He finishes the thought: "You have to be twice as good as them to get half of what they have"—searing words familiar to many people of color. Being the mistress of a spoiled white-boy president is *not* what Eli Pope had in mind for her.

Olivia seems to be very much a product of her father's decisions—to protect her from her dangerous terrorist mother, to send her to the best boarding schools, to pay for her law degree in exchange for weekly Sunday dinners. Eli is frustrated by his lack of control over his daughter's life, which makes him a bit like Emily Gilmore, if Emily had a black-ops intelligence agency at her command. Although Olivia is constantly affirming her independence, she spends much of the show bouncing among an array of men who want to make choices for her.

"I don't need protecting!" she tells her patronizing lover Fitz, when he promises to whisk her away to a dream home in Vermont. "I am not the girl you *save*! I am fine. My father runs the nation's top-secret spy organization." In fact, Olivia finally understands, she is the contagion at the heart of the show. As the black mistress of a conservative president, she is *the scandal*. This realization brings *Scandal* to increasingly bleak places, and Eli regularly reminds his daughter that no matter how high she rises, "Those people that you've chosen over me" do not see her as an equal. "You will never be one of them."

In the summer of 2014, Rhimes watched the news coverage of protests in Ferguson, Missouri, over the police killing of eighteen-year-old Michael Brown, the latest in a string of unarmed young black men fatally shot by police around the country.

"I kept waking up in the middle of the night with that image in my head of a father sitting in a lawn chair over his son's dead body in the middle of the street, with a shotgun on his lap. It had been a year of very brutal police killings and it was driving me insane," Rhimes says. She asked African

American staff writer Zahir McGhee to write an episode that begins with the standoff between the DC police force and the father of a teen who lies dead in the street, just blocks from the Capitol. The boy's father (played by Courtney B. Vance), shotgun in hand, demands justice. A local black activist named Marcus Walker (Cornelius Smith Jr.) arrives with a lawn chair, so the father can stand guard over his son's corpse. The police ask Olivia to de-escalate the situation—presumably because she is African American—but her attempt to play both sides doesn't impress Marcus.

Rhimes set out to provoke a confrontation between Olivia and Marcus, "a very woke black person, an activist, who is basically saying, 'You consider yourself to be very down with the cause, but when was the last time you've ever been anywhere in a neighborhood full of black people or cared anything about what is going on over here? You are busy helping a white Republican president maintain his job and stay elected.' It was so uncomfortable for Olivia Pope to have to face that piece of herself."

The script emerged, Rhimes says, from real conversations between Rhimes and McGhee: "He was Marcus, and I was Olivia Pope, and we were basically having these arguments in my office." It's an episode that flags Olivia's double consciousness and the limits of her power: the closest this fixer can come to fixing things is to prove that the boy was not holding a gun. He was clutching a cell phone receipt. Some viewers were disappointed by the unrealistically upbeat resolution: cop arrested, protests and violence averted. Rhimes defended the decision on Twitter, noting that the writers heavily debated this ending: "[W]e went with showing what fulfilling the dream SHOULD mean. The idea of possibility . . . And NOT the despair we feel now."

The episode was filmed in the fall of 2014. Rhimes worried that it might seem dated by its March 5 airdate, but it turned out to be all too relevant. A damning Department of Justice report on Ferguson was published on March 4, 2015, and fatal encounters between police and young black men continued, a steadily unfolding tragedy that catapulted the Black Lives Matter movement to the national stage.

There is one scene from *Scandal* that is forever seared in my mind. It's not a shocking double cross or a steamy tryst. It is the image of Olivia Pope trying to escape after she has been kidnapped as part of a political maneuver aimed at Fitz. Using the underwire from her bra, she has loosened a pipe from under the bathroom sink to beat back her captors. Her black hair, normally sleek as record vinyl, has exploded into a wild, natural frizz-halo. Running for her life, she hears her father's words thrumming in her ears: *You have to be twice as good.*

Olivia, it's suddenly clear, constantly carries the burden of representing, to her white colleagues in the White House and to her white TV viewers, an ideal of African American womanhood, just as Rhimes does behind the scenes. Encased in her elegant wardrobe and her flat-ironed head of hair, she must be perfect, or at least twice as good. And she is.

The word *melodrama* usually comes with a kind of lowbrow stench attached to it, and it's often (though not exclusively) applied to soap operas or other entertainment aimed at women. Pop-culture scholar Linda Williams notes in her book *Playing the Race Card* that *melodrama* means more or less the same thing now as it did in the nineteenth century: a work that inspires an "excess of sensation and sentiment, a manipulation of the heartstrings that exceeds the bounds of good taste." All that applies to *Scandal*. But Williams also sees melodrama as "the fundamental mode by which American mass culture has 'talked to itself' about the enduring moral dilemma of race," placing both the televised OJ Simpson trial and (intriguingly) *The Wire* within this framework. *Scandal* tests the limits of melodrama's capacity to contain these extremes of salaciousness and seriousness. Rhimes's fundamental desire may be to entertain, but she is also a provocateur, stringing cultural trip wires through her "mindless" entertainment.

Rhimes and Beers once fought the network over allowing women on *Grey's* to be unlikable, difficult, or slutty; now the duo took it as given. So Quinn, who had started out as the average white viewer's proxy, evolves into a sadistic killer who'd rather torture a guy than settle down with one. In *Scandal*, First Lady Mellie Grant, a big-haired stay-at-home wife, mutates into a formidable political player. After being elected senator, she filibusters to maintain funding for Planned Parenthood. In the very same episode that sees Mellie defending that organization, Olivia walks away from her perfect ending with the president and decides to get an abortion. The camera zooms in tightly on her face as a doctor performs the procedure. She looks resigned, or perhaps relieved. There is no dialogue, just Aretha Franklin singing a rendition of "Silent Night," her "hallelujah" ringing softly in the background.

Rhimes says there was no outcry from the network or the public about the issue of abortion in the abstract—but many viewers were unhappy about Olivia's choice.

"There is a deep belief that people really have been raised with, a fairy tale that needs to be maintained at all costs. I had a lot of conversations that involved me being told that Olivia wanted children. And I would say, 'Can you tell me anywhere in any script or any episode where Olivia Pope has said the words "I want children"?' And there would be this silence. It had never occurred to them that she had never said it." Rhimes says she would tell these people, "You have imagined that because maybe that is your fantasy of what life she should be living. But she is pretty suffocated. This is her act of freedom."

The showrunner lets out a deep sigh. "It truly was for me a very interesting instance of going, 'Wow, the character is actually exercising her right to choose, and nobody can take it.'" At the very least, people were hoping for a big fight when Fitz found out the truth. But Rhimes refused to give in to this desire for Olivia to pay for her decision. "So I wrote [a scene of] him finding out, and he has this sort of great acceptance. People were just so freaked out that he could know and be okay with her choice. And that a woman wouldn't be punished for not wanting to live out the fairy tale."

Rhimes came up against the same problem when she devised an exit route for Dr. Cristina Yang after Sandra Oh decided to part with *Grey's*

Anatomy in its tenth season. Offered the chance to run her own hospital in Switzerland, Cristina leaves behind her romance with Owen, infuriating many fans.

"The demographic of *Grey's Anatomy* truly is age twelve to seventy-two," Rhimes explains, adding that she was astonished "to hear that many people across that many age groups have such an outcry, to say to me, 'Why doesn't she get her happy ending?' And I said, 'She does!'" Rhimes says it makes her stomach turn that so many fans equate a happy ending with marriage: "A man is a partner on a journey that you can go on in life, but a man is not the be-all and end-all of your existence." Here Rhimes is drawing on her own experience and her ambivalent attitudes toward marriage. In her memoir, she reveals that she broke her own engagement to preserve her independence.

Cristina was very much modeled on Rhimes in this respect: "I gave her my passion for work. I gave her my love for something greater than any romance, something that draws her focus more than any guy, a creative genius floating forever out of reach that she will never stop trying to capture."

As she walks out of the hospital for the final time, Cristina drops some parting wisdom for twisted sister Meredith about her relationship with McDreamy (who is, by this point, her husband): "You are a gifted surgeon with an extraordinary mind. Don't let what he wants eclipse what you need. He is very dreamy, but he is not the sun. You are." It felt like Shonda was looking through the screen and talking directly to the women in her audience.

By 2014, ABC regarded Rhimes as their most valuable player, one of the few showrunners with a lock on the eighteen-to-forty-nine demographic. She signed a deal with the network described by the *Hollywood Reporter* as "easily one of the richest deals in television," said to be worth tens of millions of dollars. Thursday nights on ABC were soon devoted entirely to Shondaland series, topped off by *How to Get Away with Murder*, a new legal thriller starring Viola Davis as Annalise Keating, a high-powered defense attorney and law school professor with a briefcase full of secrets.

Annalise is very much in the tradition of previous Rhimesian heroines (brilliant, ambitious, and vaguely inscrutable), but she is the creation of Peter Nowalk. Hired as a fledgling writer on *Private Practice* in 2007, he had worked his way up through years at *Grey's Anatomy* and *Scandal* before pitching the idea for the show to his bosses. Beers says what immediately appealed to her about *How to Get Away with Murder* was that while Annalise Keating is at the top of her professional game, "she is wrestling demons on a regular basis. She is publicly walking a crazy tightrope between all these responsibilities and her own deep issues." At the same time, as a powerful African American woman, she must be a sterling representative for her race. Keating's world, like Olivia Pope's, is one with no black-and-white answers. Says Beers, "It is *all* gray."

As Shondaland characters increasingly wove together fever-pitch craziness with recognizable reality (as when *Scandal*'s First Lady, Mellie Grant, runs for president against a Trump-ish businessman), Rhimes herself dipped a toe into the actual political maelstrom. In March 2016, Annalise, Olivia, and Meredith—or was it Viola Davis, Kerry Washington, and Ellen Pompeo?—appeared in a television ad on behalf of then-Democratic primary candidate Hillary Clinton, a spot directed by Fitz himself, Tony Goldwyn.

"Every day, I wake up and play a brilliant, complex, overqualified, get-it-done woman who obsessively fights for justice, who cares, who gives a voice to the voiceless, who gets knocked down and always gets back up . . ." the actresses intone, along with Rhimes. "Our characters are on television, but the real world . . . the real world has Hillary Clinton. A bona fide, rolls-up-her-sleeves, fights-for-what's-right, in-it-for-you, won't-back-down champion for all of us."

Katie Lowes remembers the day Clinton dropped by the set of *Scandal* during a late-evening shoot. "This whole security team shows up, and Hillary walks onto stage twelve, and we are taking a tour of the Oval Office, and she's telling us about the differences between the real Oval Office and our set. It was completely surreal."

A few months later, Rhimes and Beers canceled their summer vacations when they were asked to create the short film about Clinton's life that would run at the Democratic National Convention, officially introducing her as the first-ever female major-party nominee for president. Rhimes told *People* at the time, "Given the Trumpiness of the world today, we felt like we were doing the work of angels."

And, she added, "The best part? I didn't have to add a plot twist!" The American public did that for her.

Betsy Beers can tell you to the minute how long it takes to get from the set of *Scandal* at Sunset Gower to Prospect Studios, where *Grey's* is shot. Few male showrunners in TV history have had so many shows in production and development simultaneously, and it's definitely a first for an African American woman. Rhimes has felt enormous pressure overseeing a multimillion-dollar realm. "As the shows got more popular, I was acutely, painfully aware of what was at stake. . . ." she wrote in *Year of Yes*. "Failing would be bigger than just me. Blowing it would reverberate for decades to come."

On a more practical level, the cast and crew of her shows have all wanted to see her more. Chandra Wilson talks about feeling the absence of their "matriarch" on the set of *Grey's*. "I know it's hard when you have an empire; she can't be everywhere all the time, but when Shonda steps on set, it elevates everything happening on the floor. Then she feels like she is in the way because everyone is like, 'Do you want to sit down? Can I get you some water?' And that makes her nervous! . . . But she's got a lot of children, and they all want to see her."

Within what Beers calls their "repertory company," Rhimes tries to maintain a kind of intimacy. As Quinn, Katie Lowes has been subjected to some horrifying experiences; in one *Scandal* scene, she was tortured, her teeth pulled by a rogue colleague. (Things like this happen a lot to associates of Olivia Pope.) Immediately after a rehearsal in which she practiced having dental tools inserted in her mouth, Lowes got an email from Rhimes. "She said, 'How did you feel? Are you okay? Please tell me how you are.'" The showrunner knows she can't persuade actors to make themselves utterly vulnerable unless, Lowes says, "you feel safe and taken care of."

Krista Vernoff says that she came to understand Rhimes in the early years of *Grey's Anatomy*, when they were in the midst of a fight. "I said, 'Why are you so mean to me? If I were to talk to people the way you talk to me sometimes . . .' And she said, 'Krista, haven't you figured out yet that I am Cristina?'" Vernoff dissolves in laughter at the memory. But the other side of the Cristina Yang coin, Vernoff continues, is "powerful loyalty to women. She is still the person I would call if I killed somebody and needed help burying the body. It's like we went to war together."

CHAPTER 5

Sitcom and the Single Girl:

Tina Fey's *30 Rock*, Liz Meriwether's *New Girl*, and Mindy Kaling's *The Mindy Project*

Left: Tina Fey on the *30 Rock* set in October 2011.
Center: *New Girl* showrunner Liz Meriwether in September 2011.
Right: *The Mindy Project*'s Mindy Kaling in September 2014.

In December 2006, professional contrarian Christopher Hitchens launched an unprovoked assault on half the population. In "Why Women Aren't Funny," a three-thousand-word *Vanity Fair* feature, Hitch proposed the title's sweeping statement as a self-evident truth. The argument was addled at best: something to do with human bodily functions being the root of humor, which meant that women weren't able to enjoy playing with "filth" because, as child bearers, they had to be the designated grown-ups. But rather than nail the case for why 50.4 percent of humanity was constitutionally unamusing, Hitchens inadvertently pinpointed why funny women threaten so many men: "Precisely because humor is a sign of intelligence. . . . [I]t could be that in some way men do not want women to be funny. They want them as an audience, not as rivals."

The strangest thing about the Hitchens salvo was its timing, published as women were establishing an unprecedented prominence in television comedy. Tina Fey had overseen an *SNL* renaissance, fizzing with funny ladies such as Amy Poehler, Maya Rudolph, and Kristen Wiig. Fey's own series, *30 Rock*, which premiered just a few months before this issue of *Vanity Fair* hit the newsstands, was itself a counterargument to Hitchens's condescension.

NBC's *30 Rock* took *The Mary Tyler Moore Show* as its rough template: the life of an unmarried female TV producer and the behind-the-scenes hijinks of her mostly male colleagues. But where Mary Richards personified the sweet, network-friendly version of 1970s female liberation, Liz Lemon (as played by Fey) was an ambivalent metaheroine for a postfeminist era. In place of Mary's famous spunk was Liz's cranky skepticism. "New York third-wave feminist, college-educated, single and pretending to be happy about it, overscheduled, undersexed, you buy any magazine that says 'healthy body image' on the cover, and every two years you take up knitting . . . for a week." That's how Liz's new boss, network executive Jack Donaghy (Alec Baldwin) sizes her up the first time they meet, slotting her into a microdemographic with cruel accuracy.

How do you solve a conundrum like Liz Lemon? Is she the brilliant producer of a network TV show or a corporate flunky in thrall to her paternalistic boss? A paragon of womanpower or one of the guys? A frumpy, bespectacled loser who hoards cheese, or a woman who wouldn't be out of place on the cover of a magazine? Fey and her writers set about systematically dismantling the sitcom stereotype of the single woman. In the process, *30 Rock* opened a door that *New Girl* and *The Mindy Project* would soon walk through.

———————

A virginal straight-A student, Tina Fey amused herself as a teenager by coming up with sick insults about the popular kids and the rule breakers. At the University of Virginia, she turned her wordplay toward theater. She wrote, directed, and acted in plays, such as her senior-year one-act drama *Sunday*

Girls, which reunited a group of female friends at the wedding of their mutual ex-boyfriend. After graduating in 1992, Fey drove her father's old Pontiac to Chicago. By day, she worked at the Evanston YMCA; that left nights free to study improv at the Second City, the spawning ground for many of her comedy idols. There she met her future husband, Jeff Richmond, as well as future partner-in-crime Amy Poehler. Fey and Poehler became part of one of Second City's touring companies.

Fey dreamed of "a gender-blind meritocracy" within comedy, but she found no such thing at Second City: their touring companies each had a token number of women. Things were no better at *SNL* in 1997, when she was hired as a staff writer. Just three out of twenty-two writers at the time were women, and there were three female cast members out of eleven. Over the next few years, a growing posse of female performers (Molly Shannon, Ana Gasteyer, Rachel Dratch, Maya Rudolph, Amy Poehler, Kristen Wiig) rose up through the ranks, in part thanks to the attention of Fey and writers such as Paula Pell. They wrote sketches such as "Old French Whore!" a game show that matched syphilitic prostitutes with American high school boys, and "Talkin' 'Bout 'Ginas," a *Vagina Monologues* rip-off performed by Anna Nicole Smith, Gayle King, and Joan Rivers. ("The last time I went near my vagina, bats flew out! Can we tawk?") There were parodies of maxi pad commercials and the daytime TV show *The View.* Fey saw it as part of her mission to write stellar material for female members of the cast—a covert affirmative-action campaign.

J. J. Philbin, a twenty-one-year-old writer's assistant when Fey came on board, describes *SNL* as "a tough place" for women. "When Tina got there, she demanded respect in a way that was really admirable. She wasn't scared to do things that seemed like *lady comedy*, like *The View*, but she did it with such edge and such wit that guys couldn't help but respect it. Eventually, Lorne [Michaels] knew that he had someone very special on his hands and put her in a position of power."

In 1999, Michaels promoted Fey to head writer; she was the first woman to hold the job in *SNL*'s twenty-five-year history. With Fey at the helm, the show quickly veered back into the Zeitgeist. A year later, after seeing her perform an audacious two-woman live show with Dratch, Michaels suggested Fey audition for *SNL*'s most enviable job: coanchor of "Weekend Update," alongside Jimmy Fallon. In an instant, at age thirty, Tina Fey became a recognizable face, with her librarian glasses and deadpan manner. But it was in 2004, while coanchoring "Weekend Update" with her old improv pal Poehler, that she really came into her own. The affection between them shimmered, and it gave the duo a comfort zone to play in—not just on *SNL* but later, as cohosts of the Golden Globes and in movies such as *Baby Mama* and *Sisters*. Having a soul mate in the tank with her made Fey more fearless.

After eight years at *SNL*, Fey pitched NBC's Kevin Reilly a sitcom about a female cable news producer. Reilly urged her to base it on her own *SNL* experience, and by 2005 she had drafted a pilot for *30 Rock* focusing on the triangle of Liz Lemon, conservative CEO Jack Donaghy, and ornery superstar Tracy Jordan. Alec Baldwin and *SNL* star Tracy Morgan signed on for those last two roles; Dratch was cast as Jenna, the star of *30 Rock*'s *SNL*-like sketch-show-within-a-show, *The Girlie Show*. One final question lingered: Who should play Liz Lemon?

Pregnant with her first child, Fey wasn't sure she could carry a starring role. Poehler egged her on: Did male comedians such as Jerry Seinfeld or Ray Romano worry they weren't good enough to star in a network show? When it was framed that way, Fey knew she had to play Liz. After all, the show would be a funhouse mirror version of her own experiences within comedy's boys' club. Fey once compared an *SNL* scene to the way Jessica Seinfeld's cookbook, *Deceptively Delicious*, hid spinach in children's brownies: "You all watched a sketch about feminism and you didn't even realize it because of all the jokes." With *30 Rock*, she would hide a complicated feminist heroine in a puff pastry of zany absurdism.

Fey had learned from Lorne Michaels that *SNL* benefited from a Spock-and-Kirk combo: the writers' room intermingled *Harvard Lampoon*–style brainiacs who knew how to build a well-structured sketch and tap into contemporary politics with Second City–ish improv experts, who thrived on comedic instinct and could feed on one another's uninhibited wackiness. From the Harvard camp, she hired Robert Carlock, who would become Fey's co-showrunner and consigliere. A former *Lampoon* editor and an *SNL* alum, Carlock had worked on *Friends* and *Joey*. Joining him in the writers' room were TV comedy veterans such as *Frasier* scribe Jack Burditt, as well as Matt Hubbard, Dave Finkel, and Brett Baer, who had all worked on *Joey*. There were also more inexperienced writers, such as improv performers Kay Cannon and Donald Glover, the latter such a recent college graduate that he was still living in an NYU dorm during his early days on *30 Rock*.

"I remember Tina sitting at the head of the table, and Donald and I were at the other end of the table, both super wide-eyed, like, *What are we doing here*?" says Cannon. Both would ultimately vault to independent successes rooted in their off-kilter sensibilities. Cannon wrote the *Pitch Perfect* movies and Netflix series *Girlboss* after a stint on *New Girl*; Glover jumped from *Community* to creating and starring in the unorthodox dramedy *Atlanta*. Since the heart of *30 Rock* was a sketch show, Cannon and Glover were able to inject their playful, improvising energy into the scripting process. Cannon suggests, "We were kind of the appointed goofballs of the group."

Starting in the early nineties, NBC advertised its Thursday-night comedy lineup with the slogan "Must-See TV." *Seinfeld, Will & Grace, Frasier*, and *Friends*—these shows were such ratings monsters that other networks barely bothered to compete on Thursdays. But by 2006, NBC's comedy slate was in tatters. *Will & Grace* and *Friends* were done, and *Friends* spin-off *Joey* had flopped. The network's only "Must-See" hopes were the quirky blue-collar sitcom *My Name Is Earl*; an American adaptation of the British mockumentary *The Office*; and *30 Rock*.

While *30 Rock* was coalescing, though, NBC had also signed up another series about a live *SNL*-style show. *Studio 60 on the Sunset Strip* wasn't *exactly* the same as *30 Rock*: this one was a drama about backstage machinations and interpersonal frictions. But it was too close for comfort, especially considering the powerful people behind it. Creator Aaron Sorkin had recently triumphed with *The West Wing*, while the lead actors included *Friends* star Matthew Perry and *West Wing's* Bradley Whitford. NBC insisted that these very different shows could coexist. Fey, far from convinced, complained to the *New Yorker*, with barely concealed bitterness, about the "bad luck" of having to go "up against the most powerful writer on television" in her first run at prime time. Further disappointment followed when Fey's friend Rachel Dratch was dropped from *30 Rock*. In her place, the more glamorous Jane Krakowski was cast, changing Jenna's character from a dowdy loon to a hilariously vain showbiz has-been.

Studio 60 premiered in September 2006, with *30 Rock* following a month behind. But in an early sign that the battle would go Fey's way, many critics preferred *30 Rock*. *Studio 60*, wrote *Entertainment Weekly's* Ken Tucker, "may have the classier ensemble and fancier verbiage . . . but at half the length and twice the amusement, *30 Rock* has Alec Baldwin . . . playing Fey's new boss as only a smidge more impish than the ruthless corporate soul-crusher he was in the movie version of *Glengarry Glen Ross*."

The pilot found dashing right-wing network exec Jack Donaghy seeking to improve the ratings of Liz Lemon's ailing women's comedy program by making *The Girlie Show* less . . . girlie. To attract that ever-crucial eighteen-to-thirty-four-year-old male demographic, Donaghy recruits Tracy Jordan, the irrepressible African American star of Tyler Perry-ish classics such as *Who Dat Ninja?* and *Sherlock Homie*. From his first moments on-screen, Alec Baldwin exudes monstrous magnetism; Tracy Morgan's bratty but lovable intensity is equally apparent. But the rest of the comic elements took longer to fall into place.

"That first year, it was very difficult figuring out [what the show was]," Cannon remembers. "The intricate way scripts were constructed and written meant there were a lot of long hours. That first year, we would go to Tina's apartment on the Upper West Side, maybe three or four of us. We would see her daughter Alice go to bed, and then we would still be there at six thirty in the morning when she got up." Cannon recalls riding on the subway one day with fellow writer Jack Burditt when she touched her hair and a huge clump came out in her hand. "Burditt said, 'I think you might be stressed!'"

Stress-related hair loss sounds like the kind of ailment that might befall Liz Lemon. A workaholic Wendy constantly tending to Neverland and her Lost Boys, Liz focused on the job to the detriment of her social life. If forced to choose between a romantic date or staying late at work followed by a night at home wrapped in her Slanket eating cheese and watching reality TV, there's no question she'd pick the latter. In other words, *30 Rock* made madcap comedy out of a woman putting work ahead of her personal life, just as millions of men do without fanfare.

Liz was an asexual character by design: frumpy and absolutely fine with that. Fey wanted to go against the prevailing *Sex and the City* glam single-woman stereotype—to figure out "what is the anti–Carrie Bradshaw," says Tracey Wigfield, who started as writers' assistant at *30 Rock*, graduated to producer, and later created the NBC sitcom *Good News*. "Liz is very much a woman who is career-motivated. She just wants to start a relationship five years in," when the passion has settled into easy, companionable coasting.

The show hit its cruising altitude in December 2006 with "Tracy Does Conan." Written by Fey, the debut season's seventh episode telegraphed the show's willingness to embrace lunacy. Liz's plan to break up with her creepy boyfriend is derailed by a workplace problem: she needs to wrangle Tracy into appearing on Conan O'Brien's talk show. But Tracy is off his meds and hallucinating a blue monster (played by a hilariously unhinged Dratch, a runner-up prize for having lost out on the Jenna role). At one point, Liz finds Tracy literally pinned to the ceiling. The plot careens off the sitcom walls at maximum velocity, as Liz whizzes around Manhattan trying to juggle Jenna's jealousy and Tracy's psychosis, which his physician, Dr. Spaceman (pronounced Spah-CHEM-in), defines as "erratic tendencies and delusions brought on by excessive notoriety." At the end of the episode, poor Liz is too tired to break up with her boyfriend; instead, she conks out on the sofa clutching a cheeseburger.

After the "Tracy Does Conan" episode, Brett Baer says the writers finally grasped what Fey was going for: an action-packed adrenaline whirl buzzing with pop-satirical references. "We all looked at each other and said, 'Ohhhh!'" He sighs in wonderment. "The show worked in this super-heightened way, and we just felt, *Nobody has ever done this before.*" The antic physical comedy was matched at every turn by razor-sharp dialogue that sketched in a surprising amount of emotional detail about the characters, making you *care* about even the most ludicrous and cartoonish member of the menagerie. "We worked hard to see how much we could push the limit, and we found there was no limit, so we just kept pushing."

That testing of boundaries resulted in "Black Tie," the last of NBC's original twelve-episode order. Thinking this was their swan song, the writers unleashed a berserk half-hour set at the birthday party of Prince Gerhard, an inbred Austrian aristocrat played with pathos (and one tiny doll hand) by Paul "Pee Wee Herman" Reubens. Status-hungry Jenna pursues a romance with Prince Gerhard. Although he can't dance ("Sadly, my body does not produce joint fluid"), they do share a fairy-tale moment before he drops dead, thanks to his inability to digest champagne.

This early episode also teases us with the prospect of a romance between Liz and Jack. When Liz asks her boss if this party invite constitutes a date, Jack dismisses the idea. (He dates only models and socialites.) Yet the chemistry between the two is palpable. At the end of the evening, Jack reaches out as if to caress Liz's face—and instead removes from her neck the jewels he loaned her for the evening.

Fey informed the writers early on that Jack and Liz would never be a couple: *30 Rock* wasn't a rom-com, even if it bounced around some of the genre's conventions. She said at the time, "I want to resist the temptation to turn it into a soap opera. Will they or won't they get together? Who cares! *Grey's Anatomy* is always going to beat us at that game. We're just a comedy show." Sure, Rhimes laced her shows with humor and occasional snark, but ultimately her narratives invited viewers to immerse themselves in the all-encompassing fantasy of Shondaland for an hour. Whereas, if you glazed out for just a few minutes of *30 Rock*, you'd miss dozens of jokes and sight gags. Fey borrowed aspects of the classic screwball comedy—the witty, fast-paced banter, the mismatched cultural attitudes, the farcical situations—while ditching the consummation that traditionally awaited the couple by movie's end. Liz and Jack cycle through relationships with other people over the show's seven seasons, but none of these couplings is ultimately as compelling as Liz and Jack's friendship. They are "work spouses" who admire each other, reserving their true passion for their jobs.

While "Black Tie" was shooting, NBC's Kevin Reilly called to say that *30 Rock* had been picked up for the rest of the season, despite poor ratings. (*Studio 60*, on the other hand, was canceled.) It went on to win the Emmy for Outstanding Comedy Series. Taking the stage with her actors and producers surrounding her, Fey conveyed thanks to "our dozens and dozens of viewers."

Fey's profile escalated from cult comedian to household name when she began satirizing look-alike Sarah Palin on *SNL* during the 2008 presidential race. But *30 Rock* had a much stealthier approach to current affairs. Fey wanted "to do stories about politics in this sort of interpersonal way, about gender and economic and racial politics," Carlock told one interviewer. Jack Donaghy often involves himself in Republican escapades: he funds a Trump-ish congressional candidate who wants to reduce big government to "no government," dates former Secretary of State Condoleezza Rice (who makes a guest appearance), and briefly leaves NBC to work for George W. Bush's administration.

Liz Lemon, on the other hand, is a bleeding-heart liberal whose beliefs often don't hold up to scrutiny, or are undermined. One of my favorite *30 Rock* episodes, "Rosemary's Baby," tests Liz's cred as a feminist. She hires her hero, Rosemary Howard (played by Carrie Fisher), a radical TV writer from the seventies. But when Rosemary suggests *The Girlie Show* do a sketch in blackface, Liz stiffens: "We can't do race stuff. It's too sensitive!" Jack has no patience for Liz's new political pretensions, declaring that she is not a radical like Rosemary: "You are like me. . . . You are a suit." She realizes that Jack is right after he fires her and she gets a glimpse of Rosemary's squalid hovel. Liz returns to her well-paid corporate gig at Rockefeller Center— where Jack (as if to prove you *can* do race stuff on network TV) is helping Tracy get over his family issues by mimicking the voices of black characters from TV shows such as *Sanford and Son* and *Good Times*.

The show's run coincided with the rise of an online feminist blogosphere, with sites such as *Feministing*, *AngryBlackBitch*, and *Jezebel* casting a critical eye over everything from reproductive rights to sex toys to Hollywood double standards. In the 2011 episode "TGS Hates Women," *30 Rock* lampoons the so-called lady blogs with *Joan of Snark*, a thinly disguised version of *Jezebel*—aka "this really cool feminist website where women talk about how far we've come and which celebrities have the worst beach bodies."

The site calls out *TGS* (*The Girlie Show*) for its sexism, provoking Liz to protest that she is a good feminist: "I support women. I'm like a human bra!" To prove it, she hires Abby (Cristin Milioti), a trendy young female comic, to instigate a "fem-o-lution" at *TGS*. When it turns out that Abby uses baby talk and dresses hypersexually, Liz accuses the young comedian of undermining the women's movement. "What's the difference between me using my sexuality and you using those glasses to look smart?" Abby retorts. Fey told NPR's Terry Gross that the writers chose to explore ambivalence in the episode rather than offer a simplistic resolution. "It's just such a tangled-up issue, the way that women present themselves . . . and the way women judge each other back and forth for it."

Although she had become an idol to brainy, wisecracking young women all over America, Liz Lemon provoked soul-searching in the *real* blogosphere. After all, her character flaws sometimes corresponded closely to sexist clichés, such as the way she was tortured by her ticking biological clock. Liz was mentored by the paternalistic Jack Donaghy and surrounded herself almost exclusively with men. In fact, her "Girlie" show had very few women writers, and they never uttered a word. In a much-circulated post on her blog *Tiger Beatdown*, writer Sady Doyle critiqued "Liz Lemonism" as a kind of privileged "semi-feminism": she represents someone "content with a feminist movement dedicated to the advancement not necessarily of *women*, but of one particular woman, the Liz Lemonist in question, and perhaps a handful of the friends who agree with her most often."

Yet that critique was already embedded in *30 Rock*. In fact, it's not an accident that Liz is a privileged, mildly racist corporate sellout of a semi-feminist who is privately addicted to bad reality TV even as she publicly spouts political pieties. Indeed, the writers exploit the comic potential of her hypocrisy at every opportunity. TV industry sexism made for a bittersweet running joke, too: the de-girlification of Liz's *The Girlie Show* begins with the hiring of Tracy Jordan and ends, in the final season, with the series being revamped into a frat-boy spectacle called *Bro Body Douche Presents the Man Cave*. Its tagline? "TV for Your Peen."

Fey thrived as a woman in comedy who could hang with the boys, but she was increasingly wrapping her caustic wit around Hollywood gender inequity. "I have a suspicion—and hear me out, because this is a rough one—that the definition of 'crazy' in show business is a woman who keeps talking even after no one wants to fuck her anymore," she chided in a 2011 *New Yorker* essay, "Confessions of a Working Mother." Her solution was simple: women in power need to hire more women. "That is why I feel obligated to stay in the business and try hard to get to a place where I can create opportunities for others, and that's why I can't possibly take time off for a second baby, unless I do, in which case that is nobody's business and I'll never regret it for a moment unless it ruins my life." Fey's second baby was born later that year; it didn't ruin her life, as far as I can tell. And she continued to hire and mentor talented women directors and writers on *30 Rock*, including Tami Sagher, Nina Pedrad, and Lang Fisher.

Although *30 Rock* won 16 Emmy Awards (and 103 nominations) over the course of its run, its ratings never rallied. If NBC hadn't been doing so poorly with its overall schedule, the series probably would've been canceled sooner. As the show rolled toward its seventh and final season, Fey began imagining where she wanted these characters to end up. Liz Lemon's un-married, child-free state had been a sweet spot for comedy—and also for pathos. Kay Cannon felt one of her key roles in the writers' room was to inject emotion into an otherwise gag-heavy show. "Liz Lemon, you cared who she fell in love with. You cared if she was going to be able to have it all, and what that meant for her."

Forty-something Liz had started to settle down with a younger, unem-ployed guy named Criss Cros (James Marsden). In a season-six episode called "Murphy Brown Lied to Us," she admits to him that she's contem-plated adoption but decided against it after passing a panicked mom in the office hallway trying to get a work project done. She realizes that the eighties TV icon is just a product of feminist wishful thinking. "Murphy Brown had the whole *FYI* gang in her corner," Liz tells Criss. "Jim Dial, Frank Fontana, Corky, even Miles, in his own way"—they communally helped working mom Murphy raise her baby.

At the start of season seven, however, Fey told the writers' room she wanted Liz to adopt kids. The idea was to let her embrace some of those traditional adult milestones, she told a reporter, "but without romanticizing them" or losing "who she has been this whole time."

One of Liz's final scenes was set at a strip club, a nod to the pilot epi-sode, where Tracy and Liz originally made a pact to work together on *TGS* "to break the shackles of the white dudes who want to see us fail." Beth McCarthy-Miller, who directed the final episodes of the series, recalls how hard it was to keep the jokes snapping when everyone was feeling so raw. "We were in this strip club, and it was very personal and heartfelt. Tina started crying, Tracy started crying, and then literally the whole Video Village started crying," says McCarthy-Miller fondly. "I don't think anyone was kidding themselves that these weren't the best scripts they would ever have in their lives."

After the writers' room shuttered, its occupants scattered to the four corners of TV Land. Dave Finkel, Brett Baer, Kay Cannon, and Nina Pedrad soon reunited on *New Girl*, while Jack Burditt, Tracey Wigfield, and Lang

Fisher later found themselves collaborating on another single-woman sit-com, *The Mindy Project*.

When *30 Rock* began, Tina Fey had a unique position in the television landscape: a female showrunner entrusted by a broadcast network to create and star in her own loopy prime-time sitcom about a smart, dissatisfied feminist. By the time *30 Rock* left the air, what had been a solitary occurrence had virtually become a genre. Single women were everywhere.

In the fall of 2011, each of the major broadcast networks launched an edgy chick comedy created by a woman. CBS premiered *2 Broke Girls*, co-created by *Sex and the City*'s Michael Patrick King and bawdy comedian Whitney Cummings, who also starred in her own series on NBC, *Whitney*. ABC introduced Emily Kapnek's snarky *Suburgatory*, with Nahnatchka Khan's *Don't Trust the B— in Apartment 23* lined up for midseason. Over on Fox, there was Liz Meriwether's *New Girl*. Cultural observers spotted a pattern in this sudden spate of fem-centric comedies, but it wasn't entirely clear why networks were so in sync.

Maybe the trend stemmed from Tina Fey's success, or from TV exec-utives trying to tap into the young female demographic mobilized by the ladyblogs. Veteran producer Lynda Obst believes the movie industry's declining interest in character-driven movies and romantic comedies pushed screenwriters to look to television. Or was it the *"Bridesmaids* Effect"? Written by Kristen Wiig and Annie Mumolo, *Bridesmaids* puked, farted, and shat its way into movie history upon its release in April 2011. Starring *SNL*'s Wiig and Maya Rudolph and *Gilmore Girls*'s Melissa McCarthy, the comedy would gross (*gross* being the operative word) more than $288 million worldwide. Although most of the 2011 sitcoms were fully formed when the movie hit theaters, it's likely that *Bridesmaids* emboldened Hollywood executives to greenlight those series or give them a bigger push.

"There was nothing like [my show] in the air when I wrote it," *Don't Trust the B—* creator Nahnatchka Khan observed. "Now it's like this Zeitgeist thing!"

Most of these chick comedies capitalized on networks' increasing openness to vulgarity. *New Girl* plotted an episode around dating a guy with a micro-penis, and *2 Broke Girls* dropped so many casual references to female anatomy that Whitney Cummings would later quip, "Vagina jokes paid for my house." Within six months, guys were already complaining that the medium had tilted too far toward women's concerns. "We're approaching peak vagina on television, the point of labia saturation," Lee Aronsohn, the co-creator of *Two and a Half Men*, told the *Hollywood Reporter*. "Enough, ladies. I get it. You have periods."

Although *New Girl* dedicated a whole episode ("Menzies") to menstruation, mostly it kept female abjection under wraps. Instead, the comedy of *New Girl* came from the friction of a girlie girl dropped into a bro-lific Boy World. In the pilot, schoolteacher Jessica Day—played by Zooey Deschanel, already identified strongly with the "manic pixie dream girl" archetype—breaks up with her cheating boyfriend and moves into a loft shared by three dudes. As the show develops, gender grows more muddled: Jess becomes one of the guys, without losing her dreaminess; the men let their macho fronts slip and reveal unexpected sweetness, vulnerability, and weirdness.

"I was very focused on shocking people in my twenties; I loved saying the most outrageous thing," says *New Girl* creator Liz Meriwether, sitting at a table in her LA office. Broadcast network constraints forced her to find more original ways to jolt the audience. "There is a limited number of times you can say *vagina* or *penis* on network television, so you have to choose those wisely." She giggles when she says those words, as a teenager might, then continues, "There have been multiple times when those restrictions have resulted in something much funnier."

Meriwether's office is tucked into the Fox lot just around the corner from the *Simpsons* bungalow, which has a giant yellow Homer hand holding a pink donut out front. The *New Girl* offices look far more generic; they could easily be mistaken for an insurance company or telemarketing firm, but for the *New Girl*–branded bicycles propped in the hallway, a recent holiday gift to the staff. When Meriwether first pops her head out the door to introduce herself, she looks so disheveled that I momentarily mistake her for an intern. She has just finished shooting the sixth season and has the glassy eyes and rumpled hair of someone popping up for air after a long spell submerged in a project. "I always feel like I am getting the bends, like coming back up from working so hard to normal life, and normal life hits you in the face, and you forgot you were a person in the world," she says, every syllable shot through with vocal fry and amusement.

Meriwether grew up worshipping Angela Chase in *My So-Called Life*. A theater nerd during her high school years in Ann Arbor, Michigan, she dressed like Claire Danes's gawky teenage alter ego and honed her salty sense of humor. At Yale, she put it to use writing short plays such as *Nicky Goes Goth*, starring classmate Zoe Kazan as celebutante Nicky Hilton. After graduation, a New York Fringe Festival production of *Nicky Goes Goth* caught the attention of an Off-Broadway theater company, which commissioned her to write something even cheekier: *Heddatron*, a much-lauded futuristic version of Henrik Ibsen's *Hedda Gabler*.

By the age of twenty-six, Meriwether had New York theater world cred. But what she really wanted to do was write comedy, and that mission brought her to Los Angeles. A collaboration between the Naked Angels theater company and Fox TV resulted in a Fox deal for a 2006 Meriwether series about four female roommates in New York. She named it *Sluts*, in keeping with her self-professed love of shock and outrage. "At the time, everybody kept asking, 'Why are they even shooting this pilot?' It didn't feel like a real show to anyone," she says. Still, the pilot did open the door to other projects. An anti-rom-com called *Fuckbuddies* eventually morphed into the Ivan Reitman movie *No Strings Attached*, starring Natalie Portman and Ashton Kutcher, with Mindy Kaling and Jake Johnson as the lovers' best friends.

Meanwhile, Meriwether worked on a pitch for another television show. As with *Sluts*, it would revolve around four friends. But she'd learned from that earlier experience that networks had little interest in series about young female friends. Executives were fixated on attracting a young male audience to make it easier to sell syndication rights later. "That is the business model: if you get men to watch it, you make money," Meriwether says, shaking her head. "We had meetings where they were telling us we basically *had* to appeal to men."

So, this time, she'd make three of the roommates guys. Originally titled *Chicks and Dicks*, it would soon be renamed *New Girl*.

Mindy Kaling once created a classification system to identify female roles in rom-coms. There was the Beautiful Klutz, perfect in every way except that she trips a lot, a minor defect to make her more relatable; the Ethereal Weirdo (aka Manic Pixie Dream Girl), whose sole narrative purpose is to force the male hero to break out of the rut he's in and start doing wild and crazy things; the Career-Obsessed Woman, who goes around shouting "I don't have time for this!"; and the Sassy Best Friend, a quirky sidekick who exists only as a foil for the star. Meriwether did not have this essay in mind when she set out to write an entire series consisting only of Sassy Best Friends, but she ultimately took Kaling's point and ran with it.

Network television has no problem with oddball guys, but Meriwether worried that Fox would strong-arm her into making her heroine less goofy or insist on casting a bombshell. Instead, Fox chairman Kevin Reilly (the exec who had originally championed *30 Rock*) told the fledgling showrunner that her job was to ensure that her heroine's idiosyncratic voice stayed strong.

Jess was initially based heavily on Meriwether herself. Once Zooey Deschanel signed on in early 2011, however, the role evolved into a blend of the two women. Best known as a big-eyed, girlish ingenue from indie films such as *500 Days of Summer*, Deschanel was also in a folk-rock duo, She and Him, and had recently created HelloGiggles, an entertainment and lifestyle website for young women. She looked like bluebirds helped her get dressed in the morning, as someone would later taunt her character on *New Girl*. Although Deschanel didn't want Jess to serve as the series' resident buzzkill, reining in the wild boys, she was drawn to Jess's sexual awkwardness. "Part of the interesting thing about the character, especially in the first season, was that we establish how uncomfortable [the topic of sex] was for her, and a lot of comedy came out of that."

Deschanel sat in on auditions for all the other lead roles. Max Greenfield was cast as Schmidt, a narcissistic and neurotic jerk whose roommates make him deposit cash in a "douche bag jar" for every idiotic utterance. (Sample: "Guess whose personalized condoms just arrived!") The role of cranky bartender Nick went to Jake Johnson, and Damon Wayans Jr. played Coach, a former athlete and all-around playa. After shooting the pilot, Wayans had to drop out due to another commitment. Meriwether was forced to create a new male roommate for episode two: Winston Bishop, played by Lamorne Morris, who filled Wayans's African American actor slot but was a completely different character—an eccentric, gentle guy obsessed with pranks and his cat. For the Bechdel Test, there was Jess's best friend, Cece (Hannah Simone), an Indian American model who, despite her leading-lady looks, is nearly as silly as Jess.

Since she had little experience as a showrunner, Meriwether was paired with *30 Rock* writers Brett Baer and Dave Finkel, who assembled a writers' room and tried to manage the creative commotion that engulfed the fledgling show. While Tina Fey expected *30 Rock* actors to stick to the perfectly constructed scripts, Meriwether encouraged on-set experimentation. "So much good stuff comes out of freedom like that, to be able to just keep the camera rolling and try a bunch of things," Meriwether suggests. "What we were trying to do was different from *30 Rock*. We were trying to do a show that sounded like people were actually talking. Somebody could make a weird face, and that becomes a joke."

All that spontaneity resulted in long, chaotic days; it sometimes felt as if they were working inside a snow globe that was being continually shaken. J. J. Philbin, who wrote for *New Girl* after stints at *SNL* and *The OC*, says that for the writers who worked on the show in its infancy, "there's a little bit of the feeling of having been in 'Nam together! Liz is someone who wants to keep working on it until it is really, really great. And if that means staying awake for three days in a row, she is going to stay awake for three days in a row."

Deschanel is blunt about the first few seasons of *New Girl*. "Liz's work ethic was obviously very strong, but it was almost like . . . too much devotion! It was definitely more like working on a play in college, where everybody is staying up all night, than, say, [working for] a showrunner who has a family. I remember being like, 'Wait, you are sleeping in your office?' " In the first year of shooting, Deschanel recalls, "Everyone gave [Meriwether] blankets for Christmas."

The show's distinctive blend of sharp jokes and character-driven emotion sometimes seemed impossible to pull off week after week. "Liz was not afraid to try things, and when it worked out, we would have really cool original episodes," says Philbin. "The downside was everything is an experiment, and sometimes it didn't work at all, and we had to roll up our sleeves and come up with something completely different. There was this sense that the show could constantly evolve and adapt to turn into a better version of itself."

Before *New Girl* premiered in September 2011, big yellow billboards began popping up all over Los Angeles and other major American cities. They featured a gigantic image of Deschanel in a lime-green vintage dress making a winsome face. The accompanying tagline was SIMPLY ADORKABLE.

"I was driving home one day, and I saw that 'adorkable' billboard, and I thought, *Oh no!*" Philbin moans. "I could imagine the response to that billboard if you hadn't seen the show yet. It put the emphasis on cute and not necessarily on the other elements of the show." The writers did not want Jess to be "simply" anything. Brett Baer remembers the shared determination that "she is not going to be this pixie girl. She is going to have edges and corners and missing pieces."

Misleading as the marketing campaign was, it worked: more than ten million viewers tuned into the premiere, and *New Girl* continued to be a hit with the precious eighteen-to-forty-nine-year-old demographic. It also triggered a virulent backlash. Cute-hate erupted: *Vanity Fair* recappers classified each *New Girl* episode as "Adorkable" or "Tweepulsive," while writer and actress

Julie Klausner called Deschanel a "tabula rasa . . . able to reflect with her pale limbs and heart-shaped moon face whatever it is a bewitched boy wants."

Meriwether was taken aback by "the vitriol coming at Zooey from other women. We are trying to get a show with a female lead and a female showrunner on network television. Shouldn't that be something celebrated at some level?" she asks, rubbing her hair distractedly. "Does every female character have to be representative of some larger agenda?" Deschanel's own voice wavers as she recalls, "Women who I would be aligned with philosophically were taking shots at me for being too feminine, saying that I was bringing them down and bringing the feminist movement down."

In response, Meriwether cowrote (with Luvh Rakhe) the season-one episode "Jess and Julia," in which Nick's sarcastic lawyer girlfriend Julia (Lizzy Caplan) stands in for all the Zooey haters. She offers to help Jess get out of a parking ticket, but then is tweepulsed when Jess explains that she ran a red light because there was an injured bird in the street. "A judge might buy into this whole thing," Julia snipes. "Those big, beautiful eyes, like a scared baby. I'm sure that gets you out of all kinds of stuff." Jess holds her tongue until late in the episode, when she can stand Julia's condescension no more.

"I brake for birds. I rock a lot of polka dots. I have touched glitter in the last twenty-four hours. I spend my entire day talking to children . . ." Jess lets rip, her scared baby eyes even wider than usual. "I'm sorry I don't talk like Murphy Brown, and I hate your pantsuit and I wish it had ribbons on it to make it slightly cuter. And that doesn't mean I'm not smart and tough and strong." And with that femi-ninja wo-manifesto, *New Girl* exorcised its manic-pixie demons and moved on. The monologue distinguishes the more fluid, twenty-first-century choose-your-own-adventure feminism from the padded-shoulder assertiveness of the *Murphy Brown* era, while making clear that Jess is more than a quirked-out blank slate for nerd-boy fantasies. She's a career woman, ultimately rising to become a school principal; she has opinions and desires of her own, strange as they might be. (Take her description of an intense sexual experience: "I left my body, went up to heaven, saw my grandparents, thought it was weird that I saw my grandparents, came back down.")

As the show settled into a madcap groove, and Jess found a comfortable medium between Etsy goddess and screwball comedian, the show's writers started to prick holes in masculinity, too. In "Injured," Nick drops his hard-bitten veneer when he confronts the possibility that he has cancer; later in the season, Schmidt breaks his penis (enabling a plaster-penis-cast gag), and Winston suffers from PMS. By this point, it's becoming clear that none of these guys is what he initially seemed. Schmidt is less bro than former fat kid encasing his neuroses in the armor of a hard gym body. Nick is a damaged soul terrified of failure who carries his money around in a baggie; and Winston's an empath in search of truth and usefulness, which he will eventually find as a cop. The crisis of modern masculinity—the difficulty faced by young males who don't know what being a man is supposed to involve nowadays—is played for tender laughs.

"Dave and I think of ourselves as broken and failed men in a lot of ways," says Brett Baer, sitting next to Dave Finkel in one of the *New Girl* writers' rooms. "So there is probably a willingness to admit that, in a masculine American world, we *don't* got it going on. We definitely approach those characters as failures in their own minds who couldn't accomplish the things they wanted to accomplish."

The week I visit *New Girl*'s headquarters, the writers are working on a season-five episode in which Schmidt has a humiliating interaction that provokes him to organize a classic macho bachelor party rather than the sophisticated metrosexual soiree he'd prefer. "We joke around a lot here that Schmidt's relationship with Nick is a romance," Baer says. "Not a bromance—a straight-up romance. I can't speak for every man, but the guys I work with, my partner, Dave—it is a real marriage. That's not always something that gets elucidated on television."

———

While Tina Fey made the unorthodox choice to spurn romance between her two central characters, Meriwether quickly decided that Jess and Nick would fall in love. Jess looks like she is made of sunshine, whereas Nick looks like he never changes his underwear: perfect odd couple. Sitcoms invariably stretch out sexual tension between primary characters for as many seasons as possible, and that was the *New Girl* writers' original plan, too. The script for the season-two episode "Cooler" didn't have Nick and Jess kissing at all—but when it came time to shoot the last scene, right before Christmas break, the chemistry between Deschanel and Jake Johnson was overwhelming.

Meriwether ran on set and told them to go for it. "It felt dishonest not to do the kiss based on what we led ourselves to in that episode," Finkel recalls. "How could we *not* do it? Which I think is what made that moment really powerful for fans of the show. They were feeling what we were feeling."

A great fan of rom-coms, Meriwether nevertheless realized too late that television narratives require a kind of long-term thinking different from that of movies: "It doesn't end when they come together. Having to continue to tell the story was difficult, and it changed the tone of the comedy. Suddenly, all of Nick's flaws were very amplified. He was now her boyfriend, so all this stuff that seemed hilarious got really dark. Oh no, he's an alcoholic and he doesn't have a checking account—he's actually a really messed-up guy!"

The series' other odd coupling, Schmidt and Cece, emerged accidentally. Finkel says, "We just put them together in an episode because we thought it would be funny for her to be treating him like a dog. She literally leaves him in the car while she goes into a club. But she made him funnier, and he made her funnier. He's not just a douche bag now, he's a douche bag who falls really in love. We knew, *Oh, my God, we've got to keep doing this.*"

Meriwether enjoyed playing with the formal limitations of the comedy genre to keep the series speeding in fresh directions. But it turns out that viewers don't always want a sitcom spinning too far out of its familiar orbit. In season three, the writers' decision to break up Schmidt and Cece and have him date two women backfired. "We were very excited about that in the writers' room," Meriwether remembers. "Schmidt is going to be this evil person! And the audience just *hated* it. It didn't occur to me that if you are turning on a show after a long day of work, you don't necessarily want to see these characters radically change. You want to see the same thing. For that moment in season three, we thought of ourselves as a cable show—and it didn't work."

Ratings dropped to an all-time low that season. Some execs suggested there was not enough "guy energy" to attract male viewers; they wanted more stories about bros out in the city getting laid, Meriwether recalls. "There really was this huge pressure on: how are we going to get more men to watch this show? It was this sort of impossible task where we are all trying to brainstorm ways to get people to watch the show—people who I think were never going to watch it in the first place." By the end of that season, Meriwether says everything finally "imploded." The writers scrapped the finale script after the actors' table read, and then tossed another version of the script a few days before the episode was scheduled to shoot. "It all was sort of falling apart, and it became clear everything had to change. I was sleeping at the office a lot, and everything was down to the wire because my philosophy was if there is a minute in the day, we are going to be working and using it to work on the show."

In the end, members of the *New Girl* team mounted something akin to a showrunner intervention. The actors and writers were burned out. According to Baer, Meriwether was told that "'you can't keep doing this, you will kill us. It's jokes, alt jokes, improvisation, more jokes.'" Meriwether admits, "I am such a workaholic that it actually took people saying that the show wasn't as good anymore for me to reassess the whole process. It was hard for me to take a step back and delegate more. The crazy thing about being a showrunner is that everyone is looking to you like, 'What do you want? How do you want to do this?' And I was like, 'I don't know, I just wrote some stuff!'" she says self-deprecatingly. "I just try to keep listening to people. It's a thing that is in motion."

While *New Girl* was making its debut in the fall of 2011, Mindy Kaling was hatching a sitcom of her own. After six years as a writer and actress on *The*

Office, the thirty-two-year-old had become a "girl crush" for young women all over America. She'd shared her thoughts on fashion in her blog, *Things I've Bought That I Love*, and tossed out pop-culture bon mots on Twitter. Kaling had also published *Is Everyone Hanging Out Without Me?*, her best-selling memoir about growing up an Indian American comedy nerd. The book documents the way she kickstarted her own career by cowriting and starring in *Matt and Ben*, an Off-Off Broadway show in which she played a fictionalized version of Ben Affleck to her best friend Brenda's Matt Damon. Producer Greg Daniels had seen *Matt and Ben* and invited the young Kaling to come write for his new adaptation of a British mockumentary, *The Office*. She was the only woman on a writing staff of eight.

Sitting in a coffee shop near her Los Angeles home in November 2011, Kaling told me that she was writing a pilot for NBC in which she would star as a gynecologist. "My mom is an ob-gyn, and I have so many years of detail I can access for that job," she gushed. "Being a woman who loves other women and talks to my girlfriends every day, I think—without sounding too into myself—I would be a dream ob-gyn." Kaling dismissed the idea that network prime time wasn't ready for story lines involving stirrups and yeast infections. "I think we'd talk about that stuff as much as we talk about paper on *The Office*. It's a setting that allows a constant flow of women," she continued, rattling off a list of female comedians she'd like to have on as guest stars.

Acknowledging that it might be a bit premature to discuss her show before it had been picked up, Kaling added, "I have this tendency to get overconfident about things. I'd rather be the kind of person who'll get over-excited and be devastated"—which is exactly what happened. NBC passed on her pilot script. Succumbing to devastation isn't Kaling's style, though. Instead, she sent the script to Fox chief Kevin Reilly, who had nurtured *30 Rock* and *New Girl*. He picked up *It's Messy* (as Kaling's comedy was then called) with a few caveats: he wanted a stronger male lead, and he suggested her character be called Mindy. Industry journalists gossiped that Reilly envisaged Kaling as the next Tina Fey.

One of several new comedies about single women premiering in the fall of 2012, *The Mindy Project* pilot stuck out like a gaudy neon sign plunked in the middle of a minimalist art gallery. Nothing about Dr. Mindy Lahiri's character is quiet or understated: she is a grown-up version of Willie Wonka's Veruca Salt, grabbing what she wants with reckless glee. A curvy Indian American gynecologist, Mindy rocks sparkly, skin-tight dresses with the cockiness of a supermodel. She knows how sexy she is, and she's not afraid to flirt with NBA players. Her expectations for men are also impossibly high. Before one date, she prays, "Dear Lord, may he have the wealth of Mayor Bloomberg, the personality of Jon Stewart, the face of Michael Fassbender"—not forgetting "the penis of Michael Fassbender."

As the first woman of color to create, write, and star in her own network television show, Kaling might've felt historic pressure to make her central character a positive role model—or, at the least, *admirable*. But, nope. In the pilot, we watch Mindy have a drunken meltdown at her ex-boyfriend's wedding and ride a bike into a swimming pool. An ob-gyn at a Manhattan practice, she seems to devote very little time to patient care: at one point, Mindy asks a hospital supervisor, "Am I in trouble because I might have lost a press-on nail in that woman?"

Kaling is proud to have created the first Indian American sitcom heroine, she tells me now. "The tricky thing was that because of that, people insisted that Mindy Lahiri represent all Indian women, or all Asian women, which I resisted." Why should she, Kaling demands, when *The Office*'s Michael Scott or *Eastbound & Down*'s Kenny Powers are allowed to be their ludicrous selves without standing in for all white males? For her new show, Kaling wanted to create a heroine driven by the self-confidence, sexual avarice, and tactlessness usually available only to male characters like these. "To me, the truly pioneering thing about Mindy Lahiri as a comedic lead was not that she was Indian but that she was so flawed."

Likability has long been a requirement for female characters, and a confining one at that. When an interviewer told author Claire Messud that the protagonist of her novel *The Woman Upstairs* was not good friend material,

Messud lashed back with a litany of great male antiheroes and assholes, from Humbert Humbert to Hamlet to Oedipus. "The relevant question isn't 'Is this a potential friend for me?,' but 'Is this character alive?'"

Kaling agrees that "*likability* can be a poisonous word, because so often it's attached to outdated standards for what is appealing about female characters for men. Sweetness, being agreeable, being put upon, having straight long hair, et cetera. Those are all *likable* qualities. Who cares? What is important to me is making a character *relatable*. Being able to relate to the character is everything, whether they are sweet and agreeable or not."

Dr. Mindy Lahiri constantly imagines herself at the center of a rom-com in which all eyes are on her. That's not so different from Jane Austen heroines such as Emma Woodhouse and Catherine Morland, who trip themselves up by projecting fantasies absorbed from romantic novels onto their ordinary lives. (Austen once described Emma as "a heroine whom no-one but myself will much like.") Rom-coms are often denigrated as fluffy chick flicks, but *The Mindy Project* regularly pays its respects to the genre by winking at rom-com lore lifted from movies such as *When Harry Met Sally* and *Bridget Jones's Diary*. In one episode, Mindy hangs out at the Empire State Building hoping to meet the love of her life à la *Sleepless in Seattle*, but is instead mistaken for a terrorist. "I know it's dangerous," she cluelessly tells the suspicious security guard, "but I am a true believer."

Kaling's ambition quickly hit some stumbling blocks. *The Mindy Project*'s tiny writing staff was overstretched; she was doing double duty as showrunner and star, as was Ike Barinholtz, a writer who had also been drafted to play wacky nurse Morgan Tookers. Episodes were being scratched and totally rewritten after rehearsals.

"They were so in the weeds," recalls Tracey Wigfield. "They did twenty-four episodes their first season, and I think they were halfway through when they realized, *We just need more people in the room!*" So, when *30 Rock* came to an end, Jack Burditt moved to LA to join Kaling as a co-showrunner on *The Mindy Project*; his *30 Rock* colleagues Wigfield and Lang Fisher soon followed.

Yet problems remained. Although *The Mindy Project* was supposed to be an ensemble comedy, every other character paled in comparison to Kaling's own ultravivid personality. (And yes, they were mostly pale-skinned as well.) Macho Dr. Danny Castellano (Chris Messina) quickly fell into place as a perfect romantic sparring partner for Mindy. But the other officemates never really came into sharp enough focus. "Writing *30 Rock*, it felt much more like an ensemble show," Wigfield admits. "On *Mindy*, for me, *she* was the fun character to write. It was a show about this woman."

Even more than a doctor problem, *The Mindy Project* had a woman problem. Dr. Mindy Lahiri started out with several female associates and a best friend named Gwen (Anna Camp), but those roles soon vanished or withered to bit parts until the series was basically Mindy surrounded by handsome white men. "That was a network thing," Wigfield suggests. "They were saying: 'Now Mindy should have a bunch of friends.' 'No, now the show should be all about work!'" The female patients at the gynecology practice also tailed off late in the first season. Lang Fisher says, "*Grey's Anatomy* can get away with it because they are drama. For comedy, [the execs] were like, 'Nah, we don't want to see anyone sick, anyone hurt, anyone having problems.'" It turned out the networks really *didn't* want to partake in "peak vagina."

Fisher laughs as she recalls discussions about how to bring in more male viewers. "Hey, network, guess what? Men are not going to watch a show about a gynecologist's office no matter what you do!" she shouts. "We are never going to get the *Sports Center* crowd to tune into the show . . . but, yeah, we had to just keep adding guys."

Like *30 Rock* and *New Girl*, *The Mindy Project* unraveled the single-girl sitcom in ways that felt startlingly fresh and disconcertingly unstable. "If you don't like an episode of *The Mindy Project* . . . tune in a week later, because the show will probably be something completely different," critic Todd VanDerWerff quipped in the *A.V. Club*. The show's chameleonic urge went into overdrive midway through season three, when the writers decided to break off Mindy's budding love affair with Danny and send her on a prestigious fellowship to Stanford. So the woman more obsessed with shoes than scalpels *is* actually a talented physician?

"While she comes across as a flibbertigibbet and sometimes she says inappropriate things, when she is in the operating room delivering babies or with a patient, she knows her stuff," Fisher explains. "It was important to remind the audience, and also remind us, that she is a student who worked really hard to get where she is—that doesn't go away, and you still want to be the best."

Kaling's own immigrant parents had instilled an intense work ethic in her. She realized that her lead character's ambition ought to feel as oversize as her hunger for romance. By the end of Mindy's fellowship, she has decided to open her own fertility clinic—and discovered that she's pregnant with Danny's baby. Ever confident in her own abilities, she resists Danny's request that she stop working. "A woman can have professional ambitions and still have a family," Mindy insists. "I mean, *rich* women."

Just as *30 Rock* mocked the hypocrisy of Liz Lemon's white feminism and *New Girl* commented on adorkability, *The Mindy Project* occasionally acknowledged class privilege. Yet Mindy Lahiri is a woman of color, which means that every so often—despite her many white friends and colleagues, and her refusal of identity politics—she becomes the target of mundane racism. For instance, Danny's mom assumes she's a maid the first time she meets her, and a professor mistakes her for Nobel Prize–winning activist Malala Yousafzai (something that actually happened to Kaling at a party).

"I love when we tackle the race and sexism stuff head-on," Kaling tells me. "Mindy is such a confident character—I think she has stated that she has the entitlement of a tall white man, so when she isn't treated well, that's really fun. We did an episode called 'Bernardo & Anita,' where Mindy dates an Indian man who accuses her of being a 'coconut': dark on the outside and white on the inside. That incensed her, and it was fun exploring that with the character." The title referenced *West Side Story*'s Puerto Rican couple, but Wigfield suggests that Dr. Lahiri's "coconut" attitude was largely inspired by Kaling's own assimilated life. After realizing how many Indian American fans yearned to see themselves reflected on TV, the writers decided to delve more deeply into Mindy's cultural ambivalence.

During the 2015 Academy Awards, American Express ran an advertising spot called "The Unlikely Leading Lady." As Mindy Kaling eats gummy bears for breakfast and drives to the studio set, her disembodied voice explains that, growing up, "[I] never saw someone who looked like me reflected in anything . . . I kind of realized that I had to take destiny into my own hands, and it's the harder path and it's grueling and it's not glamorous. But then I control it and I own it. No one can stop you then."

Three months later, Fox announced that it would not renew *The Mindy Project* for a fourth season. The series had dropped from nearly five million viewers for the pilot to just over two million with its season-three finale. Yet again, Kaling refused to take no for an answer. Within a week, *The Mindy Project* arose from near-death, thanks to a deal with digital streaming site Hulu.

Like Netflix and Amazon, Hulu was itching to make a name for itself with original programming. The site had already been streaming *The Mindy Project* in syndication, and the show had done incredibly well there, according to Hulu head of original content Beatrice Springborn, "so we knew she would be a great way to brand our originals right out of the gate." What excited Springborn about *The Mindy Project* was the way its viewers, who are primarily female, "watch episodes over and over and over again. Sitcoms are typically seen as a bit throwaway, more like candy than protein. So the idea that people are consuming it over and over again—and getting something out of it on repeat viewing—is fascinating."

Working with Hulu removed all worries about ratings from Kaling's shoulders—showrunners at Hulu can't get information on how many people watch each episode, even if they want to know—and also offered more freedom in terms of length, language, and format. The writers instantly took advantage in the most exultant way. Season four opened with a *Sliding*

Doors scenario in which Mindy and Danny never fell in love and she never got pregnant. Instead, he remains her grumpy colleague, while she is married to a wealthy reality TV producer and lives in a lavish Gramercy Park apartment. When Mindy eventually snaps out of her dream, real-life Danny is kneeling by her bedside, asking her to marry him. And when she goes into labor on a subway train a few episodes later, Danny runs through the tunnel to get to her, because all the best movie heroes run furiously to get to the women they love.

Until this point, the rom-com tradition had hung over the show like a sweet, druggy haze. But in the fourth season of *The Mindy Project*, synapses began to fire in Mindy Lahiri's postpartum brain. After trying out the stay-at-home-mom life, she seethes with frustration that Danny expects her to give up her job, her old apartment, and even her heritage (by raising their son Catholic).

"Every time you disagree with something I do, it's a referendum on my character," Mindy complains. "If I want to go to work, it means I'm a bad mother. If I want another glass of wine, it means I'm out of control . . . You get to make all the definitions." It's obvious that this fairy-tale romance is a goner, clearing the way for Mindy to charge back into the dating world with her brassy self-confidence restored. And motherhood also allowed *The Mindy Project* to shamelessly exploit the physicality of childbirth and breast-feeding. (What new mom hasn't dreamed of spraying milk into a rude colleague's face, as Mindy does?)

Hulu execs didn't offer much feedback or pressure on plot or characters, so "storytelling-wise, we were able to do weirder episodes," says Wigfield. Inspired by one of Kaling's favorite sayings—that she has the confidence of a white man—Lang Fisher wrote an episode in which Mindy wakes up as a blond dude named Michael (played by Ryan Hansen). Concealed within Michael's body, Mindy giddily explores the pleasures of masturbation, manspreading, and male privilege. As a woman, Dr. Lahiri did not make it to the final round of interviews for a department head position; as a less-qualified and less-hardworking man, she gets the job. "I can tell you're a good leader just by looking at you," one of the all-male committee members exclaims.

"Mindy has confidence not commensurate with her station in life," Kaling suggests. "People are constantly telling her she's not good enough, and she tries to deflect it with the confidence of Prince Harry. Obviously, she is not always successful, and it's hard to be in her skin and always be proving herself. We thought, 'Wouldn't it be fun to see her as she has always seen herself?'" In a way, it brought Mindy Lahiri full circle, back to the audacious single woman on the prowl whom we first met in the pilot—but this time, she put the cock in "cocky."

Lang Fisher describes Kaling as the showrunner version of an Energizer Bunny, one who made her own luck and rescued her show from banishment. Although Hulu's reach remains much smaller than Fox's, Kaling's popularity keeps growing because she constantly speaks to fans through social media and her books.

"When I didn't know her, I just thought, *Mindy Kaling is the luckiest person in the world because she gets to do all of this!*" says Nisha Ganatra, who directed an episode in season five. "And then I worked on the show, and there is Mindy in meetings, and then she's shooting, and then Mindy is leaving the set to go to the edit room, and then she's waking up at four in the morning to make sure she is in the writers' room the next day." This juggling act is enabled by producer-director Michael Alan Spiller, who Ganatra says provides "a huge safety net for everybody," and current co-showrunner Matt Warburton. But, at the end of the day, the burden of the series is on Kaling.

"She is such a hustler!" Fisher says, meaning it in the best possible way. "She keeps the train moving, which is how, as a woman of color, she is able to have her own show even though we did not have great ratings. There is no one else saying, *You deserve to have this*." Fisher counts herself lucky to have been mentored by Fey and Kaling. "They are training the women in the room how to do that themselves—but they are also training the men to see us as real equals."

CHAPTER 6

A Voice of a Generation:
Lena Dunham's *Girls*

Lena Dunham huddles with Jenni Konner on the set
of *Girls* during the filming of season two.

The first time I interviewed Lena Dunham, she was twenty-five, with one foot in the indie film world and the other perched on the precipice of media clusterfuckdom. It was March 2012, and after texting apologetically that she was running late, Dunham scurried down LA's Larchmont Boulevard in a pale yellow dress, zooming past tight-bodied women carrying yoga mats and mothers pushing strollers. Sitting down at the vegan café she'd chosen, Dunham ordered a kombucha. She then pulled out a bottle of green liquid from her bag. "I'm doing a very LA thing, of drinking green juice and kombucha," she said sheepishly, explaining that she was trying to ward off illness after succumbing to junk food in Austin. She'd just been there to premiere the first three episodes of her new HBO series *Girls* at the South by Southwest (SXSW) film festival.

Dunham's overloaded schedule already threatened to wear her down.

Immediately after our meeting, she had an appointment to take her driving test. She'd failed once before, and now that she was living bicoastally between Los Angeles and New York, she felt an intense pressure to learn. Los Angeles itself seemed to exhaust her. Dunham initially rented a house in the Hollywood Hills, hoping to walk in Joan Didion's footsteps, but the isolation freaked her out: "I was hiding under the covers and imagining all these running escape routes down the hill." Her next stop was an old art deco apartment building in the middle of the city, but friends were convinced that the place was brimming with dissatisfied actors' ghosts. "I have not personally seen a ghost," she said matter-of-factly. "That being said, my sink did spit up perfect soap suds. So it could be a movie star who died in a bubble bath."

Dunham was already an indie film darling; it was at SXSW that her low-budget movies *Creative Nonfiction* (2009) and *Tiny Furniture* (2010) got their first exposure. But the year we met, SXSW was where she first experienced *over*exposure, and the controversy that comes with it. She was shocked when a guy approached her after the *Girls* screening and told her he enjoyed Hannah, the character Dunham played, but found her sex scenes off-putting. "He thought the character could be separated from her sexual behavior, like, 'She'd be so cute if she wasn't such a slut!'" Dunham trilled.

As far as Dunham was concerned, explicit female sexuality was "a last frontier" for television—especially when it was filmed from a woman's point of view—and she was fascinated by viewers like the one at SXSW who responded to the show's sex scenes with revulsion. "There are so many reactions to art that make sense to me—but 'ick' means something," she said thoughtfully, nodding with such force that the loose bun of hair atop her head wobbled. "It either means you're offended politically, or you think something was morally compromised, or you find someone unattractive. So why don't we articulate this 'ick' a little?"

That's pretty much what Dunham would spend the next six years doing.

When I was growing up in the seventies and eighties, intimate depictions of women's lives were largely nonexistent on television. Female sexual pleasure and ambivalence, contraception and pregnancy scares, periods and date rape—there was so little trace of these things in prime time that when *Seinfeld* designed a whole 1995 episode around Elaine Benes's obsession with contraceptive sponges, it felt like a revelation. (The boyfriend Elaine finally decides is *not* "spongeworthy," in the script's classic coinage, was played by a young Scott Patterson, aka diner owner Luke from *Gilmore Girls*.)

A few years after that *Seinfeld* episode, *Sex and the City* blazed a new trail into virgin territory for television: there were debates among the four pals about anal sex and pubic hair and vibrators and infertility, as well as emotional tussles over friendship, infidelity, motherhood, and power imbalances within relationships. "We were all single at the time, and we would just tell the story of our bad date the night before," *Sex and the City* writer Jenny Bicks recalls of that largely female writers' room. "We did have a rule that any idea that we had, if it seemed outlandish, we would have to check it with other people to make sure that it was really happening. The thing was, as weird as this shit was, it was happening. That was so uplifting: to be able to write about the stuff you weren't allowed to say before."

By the time *Sex and the City* ended in 2004, women's blogs had begun popping up across the Internet. Soon sites such as *Jezebel* and *The Hairpin* arrived to expand this emerging online space for young women to talk among themselves, making them increasingly comfortable about sharing frank details from their lives. Dunham was no different.

"I am constantly tweeting things and going, 'Why did I just say that to the world?'" she told me at the Larchmont café. "I wanted to capture that feeling of there being no clear boundary anymore between public and private. And also, my characters will choose to keep really strange things private. They will share some sexual humiliation but refuse to tell their friends they lost their job. It's an interesting thing in this culture, what we choose to keep secret."

As a public figure in the wake of *Girls*'s instant success, Dunham would prove to be just as unguarded and impulsive. Her tendency to toss out provocative, unprocessed thoughts and jokes was an offshoot of her candor and unwillingness to self-censor, but it ensnared Dunham in constant controversy. The briefest trip down Google Lane yields page after page of rants and listicles with titles such as "Lena Dunham and Everything Wrong with White Feminists," "Eleven Reasons to Dislike Lena Dunham," and the more traditional "Hot Mess Alert! Lena Dunham Looks Like Your Crazy Aunt on a Shopping Spree."

Dunham began inspiring Schadenfreude before she even hit high school. Her first media appearance came at the age of eleven, when she was profiled in *Vogue* as part of a feature focused on the fashion taste of children whose parents were New York City creatives. The daughter of acclaimed artists Laurie Simmons and Carroll Dunham, precocious Lena sounded like a late-twentieth-century Eloise. "I tend not to go for trends. You can only wear them for two weeks," she declared. Instead, for the photo spread, she wore a dress that she'd sewn herself.

Growing up surrounded by artists, Dunham always assumed that she would do something artistic. "My uncle's a lawyer, and I remember going to see him in court and thinking, *That's cool, too bad I could never be a lawyer*," she says. In order to distance herself from her parents, though, Dunham decided to focus on words rather than images. At fourteen, she took stand-up comedy classes; the opening line of her act was, "Hi, I'm Lena, and I'm an alcoholic. Just kidding, my dad is." As a student at St. Ann's School in Brooklyn, she began writing plays. One was set in the waiting room of an abortion clinic; another, *The Goldman Girls*, was inspired by her mother's Long Island childhood. Later, at Oberlin College in Ohio, she studied creative writing in the hope of being a poet. But she felt out of place and isolated there: "Oberlin is surrounded by cornfields on all sides. You just ride your bike and think and do weird experiments with your friends."

Some of those "weird experiments" involved making videos. "Pressure" (2006), shot in the Oberlin library stacks, presents Dunham and two female students discussing orgasms and sneezes. In "The Fountain," Dunham takes a bath in a campus fountain, clad only in a bikini. That one got more than a million hits on YouTube and, in a preview of her future, a ton of nasty comments about her chubby body.

At twenty-two, an age when the rest of us were trying to cover our zits and pen the occasional maudlin poem, Dunham made her first movie, *Creative Nonfiction*, about a college student trying to write a screenplay. Dunham's influences included Woody Allen's self-portraits of verbose neurotics and Nicole Holofcener's intimate, female-focused indie movies. Critics filed her alongside "mumblecore" filmmakers Joe Swanberg and Andrew Bujalski, then coming into the ascendant with microbudget, highly naturalistic movies such as *Funny Ha Ha* and *Hannah Takes the Stairs*.

Returning to New York post-Oberlin in 2008, she juggled internships and part-time jobs while trying to make more movies. Noticing that Swanberg had made a Web series for the hip sex website Nerve, Dunham successfully pitched them *Tight Shots*, a series about sex and dating among young filmmakers. "When I was younger I would email anyone I liked," she says. "I had no qualms about emailing a director I admired and saying, 'What boom mic do you use?'" *Tight Shots* was followed by *The Delusional Downtown Divas*, an online comedy written and starring Dunham and several of her friends as spoiled brats trawling the art world.

Tiny Furniture turned the camera even more narrowly on Dunham's surroundings: she filmed the movie in her parents' loft, and recruited her mother and younger sister, Grace, to effectively play themselves alongside her own character, Aura Freeman. A recent graduate, all Aura has to show for her college years is a video of her performance art piece shot in the college fountain. (Dunham used the actual video from Oberlin.) The movie's title refers to a strand of Laurie Simmons's feminist art, photographs of dolls and dollhouses, and in the movie, Aura obsesses over her mother's life and work. Blithely unconcerned about invasion of privacy, she reads passages from her mother's diary as a young woman, excerpted from Simmons's own journal.

More or less the chrysalis of *Girls*, *Tiny Furniture* has aimless Aura toggling between poorly paid jobs and unromantic sex. She spends much of the movie in her underwear, exposing her pasty flesh in such a casual way it feels insurrectionary. Her attempts at sexual adventure invariably misfire. One schmucky guy (played by Alex Karpovsky, later a *Girls* lynchpin as the character of Ray) is willing to sleep in her bed but draws the line at having sex. And a workplace flirtation results in a rushed, doggy-style fuck inside an outdoor sewer pipe. Afterward, Aura takes a shower on her hands and knees, as if reliving the experience, and then crawls into her mother's bed looking for comfort. The sex is consensual, but it is also humiliating.

Shot in November 2009 on a fifty-thousand-dollar budget supplied mostly by Dunham's parents, *Tiny Furniture* premiered the next March at SXSW, where it won the Best Narrative Feature prize. The film was widely and glowingly reviewed; it would eventually become part of the prestigious Criterion Collection. "It is Ms. Dunham's refusal to put on a pretty show, to doll herself up, that is the movie's boldest stroke," Manohla Dargis declared in her *New York Times* review. In its anti-aesthetic of "unlovely, unadorned, badly lighted digital images," Dargis saw *Tiny Furniture* as the vanguard of a new kind of feminist cinema verité.

Dunham started to take meetings in Hollywood. Her big break came about in an unusual way. A fan of Laurie Simmons's artwork, HBO's entertainment chief Sue Naegle watched *Tiny Furniture* while she was on a camping vacation with her kids. In the cabin next door was her friend Jenni Konner, a writer/producer who had worked with Judd Apatow on his cult series *Undeclared* as well as on her own short-lived series *Help Me Help You* and *In the Motherhood*. "I finished watching *Tiny Furniture* and I knocked on Jenni's cabin door and said, 'Do you have your laptop?'" Naegle recalls. "'You need to watch this right away; it's fantastic!'" Konner was equally captivated.

When Dunham sat down with HBO execs to discuss developing a

series, she had no idea how to pitch anything. "I went in and said, 'Here's the kind of show I want to see and haven't seen on TV,'" she says. "I went on a tirade about my friends and the kinds of problems they were dealing with as twenty-something women, trying to navigate the social landscape that was totally reliant on texting and Facebook. I overshared about my own relationship foibles, and I was like, 'Which of my friends *hasn't* been on Ritalin since they were twelve?'"

Her artfully artless TMI riff excited Naegel and her younger HBO colleague Kathleen McCaffrey; it seemed to encapsulate a quicksilver millennial sensibility. These characters, Dunham promised, are "your girlfriends and daughters and sisters and employees."

———————

Sex and the City is an obvious antecedent for *Girls*: a (mostly) female-written show centered on female characters unapologetically pursuing their desires and ambitions on the small screen. It was HBO's first Zeitgeist-defining hit, yet the network mystifyingly failed to follow the mammoth success of *Sex and the City* with further original programming aimed at (or created by) women. A decade after launching Carrie Bradshaw and Company, HBO had aired only a handful of series with female characters at the center: *The Comeback*, a mockumentary starring Lisa Kudrow, from *Sex and the City* creator Michael Patrick King; Tracey Ullman's sketch-comedy series *Tracey Takes On*; and *The No. 1 Ladies' Detective Agency*, a coproduction with the BBC. There were even fewer scripted series created by women in HBO's archives.

According to Alan Sepinwall's book *The Revolution Was Televised*, in the late nineties, HBO considered buying a TV series by *My So-Called Life* creator Winnie Holzman about a female toy executive; ultimately the network decided to greenlight *The Sopranos* instead. Who knows where the path not taken would have led, but in the early years of the twenty-first century, a rogue's gallery of wayward alpha men dominated the cable landscape. HBO largely defined the genre, thanks to melancholy Tony Soprano and his brutal mob crew; profane *Deadwood* bordello owner Al Swearengen; and *The Wire*'s gay drug-dealing outlaw Omar Little. Sure, some of these dramas had splendid female supporting characters—shout out to Carmela Soprano, Trixie the Whore, and Kima Greggs—but it was those brooding male antiheroes who dominated the dialogue and drove the story lines.

Troubled and tempestuous, the men of HBO ushered in the modern golden age: television as epic narrative that could be binge-watched; television as a creative haven for art house film directors and ambitious screenwriters; television as a force field surrounded by auteur-focused criticism and forensically in-depth reviews.

"The thing that was concerning to me was, every time there was a female-lead show that worked, no one wanted to repeat it," says Naegle, who arrived at HBO in 2008, after having been an agent to many female showrunners, including *Roseanne* scribes Eileen Heisler and DeAnn Heline and *Sex and the City*'s Jenny Bicks. Naegle says that in the 1990s and early 2000s, "Many many many times, male presidents of networks said to me, 'We won't put out a show with a lead female on the air. They don't make money; no one wants to watch them.' I would argue, 'A lot of women watch television. In my house, my mom determined what we all watched. Why wouldn't she want to see a female-lead show?'"

By 2010, HBO's big draws, *The Sopranos*, *Six Feet Under*, and *The Wire*, were done, and the cupboard was bare. Entertainment blogs frequently buzzed about female-oriented projects in development at the network from young writers such as Julie Klausner, Mara Altman, and Sloane Crosley. There were whispers of a women's studies professor drama from Theresa Rebeck; a sixties groupie series by Jill Soloway; and a comedy about an aging feminist icon created by Marti Noxon. None of them made it to air. Naegle says the lack of women on HBO wasn't for lack of her trying: "I was reconnecting with people like Jenni [Konner] and all these great female directors, trying to find shows. . . . Even if you set out to find a certain kind of programming, you can't will it."

Watching *Tiny Furniture* for the first time in her cabin that summer,

Naegle fell in love with Lena Dunham's work. And because this young woman had already written, directed, and starred in a low-budget film, HBO execs could see how her show would look and feel.

"We told them, 'This is going to be *Tiny Furniture* but funnier and with more girls,'" says Konner, who quickly jumped on board as co-showrunner to help steer an inexperienced Dunham through the process. When Judd Apatow got wind of the project and asked to be involved, Naegle hesitated for a second. "I really love Judd, and he has mentored so many incredible writers, but at that moment, I was like, 'No no no no no!'" she says, laughing. "I just thought, *Let's not mess with this too much.*" But Konner knew that both Apatow's creative vision and his marketplace clout, in the wake of *Knocked Up* and *Bridesmaids*, could only help the series.

Shrewdly, Apatow moved quickly to circumvent any expectations on HBO's part that *Girls* would be an extension of the low-budget approach of *Tiny Furniture*. "There was a moment when they might've said, 'Wow, this girl works really cheap!'" he recalls, in reference to the film's fifty-thousand-dollar budget. Instead, Apatow insisted from the start that they wanted the show "to look like *Sex and the City*. We are going to shoot in New York and we want the same budget as all your big New York shows."

The pilot of *The Untitled Lena Dunham Project* pivoted around aspiring writer Hannah Horvath and her best friends, Jessa and Marnie. An odd combination of uncrushable self-confidence and wry self-deprecation, Hannah "feels like she deserves praise she's not getting while thinking she doesn't deserve anything. It's the trademark of many Jewish comedians, but it is sort of a new thing to see in a girl that age," says Dunham, who is half-Jewish. That was the jarring originality of Hannah as a character: a sad sack quality melded with cringe-inducing obnoxiousness inside the body of a young woman.

And that body—well, the remarkable thing about it was that it was so unremarkable. Not fat, just defiantly imperfect. As in *Tiny Furniture*, Dunham was compulsive about exposing it in ways that were more mundane and ungainly than HBO audiences were used to seeing. Nudity was likely to involve unsexy scenarios such as sitting on the toilet or eating a cupcake in the bathtub.

Konner says they built something like thirty bathroom sets over the years "because we don't stop the scene when someone goes into the bathroom, we don't cut away when she takes her shirt off or puts her shirt on. We see all the awkward moments of life." The sex scenes are, if anything, even less titillating: in the pilot, Hannah shows up at the Brooklyn apartment of her eccentric sex buddy, Adam. Ordering her onto her hands and knees on his threadbare couch, Adam seems oblivious to Hannah's pleasure (or, rather, lack of it). As Hannah chatters anxiously, trying to get feedback on his desires, Adam snaps, "Let's play the quiet game."

Everything about *Girls*'s approach felt abrasively surprising, like experiencing the world from a yoga position that is both enlightening and borderline unpleasant. At the center of this attraction/repulsion vortex is Hannah and her ever-shifting relationships with her friends—love affairs of a sort, freighted with unspoken aggression, jealousy, and dependency. The audience first sees Marnie asleep, her plastic mouth guard poking out of her lips as she sweetly spoons roommate Hannah. They conked out while watching *The Mary Tyler Moore Show*, a nod to the young independent single women of the 1970s from the young can't-get-their-careers-started women of the 2010s.

Knowing that comparisons to the single ladies of *Sex and the City* were inevitable, Dunham derailed them with a metareference in the pilot. Shoshanna, originally described as "a JAP in velour sweats," sizes up Jessa as "a Carrie with some Samantha aspects and Charlotte hair." Jessa, a British wild child, proves her immense cool by disdainfully replying that she has never watched the HBO show. Despite the shared focus on four young women in New York City, ramshackle *Girls* felt miles away from high-gloss *Sex and the City*. In Hannah's Brooklyn universe, messy adventure always trumped monied glamour. There were no gigantic shoe closets or suave heroes here. As Dunham once joked at a television critics conference, "[My boyfriend] in the pilot is not Mr. Big. He literally does not have bedsheets!"

Naegle recalls having very few critiques of Dunham's pilot script: "There was a voice and a tone that were so specific, we just didn't want to play around with it." HBO's one big note, she says, involved Hannah's relationship with her parents, a pair of midwestern academics. "We all felt it needed a breaking point to propel the character forward," she says. Apatow suggested Hannah's parents announce they will no longer subsidize her, forcing their daughter to look for a job in the midst of America's deep recession.

"I think I might be the voice of my generation," she protests to them, trying to win back financial support. "Or at least *a* voice. Of *a* generation." Hannah is zonked on opium tea when she announces this, but she is at least half-serious. It was the kind of self-satirizing dialogue that Dunham tossed off gleefully, perhaps unaware that her show would soon trigger an avalanche of think pieces, many devoted to unpacking questions such as: How dare Lena Dunham suggest that she is the voice of her generation?

In the last scene in the pilot, Hannah wakes up in her parents' empty hotel room. Before leaving, she steals the tip they have left behind for the maid. We have been warned: *Girls* is going to make it hard for us to like these young women.

HBO agreed to let Dunham play Hannah, much to her agent's surprise. And she had written the role of Jessa for close friend Jemima Kirke, the delicately beautiful daughter of a rock star and an interior designer, who had already appeared in *Tiny Furniture* in a similar role. Kirke was a painter with no interest in acting, even if the part was inspired by her own personality. She also had just given birth to daughter Rafaella.

"Jemima was like, 'I just had a kid; I'm not going to be on your TV show!'" recalls casting director Jennifer Euston. Dunham eventually coaxed Kirke into shooting the pilot just six weeks after she gave birth; she would later have to coax her *again* when Kirke tried to quit just before the start of season two.

For Marnie, Hannah's conventionally pretty, tightly wound best friend who works as an art gallery assistant, they settled on recent college graduate Allison Williams, best known then for a YouTube video in which she sings over the *Mad Men* theme song, and for being anchorman Brian Williams's daughter. Shoshanna was originally written as a secondary role, a slightly older party girl. Many actresses auditioned for the part, including comedian Amy Schumer. But after watching a tape of twenty-three-year-old Zosia Mamet (daughter of playwright David and actress Lindsay Crouse), Dunham decided to change Shoshanna into a loopier, college-age virgin.

"Once Zosia took on that character, she created something that was not on the page at all," Euston recalls. "So then they decided, the show is not going to be about three girls; it's going to be about four."

When asked why the core of her cast consisted of children of famous people from the arts and media, Dunham tells me that she "didn't think about it at the time. The only thing that would make it not a coincidence is that they came in with a preternatural willingness to play and an understanding of the creative process that probably comes from being raised around it." After pausing for a moment to think, she adds, "Allison has a poise that is in the best way very newscaster's daughter," while Zosia "came in and brought all this nuance. It comes from her talent and also a lifetime of watching people make interesting things. And Jemima was my best friend in high school, and she was always the apotheosis of the coolest girl. To be able to capture that but also its flip side—the struggle of the cool girl who can't express her fears because her whole self-defense is carefreeness and nonchalance, that was an interesting thing to explore with her."

As for the boys in *Girls*, Dunham knew she wanted to cast her *Tiny Furniture* costar Alex Karpovsky as Ray. A slightly older guy, Ray would end up being the show's moral compass. Christopher Abbott was perfect for Charlie, Marnie's slavishly adoring boyfriend. But Dunham had no one in mind for Adam, Hannah's perturbing boyfriend. On the first day of casting, Jen Euston scheduled three actors to audition for the role. One of them was Adam Driver, a hulking, Juilliard-trained former marine whom Euston had unsuccessfully pushed for roles in various movies she had cast.

"Nobody would hire him because of the way he looked and because he was . . . unusual," Euston says of Driver, with his huge beak of a nose and sepulchral air. Looking at headshots before the session, Euston says Dunham and Konner held up his photo and mocked it. "I said, 'Just wait, okay?'" Driver walked in and took possession of the casting session.

"It was a tiny room full of women, and he is gigantic," Konner recalls. "He was reading the part, and he was physical with Lena; he was grabbing her. It was like one of those old recordings of the Beatles where you can't hear them because all the girls are screaming—you can barely hear the audition because we were all . . ." Konner starts pretending to hyperventilate. Although Adam was originally intended to be a fleeting character, the producers knew Driver needed to be a permanent fixture. "I said on day one, we have a young Brando, we have a young De Niro. Everyone saw it," Konner says. Sure enough, within a few years, Driver was cast as Kylo Ren in the *Star Wars* saga and starring in movies by Jim Jarmusch, Steven Soderbergh, and Martin Scorsese.

From the moment he steps into the frame in the pilot, Driver exudes a kind of mesmerizing deviance, a sense of emotions so volatile they might explode. Dunham says Adam's character was initially inspired by a macho guy she dated pre-*Girls* who "was into building things," which charmed her. "The flip side was he had a lot of unexpressed pain and anger."

Driver is such a compelling actor, Dunham admits, that he made Adam almost too loveable, such that "there is no way you are going to watch the show and not come away feeling affectionately toward him." And yet she always intended for him to have a whisper of unpredictable violence about him, which comes out throughout the show's run. "My goal was never to suggest, 'This is the kind of boyfriend you should want!' I was always urging people to think critically about the kind of character he was."

Dunham went into *Girls* with an indie filmmaker's approach: she knew how to direct actors and manage a small crew, but being a television showrunner meant learning to use a writers' room. In addition to Konner and Apatow, the team included *New Yorker* cartoonist and *Six Feet Under* writer

Bruce Eric Kaplan, *New York* magazine journalist Deborah Schoeneman, *Vice* columnist Lesley Arfin, and young fiction writer Sarah Heyward. Dunham says she initially turned to them more for their life experiences than for their writing skills. "A lot of [the scripts] came from our lives. 'This happened to me. Ohmigod this happened to you?' Why have we never seen this on television, these common female experiences? Some of them sexual . . . but also about friendship or trying to do well at your job or humiliations. Tension with friends, living in a weird cramped space with your friend and her boyfriend, and watching their relationship dissolve."

Yet Dunham found it hard to collaborate at the start. Although the writers' room spent a lot of time getting themselves into a collective mindset (absorbing female coming-of-age novels such as Mary McCarthy's *The Group* and movies such as *Party Girl*), Dunham wrote a half-season's worth of episodes mostly by herself. "I was so used to going into a cave and doing it on my own. I totally believed in the concept of an auteur. But television is a people's medium, and you want to enrich your show with other people's voices." Konner saw it as part of her job to school her young partner in the art of delegation—if for no other reason than, as Konner joked at the time, "She's only twenty-five, and at a certain point she's going to run out of stories because she hasn't had time to live them."

Arranged marriages of creative minds don't always work in television (as we saw earlier with *Roseanne*). Dunham and Konner came from different generations and different coasts. Dunham was the child of New York City artists, Konner the LA daughter of two TV writers, Lawrence Konner (*The Sopranos*) and Ronnie Wenker-Konner (*Cagney & Lacey*). Yet the women bonded immediately, forging a relationship that would reach beyond *Girls*. "It's very rare that people become close friends and they find their rhythm as creative people," marvels Apatow. "[T]here are literally zero power struggles or creative wars between them."

It helped that they'd all agreed Dunham had the final say on decisions, and that Konner and Apatow saw it as part of their job to look out for her well-being. "Lena certainly benefited from the fact that Jenni and I had so

many really difficult experiences, and so we were able to anticipate everything that could go wrong," Apatow suggests. "We were able to say, here's
what the controversies will probably be."

Dunham struggled to name the series. She wanted to signal the idea that
these young women in their early twenties did not yet think of themselves
as adults. She kept coming up with cute titles along the lines of *Girls Like Us*
or *Those Crazy Girls!* Eventually, Apatow suggested they keep it simple and
call the show *Girls*. The title stuck.

A year passed between the start of filming on *Girls* and the show's premiere in April 2012. In the interim, those edgy "girl" comedies created by
women (*New Girl*, *2 Broke Girls*, *Don't Trust the B—*, *Whitney*) materialized
on network television. But it turns out that all that worrying about "peak
vagina" was premature: *Girls* took female trouble to a new level. Instead of
using genitals as sassy punch lines, Dunham's dramedy emphasized graph-
ically awkward sex and real talk about real-looking bodies.

As if to throw down a gauntlet, the series' second episode was titled
"Vagina Panic": Jessa plans to have an abortion, and Hannah gets tested
for STDs. At one point, the camera floats upward to offer a panoramic
view of Hannah's body, splayed on a gynecologist's chair. She flinches as
the female ob-gyn inserts the speculum. "Is that painful?" the doctor asks.
"Yeah, but only in the way it's supposed to be," Hannah says (as if to wink
to *Girls*'s audience, "Yes, you're supposed to be cringing"). Meanwhile,
Jessa decides to have sex with a cute stranger rather than show up for her
abortion, and conveniently gets her period, making the whole question
moot. Although *Girls* would revisit the topic of pregnancy termination
more directly in a later season, this early episode served as a declaration of
its intent to be daring.

Apatow says that although HBO rarely pushed back on anything con-
tentious, he himself was nervous about staging an abortion at the start of the
series, worrying that "it might feel like we are just shoving that in people's
faces day one. You have to pick your moments." And the political moment
of *Girls*'s debut was a fraught one: House Republicans led an attack on the

federal rule requiring employers to provide female employees with free health insurance coverage for contraceptives. When, in February 2012, law student Sandra Fluke was allowed to testify to the importance of birth control insurance coverage for young women like her before an all-male House committee, she became a lightning rod for Republican rage. "It makes her a slut, right?" Rush Limbaugh snarled on his radio show. "It makes her a prostitute. She wants to be paid to have sex. . . . She wants you and me and the taxpayers to pay her to have sex." A few months later, the Republican Party adopted a virulently antiabortion platform for the 2012 presidential election, calling for a constitutional amendment outlawing abortion with no explicit exceptions for women's health or in cases of incest or rape.

Girls leapt right into this political battleground. Midway through the HBO pilot was the excruciating "quiet game" sex scene between Adam and Hannah, an indication to the network that this show would contain starkly realistic, deglamorized depictions of female sexuality. As Dunham puts it, "It was essential [for HBO] to understand: There is going to be sex, and it's not going to be sexy. A lot of the time girls are allowed to be a mess in an adorable way, and this is girls being a mess in a *not* adorable way."

Girls premiered to fairly universal acclaim. *Slate*'s Troy Patterson opened his review by hailing the series as "an exceptional piece of American art, as witty as *The Women*, richer in raunch than *Portnoy's Complaint*, charismatic like Sleater-Kinney." Yet almost as soon as critics anointed her, Dunham was smacked by a backlash.

That shouldn't have been surprising: women's evocations of their lives have historically been derided as trivial or whiny. The eminent Mexican poet Octavio Paz once complained of Frida Kahlo's self-portraits, "I feel I am before a complaint, not a work of art." Dunham's own mother, Laurie Simmons, recalls feeling ashamed of working with female subject matter (dolls) when she started out in the art world: "I'd come to New York when conceptual art and video and all of this very intensely rigorous, intelligent, and conceptual work was happening, and I just thought, *Oh no, this is like girl play*."

In an essay about confessional female writers, Rebecca Traister noted that in a media landscape with little space for women's voices, those roles often get filled by female writers "willing to expose themselves in a way that is comfortable, and often alluring, to many of the men who control the media, and to many of the women who consume it." But Dunham was exposing herself in a way that was discomforting and not the least bit alluring. Almost as soon as the series premiered in 2012, she became a love-hate figure in a way that echoed the polarizing impact of Roseanne and Murphy Brown.

After I wrote a *Los Angeles Times* feature about the series' debut, colleagues gravitated toward my desk to vent their repelled reactions to *Girls*—not just after the first episode but for months to come. Like many viewers in the outside world, my workmates were offended by the characters' obliviousness to their entitlement, even though it seemed clear to me that it was an intentional feature of the show rather than a mistake. And then there was the affront of Dunham's naked flesh: I was never quite sure if it was the fact that she refused to starve herself or her lack of shame over her perfectly normal, slightly flabby physique that drove haters so crazy.

Another controversy dogged the series from the start, a critique that was harder to shake off because it was true. *Girls'*s portrayal of contemporary New York City was shockingly deficient in racial diversity. Not only were the core four lily-white, but there was minimal melanin to be found in any of the secondary characters inhabiting Dunham's fictional version of Brooklyn. Questioned about the show's whiteness shortly before *Girls* premiered, Dunham seemed chastened. "I became aware of it as I was editing," she told me. "You cast this world and you don't know until you watch it if it reflects what you see around you." She had been so focused on making a pioneering step for Jewish girls and weirdos that she hadn't considered all the others who'd been marginalized. Five years later, after *Girls* had shot its last scene, Dunham answered the question again: "I was twenty-three and I was half-Jewish and half-Christian, so I invented two Jewish and two Christian characters. I wrote what I knew." At Oberlin, she says, "the big thing was: don't write experiences that aren't yours" and the New York art world she grew up in was extraordinarily Caucasian. "Even if you had a very liberal childhood, the limitations of your own experience, they will come into play."

Sue Naegle stoutly defends Dunham's casting choices. While she was at HBO, she doesn't recall ever looking at *Girls* and thinking, "God, your show is really white and privileged feeling. That's what she was writing *about*. I found so much of the criticism around that time—more than anything, the body shaming criticism—so disheartening. I had to keep reminding myself that a polarizing reaction is okay; you just want people talking about it."

Over the years, a handful of black actors popped up on the show. In season two, *30 Rock* and *Community* alum Donald Glover jets in to play Hannah's handsome new law-student boyfriend, Sandy. He is the opposite of bohemian Adam, not because he's African American but because he is responsible and Republican. Sandy is also pro-gun, anti–gay marriage, and doesn't appreciate Hannah's writing. Insulted, she provokes a political argument, during which she tosses out the fact that two out of three men on death row are black. You can see the gears turning in Hannah's eyes as she realizes she has made race visible in the room. The episode had been written before the media criticized *Girls* for its lack of diversity, but when it came time to shoot, Dunham encouraged improv vet Glover to spin his own riffs on the topic. "This always happens," he seethes quietly. "'I'm a white girl and . . . I'm gonna date a black guy and we're gonna go to a dangerous part of town,'" Sandy mocks. "And then they can't deal with who I am." Hannah protests that she never even thought about him as a black man. To which Sandy calmly replies, "That's insane, okay? You should, 'cause that's what I am."

Like so many moments on *Girls*, this scene spotlighted a young white woman being schooled in her privilege and ignorance. Dunham says now that she was absorbing lessons alongside Hannah. "When someone makes a stride on television—when you see girls who look like girls you might know, you also want to see girls who look like *all* the girls you know. I get that there are women who have been waiting in the wings a long time to see versions of themselves, and it is frustrating to see a show that only half does it," she acknowledges.

Dunham had come to HBO with her narrow, quirkily idiosyncratic tale, expecting to make the TV version of an independent film, the female version of that male curmudgeon comedy genre pioneered by *Louie* or *Curb Your Enthusiasm*. Yet *Girls* was instantly burdened with the weighty expectations of universality. Male characters, performers, and writers tend to get more leeway to be incorrigible one-offs, while a woman's story often stands in for *all* women's stories.

Girls writer Sarah Heyward giggles when she contemplates the idea that the show's mission was to capture universal truths about young modern womankind. "Something about the show made people feel like it was supposed to be inclusive and it wasn't," she says, stroking her green-tinted hair. "I know through and through how much of it is Lena. It's not even inclusive to *my* experience!"

The unbearable whiteness of *Girls* remained a talking point throughout its run. Even Shonda Rhimes was dragooned into the debate in a 2012 CNN interview. "I watch the show—I find it delightful. So why couldn't one of those girls have been Native American or Indian or Asian or Hispanic or black and been exactly the same story?" As someone accustomed to casting with an eye toward diversity, Rhimes was baffled: "I don't understand why it would have to be a different story because the person was a different color."

Rhimes's and Dunham's approaches seem almost diametrically opposed. Whereas Shondaland shows us what an egalitarian utopia could look like, Lenaland pretty accurately reflects the world its creator inhabits: a milieu riddled with unconscious racism and unacknowledged privilege. But is reflecting reality good enough? As the debate continued to rage, *Girls*'s ongoing preference not to cast actors of color in major roles began to seem like obstinacy.

Ta-Nehisi Coates suggested a way to break the cycle of skewed representations. Good writing is a "selfish act," Coates argued in the *Atlantic*, declaring, "I'm interested in [Dunham's] specific and individual vision, in that story she is aching to tell. If that vision is all-white, then so be it." For Coates, the real issue was systemic exclusion: "My question is not 'Why are there no black women on *Girls*?' but 'How many black showrunners are employed by HBO?'"

The answer was troubling: HBO had aired no long-form scripted prime-time series created by an African American since it began showing original programs in the mid-eighties. It would take until 2016 for the network to air its first series created and run by an African American woman, Issa Rae's *Insecure*.

Visibly shaking in a burgundy gown that showed off her tattoos, Lena Dunham took the stage at the Golden Globe Awards in January 2013 to accept her statue for Best Actress in a TV Comedy Series, the first of two awards she took home that night. (The other was for Best TV Comedy Series.) Dunham dedicated the honor to "every woman who's ever felt like there wasn't a space for her" and thanked her fellow nominees, Zooey Deschanel, Julia Louis-Dreyfus, and Globes cohosts Amy Poehler and Tina Fey for helping her survive middle school and other traumatic experiences in her young life.

Resuming her hosting duties a few minutes later, Fey mocked, "Glad we got you through *middle school*, Lena." Although it clearly had not been intended as a dig at aging actresses, everything Dunham said seemed to kindle a controversy.

The undercurrent of resentment was not all that surprising in the entertainment industry. Here was a young woman not just leapfrogging the line but also doing it without the compromises required of network showrunners. Jill Soloway, who had spent decades toiling on other people's series and trying to get her own pilots on the air, admits to feeling jealous of

Dunham's work. How many times had Soloway been critiqued for female characters who were too unlikable, too Jewish, too weird?

Dunham didn't set out to create unlikable characters, just recognizable ones. If it sometimes felt as though Dunham was deliberately humiliating her creations (especially her alter ego), she intended that more as a personality-revealing challenge. "My natural inclination is to put characters I play through heinous tests, and I'm never sure why I'm doing it until later, when I see what it's explaining about the character or the world. I do think Hannah courts it, but we also live in a world that's tough for a twenty-four- or twenty-five-year-old woman to navigate. There are things you're going to face that are totally debasing. Friends always say, 'That would only happen to *you*.' But I just think I'm the only one talking about it."

Some of these mortifying moments in *Girls* emerge in the work world, where our heroines' ambition collides with the restricted opportunities of New York City's postfinancial crash creative class. Marnie, with her perfect hair and chic clothes, looks like a *Sex and the City* go-getter—but that show was backdropped by the turn-of-millennium boom. Marnie gets laid off from her gallery assistant job and turns to hostessing at a restaurant. Jessa floats through a number of low-level gigs (babysitter, children's clothing store employee, caretaker for an elderly artist) before finally deciding to actively *pursue* something: a degree in social work. The most focused character, Shoshanna, graduates from college with a rigid "fifteen-year plan," which the real world promptly decimates.

Meanwhile, Hannah is her own worst underminer. At a job interview, she ruins a genuine connection with her potential boss by making an inappropriate date-rape joke. Seasons later, she gets into the prestigious University of Iowa creative writing MFA program but quickly hightails it back to New York, having pissed off her fellow students and failed to produce any writing.

"It took us a little while to realize Hannah does have some talent, but sometimes she is too busy living the life she thinks a writer is supposed to be living to actually sit down and work," Dunham explains. Hannah's whole identity is wrapped up in the persona of a confessional nonfiction writer, someone constantly chasing experience as raw material for the work. She snorts cocaine off a toilet seat and deflowers a nineteen-year-old boy in a graveyard in the hope that she can stockpile some good stories. At one point, she dresses up in a disguise to entice Adam with role play. (In the past, he involved her in his perverse fantasies of defiling little girls.) Instead of getting turned on, however, he accuses Hannah of being "outside your body watching everything" and, even worse, of exploiting him. "I'm not here to fill your life up with stories for your fucking Twitter."

Critics and fans predictably equated Hannah with Dunham. After all, both were Brooklyn-based writers with a penchant for emotional and physical exhibitionism. But the differences are just as telling: where Hannah is an unfocused, self-defeating slacker, Lena is a workaholic who, careerwise, has yet to stumble. And while Hannah invariably manages to alienate colleagues, Lena commands enormous respect on her set. "One of our crew guys got in an altercation in his hockey locker room because someone was talking shit about Lena," Konner says, laughing. "Her crew would take a bullet for her."

One thing Dunham does share with her creation, though, is a relaxed attitude toward nudity. Konner says that when Dunham is directing and acting in a sex scene, "She'll run to the monitor [naked] to watch the playback, and I literally need to remind her, 'You have to put on pants!'"

———————

By season two, *Girls*'s cultural prominence far outstripped its actual ratings, which averaged 4.6 million viewers across TV and digital platforms. (*Game of Thrones* episodes, in contrast, pulled in more than 14 million that year.) But rather than pushing the show toward more accessible material in search of a larger audience, the writers headed for bleaker terrain. Jessa trashed her impulsive marriage to a hedge-fund jerk, Marnie's overconfidence crumpled, and Hannah's childhood OCD returned.

Dunham has written of her own experience with the disorder: in her memoir, *Not That Kind of Girl*, she lists things that panicked her as a child, among them "headaches, rape, kidnapping, milk, the subway, sleep." She was fixated on the number eight and racked with fear of sex. Later, in high school, she took "massive doses" of antidepressants. Her personal travails informed the story line of Hannah's gradual relapse, which starts with repetitive gestures and graduates to hiding under her bed, plagued by uncontrollable thoughts. The OCD resurgence is triggered by anxiety: a hip publisher has contracted with Hannah to write a confessional e-book with an impossibly short deadline. What she hands in gravely disappoints him. "Where's the sexual failure? Where's the pudgy face slicked with semen and sadness?" he sneers.

She has failed at being the voice of a generation, or at this editor's idea of millennial femininity. Back at home, Hannah compulsively roots around her ear with a Q-tip, resulting in a gush of blood and a trip to the ER. The punctured eardrum came directly from Dunham's life. Apatow says that one day she came into the office wounded, claiming that she had "slipped" and popped her eardrum. He thought the story sounded unlikely; Dunham quickly admitted it had been the result of compulsive behavior and decided to weave it into a script. When it was time to film the eardrum-bursting scene, however, Konner fled the set. "It was too upsetting to me. I had lived through it with her and it was . . ." She shudders. "Just disgusting. But when Judd saw the dailies, he said, 'It's not gruesome enough!'" They ended up having to reshoot it.

Even harder to watch was another story arc running through the Q-tip episode, written by Konner and Dunham: a brutal sexual encounter between Adam and his new girlfriend, Natalia (Shiri Appleby). Over the course of the first two seasons Adam had developed from an emotionally remote, creepy dude into a sweet, complex character. *Girls* fans had grown to love him, which made what came next hurt. After breaking up with Hannah, he began to date a more emotionally grounded woman. Where Hannah hesitated to assert her needs in bed and complied with Adam's kinks, Natalia tells Adam what she likes and where she draws the line. The clarity excites

him. But a chance encounter with Hannah sends Adam, a recovering alcoholic, to the bar. The aftermath of his drinking spree is a scene as grim as
it is graphic. It starts with Adam ordering Natalia to "get on all fours" and
crawl down his dirty hallway. Her discomfort is clear as he positions her
on the bed and has rough sex with her. When he pulls out and masturbates
over her, she begs, "No, no! Not on my dress!" The camera closes in on her
disgusted face as she lies still, his fluid pooling between her naked breasts.
Natalia quietly declares, "I really didn't like that."

"Did *Girls* romanticize a rapist?" asked *Ms.* magazine's media blog,
echoing the alarm of some viewers. The situation, sex that drifts into a coer-
cive and degrading gray zone, was probably recognizable to many women.
"This one incident on *Girls* is so universal and so unspoken and so preva-
lent, that seeing it on television was incredible and revolutionary," Rae Alex-
andra blogged in *SF Weekly*. That the perpetrator, Adam, was a troubled but
basically good-hearted character only underlined the horror of the scenario.

"When people started saying, 'Is that scene rape?' I never thought that,
not for one second," says Konner. "It was an upsetting scene," she says,
one intended to ambiguously probe ideas of consent, "but we have a lot of
upsetting scenes." Like many earlier *Girls* episodes, it also seemed to high-
light how much the Internet's pornucopia of instant-access, ultragraphic,
and grotesquely unrealistic sexual imagery has warped male expectations
of sex. Dunham later told a reporter, "In some ways, all the sex on the show
is a rebuke to porn . . . My entire sex life has been against that backdrop."

The day they shot that scene "was a solemn day on set," Konner recalls.
"Shiri and Adam were incredibly kind with each other when it wasn't shooting, and it was a really safe space."

Dunham, who directed the episode, says the secret is that she always
films "with the female gaze in mind," a term that bounces off feminist
film theorist Laura Mulvey's concept of the "male gaze." Her 1975 essay
"Visual Pleasure and Narrative Cinema" describes how a camera becomes a
stand-in for the masculine eye, presenting women as objects of male sexual
desire in movies (as well as art, literature, TV, etc.). "If there is a perspective

in the scene, it is a woman's perspective," Dunham continues. "If there is a sense that somebody is experiencing something, it's usually the woman's experience—even if it's her [feeling of] distance from the act."

Ironically, the other controversial episode of that season revolved around sex so sweetly consensual and fulfilling that some viewers found it unrealistic to the point of absurdity. "One Man's Trash" unfurls like a luminous indie film in which Hannah embarks on a whirlwind fling with a debonair forty-two-year-old doctor. They meet when Joshua (Patrick Wilson) comes into the coffee shop where Hannah works to complain that someone is dumping trash in the cans outside his brownstone. She goes to his house to confess, and a casual encounter turns into a tryst. For once, Hannah seems totally at ease: she looks sensual and lovely as she wakes up in his expensive white sheets, joyful as they play Ping-Pong topless in his stylish sunroom. It's as if Hannah has stepped through the looking glass and, as she notes in the episode, into a Nancy Meyers movie (Meyers being a writer/director known for high-end rom-coms such as *It's Complicated* and *The Intern* set in beautifully chic houses). They have mutually satisfying sex, one of the few times this ever happens on *Girls*. Hannah actually asks him to make her come, and the camera stays on their faces as he touches her.

"She has a good orgasm, which we had never shown before," Konner proclaims. "Every other time, she is pretending!" Eventually, though, Hannah's anxiety intrudes, and she drains the fun out of this fantasy. As a woman who prides herself on shunning materialism in favor of experience, she feels ashamed at how much she enjoys his comfortable life. She ultimately overshares until she has broken the spell. When Hannah leaves his apartment, she throws out his trash—and never mentions the affair to anyone.

Some viewers and male recappers responded to the episode with disbelief: why would this gorgeous man want to have sex with someone who looks like Lena Dunham? Peter Martin at *Esquire* even suggested the whole story line had to be a dream sequence. No matter that there is a grand tradition in TV and movies of male nerds pairing themselves with conventionally attractive women.

A lyrical interlude, "One Man's Trash" served as a riposte to all the body shaming that surrounded the show. "I think people expected Hannah to hate her body more," Dunham says now. "Hannah has a lot of problems, but being fat isn't one of them. She always considered herself sexually desirable; she always hit on people. All that stuff about 'Could Patrick Wilson ever sleep with Hannah?' was such a boring conversation!" she continues, her voice accelerating with annoyance. "Of *course* he would. One of the sexiest things is having a positive relationship to your own body. How many women do we all know who barely eat food and are constantly working toward a better appearance who can't find a boyfriend? And how many women do we know who subsist on Big Macs and are in constant relationships?"

———————

Over the six years that *Girls* was on the air, Dunham got very good at apologizing—not for Hannah's behavior but for her own. She had talked about her characters sensing "no clear boundary anymore between public and private"; she mirrored that off-screen by casually dropping her thoughts on the Internet as if she were just another twenty-six-year-old woman with dozens of social media followers rather than millions. There was the time she tweeted (and later deleted) "a not so great molestation joke," and the podcast about reproductive rights in which she quipped, "I still haven't had an abortion, but I wish I had." Then there was her decision to defend one of *Girls*'s writers, Murray Miller, from a serious sexual assault accusation in the wake of Harvey Weinstein's downfall; after outcry on social media, Dunham quickly apologized for undermining Miller's accuser, noting in part, "As feminists, we live and die by our politics, and believing women is the first choice we make every single day when we wake up."

"Sometimes I do just want to cradle Lena in my bosom," Konner says tenderly. "There was one time two years ago when she started this Twitter war, and she would just not stop. So I took a taxi to her house and literally made her put her phone down. Part of why people respond to her is she says what she feels and what she means. So you don't want her to lose that part of herself and check every single thing she wants to say, because that is the opposite of who Lena is."

There's a thread that connects the fourteen-year-old Lena who started a stand-up act by goofing on parental alcoholism with the twenty-something Lena who attracted scandal the way streetlights draw moths. Dunham's father presciently foresaw that her disarming humor might cause problems. Before *Girls* was a speck on the horizon, Lena mentioned in a 2010 *New Yorker* profile that a joke she told friends (about sleeping in her parents' bed) turned into a rumor in her social circle because it seemed so plausible. Her father warned that this was a cautionary tale: "It's funny to say, 'I sleep with my parents,' but it's also too close to being massively weird. And you will have to navigate this for the rest of your life." This inability or refusal to pay attention to propriety enables her to be groundbreaking in her art. Yet this very same lack of boundaries constantly lands her in trouble in real life.

The biggest backlash came in response to unguarded disclosures in her 2014 memoir *Not That Kind of Girl*. Describing her childhood relationship with self-possessed younger sister Grace, Dunham recalls bribing the toddler for affection: "Three pieces of candy if I could kiss her on the lips for five seconds . . . Basically anything a sexual predator might do to woo a small suburban girl, I was trying." It is not a portrait of depravity but of a needy big sister. Then there is another scene in which the seven-year-old Dunham's curiosity about vaginas drove her to examine Grace's, and she found that her sister "had stuffed six or seven pebbles in there. My mother removed them patiently while Grace cackled, thrilled that her prank had been such a success."

Right-wing media outlets grabbed these quotes and ran with them, catapulting the anecdotes into molestation accusations. Kevin Williamson at *The National Review* declared, "There is no non-horrific interpretation of this episode." Truth Revolt posted an article entitled "Lena Dunham Describes Sexually Abusing Her Little Sister." Dunham apologized on Twitter and in statements to the press for having written something that might offend or trigger abuse sufferers. Grace used the opportunity to back up Lena and throw down a challenge: "As a queer person, I'm committed to people narrating their own experiences, determining for themselves what has and has not been harmful. [To]day, like every other day, is a good day to think about how we police the sexualities of young women, queer, and trans people."

Dunham's twelve-city *Not That Kind of Girl* US tour showcased a politically engaged, outspokenly feminist side of Dunham that was very different from the hipster narcissist Hannah Horvath. She partnered with Emily's List and Planned Parenthood, led writing workshops for young women, and engaged in lively conversations with fellow feminist culture icons such as Zadie Smith, Amy Schumer, and Carrie Brownstein. As she told *New York Times Magazine*, "I want to make clear that the utterly self-involved, politically disengaged character I play on *Girls* is not who I am."

When Hillary Clinton ran for president in 2016, Dunham campaigned for her with a sense of once-in-a-generation urgency. She made a self-parodying rap video on behalf of Clinton ("Sensual Pantsuit") and delivered stump speeches. In Iowa City, clad in a white dress emblazoned with Hillary's name, Dunham told the crowd, "I can't talk about Hillary Clinton without also acknowledging that she has survived horrific gendered attacks on nearly every single aspect of her character with tremendous grace and aplomb"—something that clearly resonated for the *Girls* creator. "The way she's been treated by the media is just more evidence of the anger that exists toward women, particularly ambitious women, and the way we are not allowed to exist on our own merits, rather than as extensions of powerful men." Her support for Clinton reached its zenith with a speech at the 2016 Democratic National Convention.

Yet the molestation chatter continued to dog Dunham's footsteps, seemingly drifting in parallel with the cloud of aspersions looming over Hillary's head. Twitter bubbled noxiously with rancid rancor from Trump supporters, jibes such as "As if Lena Dunham wasn't already repulsive enough by her 'looks' alone, oh and yeah child molestation can't forget that." Milo Yiannopoulos, then a senior editor at *Breitbart*, even publicly offered to buy

Dunham a first-class one-way ticket to Toronto after Trump was elected president.

One week after Clinton's loss, political writer Anand Giridharadas grappled with the election results on Twitter, and with the ideological chasm that split the country in half. He named Lena Dunham as an archetypal representative of the cultural elite now being demonized by heartland populists: "We just had a contest that pitted 61 million of us against 61 million of us. But now these vast, diverse camps are being boiled down . . . Joe Sixpack vs. Lena Dunham, Coors Light versus Champagne, Cheetos vs. arugula, down-home vs. out-of-touch." Giridharadas, who aligned himself with Dunham, argued that while the coastal progressives were "guilty of some out-of-touchness," this so-called elite was nevertheless "in coalition with the most vulnerable people in America . . . Black and brown people, Latinos, Muslims, women, immigrants, LGBTQ folks, the very poorest, the incarcerated, refugees, and more."

As if to make good on that description, Dunham showed up at a post-election gathering in LA organized by *House of Cards* creator Beau Willimon to inspire activism. Clad all in white, Dunham stood in front of the crowd and, in a high, wavering voice, advocated for groups that support LGBTQ teens and sex-trafficking survivors before introducing the regional director of Planned Parenthood.

The trick that *Girls* managed to pull off was allowing Dunham's feminism to inform its fictional world without seeming overtly didactic. "Everything she writes is pushing forward feminist ideals," Sarah Heyward suggests, "but that doesn't mean her characters don't sleep with someone for the wrong reasons. Because people do sleep with people for the wrong reasons! Hannah is never going to be a perfect feminist, because no one is."

———

When the series began, *Girls*'s heroines were in their early twenties; by season six, they were thirty years old. Dunham herself turned thirty in May 2016. The media reported excitedly on her birthday, the symbolic date on which a millennial female icon stopped being a twenty-something: *People* noted that Taylor Swift posted a card for her on Instagram (it paid homage to their "long talks, arts and crafts projects, and running-into-each-others'-arms-hugs"), while *New Yorker* editor David Remnick celebrated the day on the magazine's podcast.

In addition to showrunning a successful TV series, Dunham and Konner had now expanded their hub of feminist activity by creating a newsletter for young women, *Lenny Letter*, and a production company, A Casual Romance. The latter produced several documentaries (including one about the illustrator of Dunham's favorite children's book, *Eloise*) and *Max*, an HBO pilot that never aired about a feminist magazine writer in the 1960s. In her personal life, Dunham had settled into a long-term relationship with Jack Antonoff of the band fun.

Dunham could also take pride at having been in the vanguard of a TV "fem-o-lution," as Liz Lemon once called it. When she first conceived *Girls*, there was nothing like it anywhere on television. "Looking at the landscape in this current moment and then looking back to the landscape before Lena started, it's hard to deny how she's changed television," Judd Apatow says.

The landscape now changed, Dunham decided it was time to bow out gracefully. As soon as the producers and HBO agreed that *Girls* would end with the sixth season, the writers set out to discover what it might look like for Hannah, Jessa, Marnie, and Shoshanna to grow up. Konner and Dunham had begun joking about how to conclude the series before it even premiered.

"I remember being at SXSW, we were in separate hotel rooms talking on the phone. We pitched how everyone would die," Konner recalls with a throaty laugh. "I think it was inspired by the end of *Six Feet Under*, which was so satisfying—and we were like, what if we go the opposite direction and just make it really *unsatisfying*?"

Dunham says it was important to her that the ending "didn't feel like it flew in the face of the aesthetic of the rest of the show, which was not a super plot-driven, plot-heavy, finality kind of show. And that it feel authentic—

which is such an overused word—but so that you would have a sense of their growth without it being too tidy." Her hope was that viewers would see Hannah as "a more empathic, engaged, and wise person" than they had previously understood her to be. "She may not be Joan Didion, but she is able to write and share her stories in a compelling way."

The final season's shoot was riddled with problems. Dunham ticks off a litany of complaints: "I was sick, I had surgery twice, I broke my elbow, we had actors starting rehearsals for other things and being in *Star Wars* and blah blah blah . . ." On top of all that, one of the sets caught fire, and the production had to switch plans at the last minute when their Florida shooting location was infested with the Zika virus.

"There were moments when I just thought, *Does whatever is the higher power want us to get this show done?*" Dunham recalls. But, she adds, "what is interesting is that all that pain and anxiety—it doesn't show on the screen. I am the only one who knows 'Oh, that is the day that I felt like my arm was going to fall off because I did physical therapy and it made me cry.' 'That was the day that I had to totally reconfigure our entire August schedule!' " Is that a testament to their professionalism? Dunham pauses, and then admits, "I guess by the end we did get good at what we were doing."

Sitting in a downtown Manhattan lounge late in the summer of 2016 as the production enters its final weeks, Konner sounds nostalgic. "We just shot the last day in Hannah's apartment, which was heartbreaking," she says, her mouth crinkling into a frown. "We were looking at all the pictures on the walls of our sets that have been there for years—photos we took [of the actresses] before the show even started, that we used as pictures of their friendship. I looked at them and I thought, *Who are those babies?* I could barely recognize them. Six years at those ages is such a long time."

Several months later, working on the final edits for the series, Dunham confides that the last shoots were intense. "I was not quite prepared for how emotional it would be, you know? It's not like anyone is dying or anyone is breaking up, but, in a way, it is like someone is dying and someone is breaking up. We definitely had that sense of intensity and just like, every day there would be a new good-bye and every day there would be a new sense of grief."

As they moved toward the finale, each of the central characters began to grasp at maturity: Shoshanna trades stringent career goals for figuring out what she enjoys doing; Marnie begins to see her Pollyanna-ish tendencies as a liability; Jessa tries to stop chasing self-destructive thrills. And Hannah— well, like Murphy Brown and Liz Lemon before her, Hannah contemplates what it would feel like to care about someone else's problems as much as her own. She approaches motherhood in the same dysfunctional, vaguely self-defeating way she approaches everything: hoping her flawed best will be good enough. In April 2017, the characters, actresses, and fans all went their separate ways—out into a world more unstable and threatening to women than many of us could ever have imagined when *Girls* began.

CHAPTER 7

Gross Encounters:
Inside Amy Schumer and *Broad City*

Amy Schumer takes to
the streets in April 2014
for *Inside Amy Schumer.*

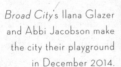

Broad City's Ilana Glazer
and Abbi Jacobson make
the city their playground
in December 2014.

"On its best day, my pussy smells like a small barnyard animal—like a goat at a petting zoo," Amy Schumer confided to me—well, to me and thousands of other people at the Los Angeles Forum.

Dressed in a short black sheath dress and swigging occasionally from a bottle of wine, she stood onstage telling a story about her college days: the time she woke up in an alcoholic haze and realized there was a strange guy between her legs, going down on her. What concerned Schumer, looking back at this moment, wasn't the horror of blacking out and losing control of her body, but the olfactory ordeal this guy was going through. Having hooked the crowd with her body shame, she then flipped it into the stand-up version of a teachable moment.

"Men are not raised to hate themselves," Schumer told the audience. "They are raised to think everything that comes out of them is a miracle!

Guys never ask, 'Did it taste okay?'" she said, voice high and squeaky in mock mortification. The women in the seats around me at the arena laughed appreciatively. The men seemed to squirm a little.

The goddess of grossness, Amy Schumer is in the vanguard of an ever-edgier strand of confessional female humor. It's a genre fed by a decade of women's intimate memoirs and online essays that replaced private consciousness-raising with public self-disclosure. Consciousness-raising emerged out of the women's movement's drive to "tell it like it is." Pioneered by radical feminists in the late sixties, consciousness-raising groups proliferated in the seventies: women opened up about their private lives in order to draw broader political conclusions from their own experiences. So women asked themselves questions such as: Are you a "nice girl"? Have you had an abortion? What does it mean to you to earn your own money? When did you first notice you were treated differently from boys? Do you ever feel invisible?

Forty years later, these questions still vibrated under the surface of pop culture made by women. But the emphasis shifted: rather than vigilance over the way that behavior, relationships, and desires were all linked to structures of control and conditioning, the impetus now was a carnivalesque fuck-you to double standards—specifically, the way that male mischief was seen as cool and wild, whereas women behaving badly were seen as pathetic and out of control. Lena Dunham and friends flaunted their imperfect bodies and messy lives on *Girls*; Edie Falco popped pills as *Nurse Jackie*; Mindy Kaling tested the audience's tolerance for unlikable women on *The Mindy Project*; and the roommates of *2 Broke Girls* spouted dialogue that was so smutty, viewers complained to the FCC. There were so many trend pieces about these new "funny women" of TV that actresses began complaining about being asked what it was like to be a funny woman on TV.

One place you would not find many funny women, strangely enough, was on the cable channel specifically designed to make you laugh. For much of the network's history, Comedy Central's programming felt like a giant bro bubble, something that only got worse with its 2011 rebranding, which focused on luring in tech-savvy eighteen-to-thirty-four-year-old men. But as an increasing number of cable competitors such as FX, IFC, and TBS targeted that same demographic with their own quirky comedies, Comedy Central began to look for new ways to expand its audience.

The result was an estrogen infusion: the 2013 premieres of *Inside Amy Schumer* and *Broad City*. Both shows revolved around women who didn't seem the least bit concerned about propriety. Bodily fluids, casual sex, farting, and getting drunk and stoned were a few of their favorite things. Schumer and *Broad City* creators Ilana Glazer and Abbi Jacobson embodied a new kind of feminism: foulmouthed, physical, and filthy.

Early in life, Amy Schumer learned how to use her body to provoke a reaction. Once, when a high school teacher wouldn't let her leave the class to go to the bathroom, she loudly announced, "That's cool, Mr. Simons. I'll just stay here, even though I can feel my period blood leaking out of my vagina and about to seep through my pants and onto my chair." As Schumer writes in her memoir, *The Girl with the Lower Back Tattoo*, making people laugh "dismantled the power structure within seconds." Her favorite children's book was *Eloise*, a cosmopolitan fairy tale about a little girl left to her own devices who wreaks havoc on the genteel aristocrats of the Plaza Hotel.

Born on the Upper East Side of Manhattan, Schumer lived in relative luxury (if not quite Eloise-level wealth), until it all fell apart: her parents lost their business, they divorced, and her dad was diagnosed with multiple sclerosis and became an alcoholic. Schumer's persona as a tough-talking blue-collar chick was forged during those bumpy later childhood years on Long Island. She sometimes tells an anecdote about the time her dad pooped in his pants while they were at an amusement park. One of several involuntary defecation stories, it suggests Schumer learned to make grotesque trauma bearable through humor. After high school, with aspirations of being a serious actress, she left home to study theater at Towson University in Baltimore.

It was during a women's studies class at Towson that Schumer first encountered feminist ideas, specifically the concept of the male gaze coined by theorist Laura Mulvey that would later be absorbed by Lena Dunham and other forward-thinking TV writers and directors. Schumer wrote a paper on the effect of the male gaze in movies and books such as *Madame Bovary*, analyzing the way it framed women as passive, erotic objects rather than active participants. "It was pretty sophisticated for somebody who was just getting blackout drunk every night," she tells me, chuckling quietly at her younger train-wreck self. "I delivered my thesis, and I was shaking from being so hungover, and the professor thought I was nervous. I was just really interested in how every movie we were seeing was this kind of slow pan from the shoe to the woman's upper thigh."

After graduation, Schumer studied acting and cofounded New York City theater company The Collective. She also made her first forays into stand-up comedy, joking her way to fourth place on the reality show *Last Comic Standing* in 2007. This led to a tour with the other top contestants (all older men) and then stints on a variety of low-level TV shows. Schumer's second major break didn't come until 2011: She pitched material in the hope of writing for Comedy Central's Charlie Sheen roast but, instead, was invited to perform on the dais with Mike Tyson, William Shatner, and *Jackass* star Steve-O. The network recognized Schumer's disruptive talent, the distinct cognitive dissonance between her cute blond appearance and her potty mouth. She made headlines at the roast with her vicious riff on Steve-O, whose costar Ryan Dunn had recently died in an accident: "I know you must have been thinking, *It could have been me*, and I know we were all thinking, *Why wasn't it?*" The joke attracted a ton of media attention and even some death threats. This was just a taste of the hate to come.

At thirty-one, Schumer recorded the Comedy Central special *Mostly Sex Stuff*. Onstage at San Francisco's Fillmore, with her shiny blond hair, apple cheeks, and baby doll minidress, she fired off raunchy jokes about dating in her persona of a bubbly, slutty white girl. "I finally just slept with my high school crush," she said sweetly. "But I swear, now like he expects me to go to his high school graduation. Like I know where I'm going to be in three years!" Responding to some members of the audience who looked startled at the pedophilia joke, she assured them she would never have sex with kids, then interrupted herself: "I shouldn't say *never*! You don't know." Of the decision to call the special *Mostly Sex Stuff*, Schumer told NPR's Terry Gross, "I didn't grow up hearing any women really delving into that side of themselves, and so I thought, *Okay, maybe I can be this person for women and for men just to hear the woman's perspective in, you know, a less apologetic, honest way*."

Comedy Central offered Schumer a deal to make a pilot of whatever kind of show she wanted—a rare offer for a relative unknown. "Comedy Central hinted at the fact that there was a hole in late night at the time and that maybe they might be looking for something that had a kind of *Chelsea Lately* vibe [invoking the comedian Chelsea Handler's popular late-night show on E!], a studio-based talk show kind of thing," says Dan Powell, who was brought in to produce the pilot. That didn't exactly interest Schumer; she dreamed of making a boundary-stretching sketch series that played on her acting and stand-up skills. Yet Schumer had seen many previous projects fall through, and figured this one was doomed because, as she says with a sigh, "Comedy Central was such a boys' club. I just wanted to get some money for the pilot and then focus on doing a show somewhere else that seemed more *possible*."

Just hours before she had to present the network with details about the show, she went out for drinks with Jessi Klein, a comedian and former Comedy Central executive. Shocked that Schumer seemed all set to squander the carte-blanche opportunity offered by Comedy Central, Klein urged her to think boldly. What would Amy Schumer's dream show look like?

"Amy texted me late at night after talking to Jessi and said, 'Scrap the treatment we have! I want to make my *Louie*!'" says Powell. The first person they hired for *Inside Amy Schumer* was Klein, who became head writer.

As the show developed, Klein says, "A lot of sketches fell into two categories. There was Amy as a 'monster' version of herself and Amy as a 'victim' version of herself. Those were two comedic poles we bounced around. We were just constantly trying to think: *What are the things from her stand-up and from knowing her that just felt most . . . Amy? How do we make the show feel like her?*"

Some of the earliest sketches involved the dichotomy between male expectations of women and the drab reality of female existence. In "Sexting," Amy sits on her couch in cat pajamas eating pasta with her hands and texting a guy. He wants to talk dirty, asking what she'd like him to do to her. She bluntly responds with lines like "Tell me I'm safe in my apartment." After he informs her that he's ejaculated, she returns to shoveling spaghetti into her mouth and watching a rom-com. "I thought, *Oh, these are little moments from a woman's point of view that are so relatable to women*—and, I think, to everybody—but I hadn't seen anybody really do it," says Klein.

When asked which early sketch best conveyed what she wanted to do, Schumer giggles and mentions "Third Date," in which a woman (played by Schumer) goes out on her third date with a guy. After telling him she's ready to sleep with him, he mentions he has AIDS. "We just played out truthfully how it would go if a guy, on the third date, told you he had AIDS," Schumer says. "It's such an awful thing to think about and could be deemed insensitive but . . . what would this look like if it happened? I think there's room for comedy there."

Schumer is riveted by things that make other people shudder. Even when she was a schoolgirl, she says, "When I was in class or whatever, I always thought, *What is the worst thing I could say right now? What would ruin this moment and this time for everyone?*" She likes to play with that part of her character—"*that* girl, who would say the most annoying thing, you know?"

Once Comedy Central ordered a full season of *Inside Amy Schumer*, the question became: how do you create a successful comedy show from a female perspective on a network watched mainly by dudes? In 2012, 65 percent of the network's audience skewed male, with a median age of twenty-nine.

Not only that, but *Inside Amy* would be following *Tosh.0*, a snarky compendium of Internet video clips hosted by Daniel Tosh, a comedian specializing in ironic frat-boy humor. It was the top show that year in prime time among eighteen-to-twenty-four-year-old men.

"At first, we were like, 'How do we suck in the guys that watch *Tosh*?'" Schumer asks. "Someone told me our show was the equivalent of putting shaved carrots into brownies so kids will eat them," she says, echoing Tina Fey's comparison of sneaking feminism onto *SNL* to Jessica Seinfeld's recipe for spinach hidden in brownies. "Yeah, in that first season, we didn't necessarily say what we wanted to say." For Schumer and her team, the brownie was sex, a reliable lure to the dudes out there. But mixed in was always a little bit of mind-nourishing feminism (the shredded carrot/spinach element). The "2 Girls 1 Cup" sketch, for instance, follows Schumer's ordinary-girl character as she goes on a casting call for the notorious shock-porn video that involves two women pooping in a cup, eating it, and then vomiting into each other's mouths. She remains unruffled as the director lists the ways Schumer will have to debase herself, not least of which is that she has to lose weight—"mainly in the face."

In another sketch, she announces pleasantly, "I'm Amy Schumer, and I'm proud to say I'm a feminist. That's why I'm hosting my very own gang bang." Standing in her own living room, she watches queasily as a horde of average Joes shuffles in, prepared to pound her. "I was in a phase of watching a lot of porn, and I thought, *That would just suck*," Schumer says, dragging out her consonants like a Valley girl. "What if you went [to a gang bang] and you're just not in the mood? I would never really want any porn or fantasies I have to really happen, which is very different than men, who I think would very much like them to happen."

Some of the most original *Inside Amy* sketches didn't involve men at all, focusing instead on the mind games women play with themselves and one another. In "Compliments," a bunch of young female friends converge on an East Village street and flatter each other in passing. "Look at your cute little dress!" one says enthusiastically. "Little?" the other replies sarcastically. "I'm like a size one hundred now. . . . Anyway, I paid like two dollars for it." The deflected compliments escalate into a self-abasement circle jerk, until finally a friend passes by and they all coo over her jacket. She thanks them—and the shock is so severe, the friends all lose their minds and commit suicide on the spot. As Schumer told *A.V. Club*, "One of the things women are taught is that it makes you more attractive when you hate yourself. To be accused of having any sort of an ego is really frowned upon."

"Compliments" was the first *Inside Amy* sketch to go viral, but it would be far from the last. Klein says, "When we were writing it, I thought, *Oh yeah, this is what women spend seventy percent of our day doing with each other. How has this not been written about before?*" That became their modus operandi going forward: find moments in women's lives that hadn't been exposed to the light and "take them to the point of absurdity," while keeping the emotional reality intact.

As the tone of the show cohered, Klein had an epiphany: "We are in charge and we can write about whatever we want, even if it seems like a really marginal female experience. There are so many things that, on another sketch show, you might not even have had the guts to pitch. Because there's a sense that if men won't get it, it's not worth doing."

On April 30, 2013, *Inside Amy* premiered to three million viewers. Comedy Central's most-watched debut of the year, it topped its time slot in the male eighteen-to-thirty-four demographic. Comedy Central president Kent Alterman praised Schumer in *Vanity Fair*: "She kind of transcends gender—ironically, because a lot of her stuff is about gender. But it's never alienating."

Perhaps it *should* have been alienating to Comedy Central's male viewers; sometimes the show took direct aim at them. In the season-two sketch "Focus Group," a moderator asks a roomful of men if they would watch *Inside Amy*. "I would bang her, if that's what you mean!" one guy jeers. A few seasons later, Schumer expanded this idea into one of the series' masterworks: the episode-long "12 Angry Men," directed by Schumer. A parody of the classic film, it is shot in black and white. Twelve great character actors (i.e., guys who aren't leading-man handsome) prowl around a jury room debating a crucial issue: Is Amy Schumer pretty enough to star in a TV show? After hours of deliberation, John Hawkes (wrinkled, beaknosed) holds up a giant poster of Amy for examination. "Do we really need to look at her again?" seethes Paul Giamatti (balding, puffy). "She's built like a lineman and she has Cabbage Patch-like features. Her ass makes me furious!" Hawkes asks Vincent Kartheiser (receding hairline, pasty faced) if he might be inspired to masturbate to Schumer if he got drunk and took off his eyeglasses. Kartheiser concedes he might.

Schumer conceived the "12 Angry Men" idea, and she insisted on writing the torrent of insults herself. Just as Lena Dunham made Hannah Horvath say or do the worst thing as a kind of defensive reflex, Schumer sometimes seemed intent on imagining the most horrible slurs anyone could say about her (or women generally) and exorcising them.

"It was really hard, and then it was really empowering," she says. "I was kind of checking in with myself while I was writing it, like, *Am I hurting myself? Is this healthy?* It never got to be too much, and I said everything I wanted to say." She insists there was no masochism at play—or, at least if there was, it was purposeful self-flagellation. "I told them that I would write it on my own because that made it feel like I had control. I didn't want the writers to come up with new insults I hadn't thought of myself. And there is nothing about my physical appearance that bothers me. I have days where I feel like I am really gross and I can't believe that anyone wants to have sex with me, but for the most part, I'm fine."

Like "Focus Group," "12 Angry Men" skewered the entertainment industry, with its male decision makers eagerly courting male audiences. My favorite *Inside Amy* sketch, "Last Fuckable Day," takes that critique of Hollywood further. Directed by filmmaker Nicole Holofcener, the season-three sketch stars Tina Fey, Julia Louis-Dreyfus, and Patricia Arquette as themselves—actresses over forty out for a picnic to celebrate Louis-Dreyfus's waning Hollywood appeal. Klein came up with the idea early in the show's run, but it took several years to realize because older actresses kept turning them down. It was Holofcener who got the fifty-something Louis-Dreyfus on board, who in turn attracted the other stars.

Filmed at a bucolic ranch in Southern California, it opens with Schumer innocently stumbling upon the older women carousing in the grass. "Are you that girl from television who talks about her pussy all the time?" Louis-Dreyfus asks her. The older women regale Schumer with some of the telltale signs that an actress's sell-by date is approaching—for instance, when they cast you to play Tom Hanks's mother instead of his wife, or when your movie poster features a kitchen and has an uplifting title such as *Whatever It Takes* or *She Means Well*.

Schumer finally asks, quite innocently, "Who tells men when it's *their* last fuckable day?" The older women roar with laughter.

———————

Amy Schumer ekes comedy out of constriction; she makes us laugh at the ways women succumb to the grim traps man-made civilization has set, or how they try to crawl out of them. Lurking behind all those confrontational jokes about body parts and physical imperfection, though, are hints of real self-loathing that resonate with most women at some level. Even the silliest sketch never strays too far from the malevolent real world.

What's so exhilarating and, arguably, subversive about *Broad City* is that its comedy is *shameless*. The twenty-something characters played by Abbi Jacobson and Ilana Glazer joyfully caper through a carnivalesque version of New York City in which those man-made traps are irrelevant. Pitched somewhere between superheroines and cartoons, they seem to exist in a world built for them alone. The city is not so much an urban jungle as a giant, sweaty jungle gym supplying the duo with nonstop adventures and an endless supply of weed. Men are, at best, coconspirators, sex toys, and love objects; at worst, they are ineffectual fools who stand between the women and their fun.

Chief mischief-maker Ilana Wexler (Glazer) is a polymorphously per-verse hedonist who dresses like a dancer in a nineties hip-hop video. A perpetual motion machine, she frequently busts into impromptu cartwheels and keeps a supply of marijuana tucked into her nether regions. (While Amy Schumer worries about her stinky pussy, Ilana proudly calls her *va-yine-ya* "nature's pocket," explaining that its strong natural odor "masks the smell" of weed, throwing any nearby sniffer dogs off the scent.) Ilana exasperates workmates at her Internet sales job with her laziness and insubordination. One colleague keeps a daily record of her misdeeds: "Day Two-seventy-four: Five hours late. Wearing a napkin as a shirt. Violently high."

In the tradition of odd couples, Abbi Abrams (Jacobson) is the yin to Ilana's yang. A more hesitant, earnest soul, Abbi schedules time to mas-turbate, moons awkwardly over her hot neighbor, Jeremy, and dreams of becoming a trainer at Soulstice, the fancy gym where she works as a janitor, mopping up other people's pubes and vomit. (Paul Downs plays her boss, Trey, a zealous trainer with a secret porn-star past.) A former jam-band obsessive, Abbi worships at the altar of Oprah—she even has an Oprah lower-back tattoo—while Ilana reveres Rihanna. In fact, sometimes Ilana seems convinced that she is an African American drag queen, rather than a frizzy-haired nonpracticing Jewess from Queens.

It's usually Ilana who lures Abbi into madcap hijinks, such as answering a Craigslist ad to clean the apartment of a man in a diaper, or swapping identities so that Abbi can take Ilana's shift at the local food co-op. Abbi's impersonation perfectly embodies Ilana's manic overconfidence as she twerks through the food co-op's produce aisles, blurting politically correct catchphrases at random, such as "Rape culture sucks!" Ilana dates a doting African American dentist named Lincoln (played with slow-burn mellow-ness by stand-up comedian Hannibal Buress), but the true love of her life is Abbi. They support each other's ambitions (or lack of). As Ilana announces in the opening moments of *Broad City*'s pilot, "Today is the day we become the boss bitches that we are in our minds."

Jacobson and Glazer first met at improv hub Upright Citizens Brigade.

Just as Tina Fey and Amy Poehler were the only women in their Second City touring group, Jacobson and Glazer found themselves as the only broads on a UCB practice team called Secret Promise Circle. They bonded over shared influences such as *SNL*, *Curb Your Enthusiasm*, and *Roseanne* and decided to make a Web series based on their own experiences.

This was 2009, the same year Lena Dunham launched her second Web series, *Delusional Downtown Divas*. Creating shows on the Internet was starting to look more like a calling card than a hobby. A growing audience watched these videos, and conventional television networks were trying to figure out how to tap this new talent pool and win back viewers. ABC adapted MSN's *In the Motherhood* (executive-produced by Jenni Konner); Nickelodeon swooped up YouTube star Fred. Neither fared very well when transferred to TV schedules, but it seemed likely this medium would eventually yield some stars. For creators, the appeal was the low bar to entry: all you needed was a friend to film you.

Jacobson and Glazer began shooting short lo-fi videos around town featuring exaggerated versions of themselves: two broke single girls with crappy jobs and few responsibilities. No complicated plots were required, as most of these YouTube videos didn't run more than five minutes. They were grubby, believable slices of life enlivened by the chemistry between these two women. Episodes pivoted around mundane activities such as a sleepover or a Skype conversation. A brunch with their mothers (played by their real moms) begins with the older women wondering if their daughters are lovers and culminates in a physical altercation.

Filmed over the course of a year and a half, the episodes grew more polished. Jacobson and Glazer had day jobs at the Groupon-ish website Lifebooker along with their fellow UCBer Lucia Aniello, but they decided it was time to take their Web series more seriously. They began writing episodes in advance, paying directors, feeding their crew, creating merchandise, and doing self-promotion. Those more rigorous production values are evident in the penultimate episode, a joyous homage to the opening sequence of Spike Lee's *Do the Right Thing*. After a string of creepy neighborhood guys sexually harass Abbi and Ilana, the two women reenact Rosie Perez's ferocious dance sequence from the movie, gyrating to Public Enemy's "Fight the Power." It's a taste of what *Broad City* would become: two young Jewish women as agents of gleeful mayhem, an explosion of irrational exuberance.

With their cult following growing, the women decided to reach out to one of their idols, UCB cofounder Amy Poehler, to ask if she'd appear in the last episode of season two. She not only made a cameo but also agreed to executive-produce a series for them, and set about finding them a network deal.

When Brooke Posch took over as Comedy Central's VP of original programming and development on the East Coast in May 2012, she had no plans to transform the network into a hive of female comedy. The pilot for *Inside Amy Schumer* was delivered about a week into her tenure, and she would oversee its birth. But, she says, execs gave her no mandate to bring in more women's voices.

One of the first people to congratulate Posch on her new job, however, was Amy Poehler. Posch had worked as an assistant at *SNL* for a while, and the women had remained friends. They went out for drinks, and Poehler raved to her about a show she was producing with Abbi Jacobson and Ilana Glazer. "The girls and Poehler came into my office the first week I started. I had nothing on the walls, I had no staff. It was me, an assistant, and a lamp," Posch recalls. This was the first pitch she had heard at Comedy Central, and she was instantly smitten. "Abbi and Ilana were just like lightning in a bottle." The two women effervescently bounced off each other, every new sentence an unexpected adventure. Posch had never related to the high-end heroines of *Sex and the City*, but in *Broad City*, she saw women she could adore.

"They are not rich, they are struggling to get by, and they put each other first. These are girls who love each other, who are best friends. That is the DNA of *Broad City*." The moment they left the room, Posch continues, "I called Kent [Alterman] and said, I am *obsessed* with them. I want this to be the first thing I buy."

Although there are plenty of similarities between the creators and their lead characters, Jacobson and Glazer are anything but slackers. "We are writing versions of ourselves without drive, without knowing what they want to do," Jacobson tells me. They came to Comedy Central with a very sharp vision for their series. For starters, they knew they wanted the pilot to be directed by Lucia Aniello, their UCB and Lifebooker colleague, who'd already worked on some episodes of the online *Broad City*. With partner Paul Downs, Aniello had been creating her own online comedy videos, loopy pop-culture parodies such as "The Real Housewives of South Boston" and "Diary of Zac Efron." Hiring her was something of a risk—Aniello had never directed anything for conventional television—but Posch acceded to Jacobson and Glazer's choice: "She knew the girls, she got their comedy." Aniello's visual aesthetic was gracefully anarchic, crammed with "big pants-down moments that feel very real," as she describes it.

Comedy Central picked up the show for a full season, and Jacobson and Glazer filled the writers' room with friends such as *SNL* writer Chris Kelly, Aniello, and Downs. "Lack of experience was our North Star," Downs says. "And because we were all best friends, it was easy to tell stories that were truthful to us. Everyone in that room had experience with locking themselves out of their apartment for the ninth time or . . ." Aniello jumps in: ". . . having to pick up a package at a FedEx office that was so far away from your apartment it was like another world." That's a reference to an early *Broad City* episode written by the couple in which a missed delivery sends Abbi on a Kafkaesque search to a dilapidated island where an old crone sits in a warehouse guarding unclaimed packages.

Because Jacobson and Glazer had no television experience, Comedy Central partnered them with a showrunner: TV writer Tami Sagher, a veteran of *30 Rock*, *Psych*, and *How I Met Your Mother*. "Abbi and Ilana respected her, but you could say we created a bad arranged marriage," Posch admits. "Tami had all these credits, they had their voice, and it lasted for . . . three months?" The *Broad City* creators bridled at having someone else in charge of their brainchild. "Abbi and Ilana came to us and they were like, 'We know the voice of our show. We don't want to make an old-fashioned sitcom. We don't want every act tied in a perfect bow. We want this to be its own beast and not follow any rules.' "

Soon, Jacobson and Glazer were showrunning *Broad City* themselves, with all the juggling that entails: conceptualizing, writing, acting, producing, and editing episodes. Amy Poehler weighed in on every script treatment and joined them for meetings and table reads. Her influence is evident in the show's joie de vivre. Even when Abbi and Ilana are doing something vile or debauched, their fundamental sweetness shines through.

"She always encouraged us in terms of having women who are unpolished and fart and have sex casually," Downs says of Poehler. In her own work, Poehler is a genius at infusing zany physical comedy with empathy. "She also steers us toward the heart of relationships," says Downs. "Whether it's Ilana and Abbi, or Lincoln and Ilana, she wants them to feel real and grounded."

Aniello recalls a conversation about creating a scene where one of the women has a guy in her bed. Poehler suggested they just show the man without further discussion: "We would make it clear he wasn't the heart of the story. I remember her saying, 'It's not about the guy; it's about the rest of her day.' " That played out in the very first scene of the series: The two women are chattering away over Skype, until Abbi realizes that Ilana is nonchalantly having sex with Lincoln while they speak. Lincoln appears to be a model boyfriend, and a perfect foil for Ilana: calm where she is hyper, steady where she is capricious, a hardworking dentist where she is a recalcitrant slacker (at a workplace directly modeled on Lifebooker's). Yet Lincoln remains little more than a plaything for Ilana, because Abbi is her priority. On *Broad City*, hos always come before bros. As Poehler once told the *New Yorker*, "There aren't enough like them on TV: confident, sexually active women, girlfriends who love each other the most."

Just as it was inevitable that *Girls* would be measured against *Sex and the City*, *Broad City* was doomed to be held up against *Girls*—as if only one show about white boho twenty-something women could thrive at a time.

IndieWire offered a primer on "Why *Broad City* Is the Anti-*Girls*," while the *New York Post* offered "5 things *Broad City* offers that *Girls* doesn't."

In almost every head-to-head comparison, *Broad City* came away the conqueror. That's probably because *Broad City*'s version of youthful urban life simultaneously feels more realistic than *Girls*'s—the cast is multiracial, the streets are dirtier, and the cash-poor central characters are far less cocooned in privilege—while also being dreamlike. The essence of *Broad City* is antic surrealism. Abbi and Ilana romp through one misadventure after another without real responsibilities or serious consequences, just like dudes in a nineties buddy movie. Sure, they might lock themselves out of their apartments and get Maced by a suspicious neighbor, or they might end up vomiting after a night of partying, but we never see them dealing with unfunny *Girls*-caliber traumas such as OCD, drug addiction, or abortion. With the brief exception of a few 2017 episodes dealing with seasonal affective disorder, Abbi and Ilana levitate in a glorious bubble of laughing gas. Really, these girls just want to have fun.

As Hannah and her soul sisters fumblingly try to grow up, they can't seem to stop hurting and outgrowing one another. Dunham's vision of volatile friendship is closer to my own youthful experiences, but that makes it all the more pleasurable to revel in the idealized girl-buddy fantasy that is *Broad City*. While the *Girls* pick at one another's flaws, Abbi and Ilana delight in each other like voracious lovers, with each going to absurd extremes to help the other. After Ilana has an allergic reaction to shellfish at a fancy restaurant, Abbi morphs into the Incredible Hulk (crossed with Richard Gere in *An Officer and a Gentleman*) and carries her ailing friend to the hospital. In another episode, after the water shuts off during a party, Ilana removes Abbi's turd from her nonworking toilet and duct-tapes it to her stomach to smuggle it out of the apartment without anyone knowing. She proudly declares herself Abbi's "doo-doo ninja."

Each is equally elated when something goes right for the other. When Abbi's crush Jeremy asks her to peg him (i.e., penetrate him with a strap-on dildo), she turns to her friend for advice. The sexually omnivorous Ilana breathlessly encourages her friend to seize life by the balls—or, in this case, by the shaft. The camera watches Abbi from behind as she swaggers into the room, the green plastic penis substitute swinging between her legs. Afterward, Abbi calls Ilana to give her the play-by-play. Although Ilana is sitting shivah for her own grandmother, she shrieks, "This is the happiest day of my life!" Somehow this anal sex-capade is transformed into a sentimental moment, more about sisterhood than about Abbi scoring with her next-door neighbor. Upon hearing of the pegging adventure, Ilana's equally openminded mother, Bobbi (Susie Essman), kvells like a proud Jewish mother: "Good for you for trying something new!"

Sexuality in *Broad City* is female-centered, casual, and played for giggles; it takes gender conventions and makes Silly String out of them. Abbi and Ilana openly lust after guys; they even guess at guys' genital endowments while watching a pickup basketball game in the park. (One of the players politely tells the duo their female gaze makes them uncomfortable.) In another episode, Abbi worries that she has raped a guy (played by Seth Rogen): he fainted from heat exhaustion mid-intercourse, but she kept grinding on his unconscious body.

Although Abbi and Ilana frequently get naked, their bits and pieces are always blurred or covered by bars. Glazer and Jacobson insist they aren't trying to make a political point about women's bodies; they just want to make people laugh. Some of the show's most extreme scenarios start out as dares in the writers' room, as the friends egg each other on. "It's very deceptive, because we are so comfortable in the writers' room, and when we are writing scenes, it all sounds so funny. But when it actually comes upon you, it really is scary," Glazer tells me. Jacobson adds forlornly, "Once we start shooting, we realize, *We are the people who have to be in this. What were we thinking?*"

Part of *Broad City*'s brilliance is the way it short-circuits rational thinking. So much ambient amusement emerges from the nonstop physical comedy: tiny, ridiculous facial gestures or grand moments of anarchic release, such as Abbi wildly hallucinating her way through Whole Foods on painkillers after having her wisdom teeth removed. Tightly scripted chain reactions often propel the duo through zany escapades. In one episode, Ilana's mother's search for a counterfeit purse in Chinatown leads them on a journey into the sewer system. In another, Abbi's need to pee triggers a haywire series of events that includes Abbi's getting trapped in a flying Porta Potty and Ilana magnetically sticking to the back of a truck that's whizzing through New York City traffic.

That slapstick attitude radiates from the split-screen montage that opens season three, directed by Aniello. A visual manifesto for *Broad City*, it jump-cuts across six months of activity in each woman's bathroom. We watch them check breasts for lumps, fart, puke, shave, and stare at pregnancy tests. At one point, Lincoln goes down on Ilana on one half of the screen while Abbi reads Hillary Clinton's memoir on the other side; a moment later, Abbi is flushing a dead fish down the toilet while Ilana reads the same book. The minute-and-a-half-long sequence ends with them puffing on their bongs and rushing off to meet each other. *Broad City* had made a feminist statement out of toilet time, officially reclaiming bathroom humor from the boys.

———————

Amy Schumer dropped some toilet humor of her own into the third-season opener of *Inside Amy*. A parody of a rap video, "Milk Milk Lemonade" mocks pop culture's booty obsession by stretching it to its limits. Accompanied by Amber Rose and Method Man, Schumer chants "Milk, milk, lemonade / 'round the corner fudge is made" as the camera pans over a sea of gyrating asses. "This is where our poop comes out," Schumer confirms flatly late in the song, "This is what you think is hot." Released in advance of the season-premiere episode in April 2015, the vibrant, candy-colored video quickly went viral.

A few months later, Tina Fey presented Schumer with the prestigious Peabody Award. After attempting to "suck her soul out in a very awkward staged lesbian kiss," Fey paid homage to a more serious side of the younger comedian's work: "Many people will tell you that you can never, ever joke about rape, but it is all about context and point of view, and Amy and the

Inside Amy Schumer show's brilliant sketch about sexual abuse in the military as filtered through violent combat video games was inarguably funny and so, so rapey."

Fey was referring to the season-two sketch "A Very Realistic Video Game," in which Schumer's clueless character sits with her boyfriend trying out his *Call of Duty*–style shooter game. After she chooses to play as a "girl soldier," her avatar is raped in the barracks. The camera stays tight on Schumer's shocked face as she registers what is happening. The game tries to persuade her not to report the assault. "Are you sure?" it asks. "Did you know he has a family?" The next level of the game is a military trial, where she enters a stage of battle her boyfriend didn't know existed: a panel of men attack her character. The game is over when the rapist is found guilty—and his commanding officer dismisses the charges.

"The woman who made rape funny" is probably not something most comedians yearn to see etched on their gravestones, but it's a topic Schumer returns to again and again. In some ways, it's the inevitable flip side of her drunken slut persona. Both the alcohol abuse and the sexual assault material emerged to some extent from her own experience. Schumer channeled the boozing into the script for *Trainwreck*, which was loosely based on her pre-fame life. The nonconsensual sex she chronicles in her memoir: the involuntary loss of her virginity, age seventeen, when her boyfriend penetrated her while she was sleeping. Schumer kept dating him afterward and told no one what had happened to her. She wasn't even sure how to think about what had happened because it didn't fit into her preconceived notion of rape (dark alleys, strangers, knifepoint, etc.). Schumer suggests the experience warped her later sexual responses, making her either too guarded or too blasé—"as if the act of sex didn't matter to me."

Rape jokes have long been standard fare in the comedy world; in the summer of 2012, a public discussion arose in response to a stand-up performance by Daniel Tosh at Hollywood's Laugh Factory. A woman who was in the audience said he responded to her complaint about his rapey humor during the show by goading his audience, "Wouldn't it be funny if that girl got raped by, like, five guys right now?" After the "girl" in question blogged about the upsetting experience, Tosh's fellow comedians lined up to defend him. Writer Lindy West weighed in on *Jezebel*, and later in her book *Shrill*, arguing that feminists are not just being censorious killjoys when they complain about rape jokes. In a society that shrinks the definition of sexual assault, blames the victim, makes it difficult to report, and rarely convicts perpetrators, telling a rape joke is a distinctly hostile act. And, as West asserts in *Shrill*, "it reinforces the idea that comedy belongs to men."

It was against this backdrop that Schumer made the story of her "gray rape," or "grape," a regular part of her stand-up act. She told one reporter she hoped "maybe a guy will hear that joke and know that this isn't okay . . . And a girl will hear it and feel less alone, because she knows that it happens to other people."

Tami Sagher, who joined Schumer's staff after her stint on *Broad City*, compares writers' rooms to dinner parties and says at *Inside Amy*'s version of the party, "A lot of the conversations would be about feminism. It's reflective of who Amy is as a person, and how Jessi and Dan and Amy ran that room." Sometimes they'd find themselves chatting about current events, like the Bill Cosby rape charges. That turned into a segment in which they put the actor on trial; his defense lawyer (played by Schumer) shows the jury a scene from his famous sitcom and asks, "Did anyone feel raped by that? How about drugged? Me, neither. I felt comforted by a familiar father figure."

Then there was the 2012 news story about two high school football stars in Steubenville, Ohio, convicted of raping a drunk, unconscious sixteen-year-old girl at a party. Fellow partygoers circulated photos of her naked body on social media; one athlete who was at the party tweeted, "If they're getting 'raped' and don't resist, then to me it's not rape. I feel bad for her, but still." Staff writer Christine Nangle proposed a Steubenville-inspired scenario set in the heartwarming world of TV drama *Friday Night Lights*, with its beloved high school football coach. The resulting sketch, "Football Town Lights," features actor Josh Charles as the new coach in town laying down his rules for the players. NO RAPING, he writes on the locker-room whiteboard. Stunned, his players press him for exceptions: "What if my mom is the DA and won't prosecute?"

That summer should have been a pinnacle of Schumer's career. *Inside Amy* had just finished its third season, with at least half a dozen of its sketches going viral. She had been named one of *Time*'s 100 Most Influential People, her face was splashed across the cover of multiple major magazines, and her movie *Trainwreck* (written by Schumer, and directed and produced by Judd Apatow) had grossed $110 million in the United States. The transformation of Amy Schumer from feminist stand-up comic to international superstar was complete.

But ten days after the movie's release, a fifty-nine-year-old white man walked into a theater in Louisiana and started shooting during *Trainwreck*. Two women died, and nine people were injured. "It felt a little bit like something that I had done, that there was a connection to me actually hurting people," a devastated Schumer recalled in an interview with Lena Dunham in *Lenny Letter*. Schumer started to appear alongside Senator Chuck Schumer (a cousin) to jointly call for stronger gun-control legislation.

When she returned to work on the new season of *Inside Amy*, a bodyguard stood by as the writers' room churned out increasingly direct political material. Season four's second episode was called "Welcome to the Gun Show." In the title sequence, Schumer plays a Home Shopping Network saleswoman hawking handguns as stocking stuffers—perfect for the person in your life with violent felonies! She promises that, in the next segment, you can buy lawmakers "whose influence can be purchased for much cheaper than you think," and then scrolls a real list of members of Congress who get the most money from the gun lobby. The fake network's 800 number also leads viewers to a real place: a gun-control advocacy group. Another sketch, a bleak parody of injury-attorney TV ads featuring a guilt-ridden lawyer who warns viewers he can do nothing to help victims of gun violence, was deemed too edgy to run on the show. *Inside Amy* released the video online two months later, however, after Congress failed to pass gun-control amendments in the wake of the massacre at Orlando's Pulse nightclub.

"The thing is toeing the line so that people don't feel you're getting too preachy," Schumer tells me. "And because I am a celebrity now, people are watching and thinking, *Oh, she thinks she's so important now that she's going to help with the gun violence.*" Despite the danger of being seen as pompous, Schumer went into the new season determined to slip some education into the show. At one point, she tried to adapt the 1985 movie *Clue* into a half-hour argument about gun control, along the lines of the "12 Angry Men" episode. She even got some of the actors from the original film to commit, but, she says, "it just never got funny, so we walked away from it. No one's going to watch and say, 'Wow, they had such good intentions here!' You have to have the laugh."

In the same "Gun Show" episode, *Inside Amy* threw in a bit about online trolls harassing women. The VP of a social media site announces a bold new feature: in addition to the "Like" function, there would now be an "I'm going to rape and kill you" button. It might've seemed didactic to some viewers, but Schumer herself had become the target of a fusillade of rage, on Twitter and elsewhere on the Internet. The backlash struck hard, just as it had for Roseanne Barr and Lena Dunham.

Once seen as a ballsy girl who could drink and swear like an average Joe, Schumer had now mutated, in some quarters of the public imagination, into a ballbusting hypocritical feminist fame monster. The hits came from all sides and many angles. She was reviled as a fat-shamer when she complained that *Glamour* magazine included her in a "plus-size" issue without telling her. She was reviled for being obese when word leaked out that she was in talks to play Barbie in a movie based on the doll. She was reviled for stealing jokes from other comedians. She was reviled for telling racist jokes in her past stand-up. And the reviling only got viler when Schumer began campaigning for Hillary Clinton. At an October 2016 stand-up performance at a Tampa, Florida, arena, a few hundred fans walked out after Schumer called Trump an "orange, sexual-assaulting, fake-college-starting monster."

She joined Lena Dunham as the alt-right's favorite feminist bêtes noires. Denizens of right-wing Reddit boards rushed to ding her book, *The Girl with the Lower Back Tattoo*, with poor ratings on Amazon, seemingly using a similar tactic in March 2017, when Netflix released *The Leather Special*, a new Schumer stand-up act. On Instagram, she trolled her trolls with backhanded thanks for the attention: "It makes me feel so powerful and dangerous and brave. It reminds me what I'm saying is effective and brings more interest to my work . . . their obsession with me keeps me going."

Schumer once observed that people don't "want to hear a woman talk for too long. A lot of people project their mom yelling at them. My [career] has been about tricking people into listening." For female comedians, that has often meant acting like a cool girl who can hang with the guys.

Gillian Flynn defines the mythical "cool girl" in her novel *Gone Girl* as "a hot, brilliant, funny woman who adores football, poker, dirty jokes, and burping, who plays video games, drinks cheap beer, loves threesomes and anal sex . . . while somehow maintaining a size 2, because Cool Girls are above all hot. Hot and understanding." Like the adorable manic pixie dream girl, the cool girl is an impossible archetype for any real woman to fulfill. Schumer skewers this fantasy in a sketch called "Cool with It," written by Jessi Klein. Playing a woman who pretends to be wildly "cool" with anything her male colleagues suggest, Schumer hangs with them at a strip club, knocks back shots, and then single-handedly digs a grave for the stripper one of her workmates accidentally choked.

What seems to particularly enrage some men is a female performer who doesn't resemble a supermodel but is undaunted by that, who moves through the world with self-confidence. In fact, one of Schumer's favorite *Inside Amy* characters is Merryweather Sherman in the sketch "Babies & Bustiers," a monstrously cocky six-year-old beauty-pageant girl who is convinced of her superiority over the smaller, daintier competitors. The character harks back to Baby Snooks, the bratty toddler character created by

Fanny "Funny Girl" Brice that allowed the saucy vaudeville star to say all kinds of ornery things that adult women couldn't get away with on American radio in the 1940s.

When I ask Schumer why her own self-assurance infuriates others, she just laughs. "What is that about? Lena, Mindy, and I are aligned for a bunch of reasons, but I think it's just our unbridled, unapologetic confidence that scares people. That's maybe also why women didn't vote for Hillary." She says that if people voted on comics, "I might be out of a job."

Like Schumer, Jacobson and Glazer aligned themselves with Hillary Clinton's campaign. The candidate made a cameo on *Broad City* in 2016, hoping to prove to hip American millennials that she had a sense of humor. The writers proposed having Clinton utter, "Yas, Queen" (Ilana's favorite catchphrase), but instead, the brief scene mostly involves Clinton beaming at campaign volunteers Abbi and Ilana as they hyperventilate with excitement. Jacobson insisted at a SXSW panel in March 2016 that they were not trying "to make a political stance here. It was really more that this is something Ilana's character would do. Hillary, even regardless of where we stand—and we love Hillary—is such an iconic figure."

Where *Inside Amy* was increasingly pointed in its messaging, *Broad City* maintained its sunny, optimistic drift. Glazer told one reporter that Schumer's "message is more transparent than ours, I think. Each one of her sketches has a message, and she just happens to make it so funny." That kind of serious intent wouldn't really fly in *Broad City*'s romper room. While the painful comedy of Schumer exorcizes real-world demons, *Broad City* presents a triumphant portrait of women creating their own reality. Perhaps what's really subversive about *Broad City* is the way that Abbi and Ilana are radically carefree; male opinions and desires are irrelevant to them. Guys remain peripheral figures: crushes, creeps, or authority figures who are ineffectual and easily outfoxed.

Glazer and Jacobson's challenge now is finding a way for their heroines to evolve without losing the fundamental goofiness and ribaldry that make them so lovable—to bridge the gap between the show's scrappy twenty-something characters and the hardworking thirty-something creators who play them. As Glazer puts it, the paradox of the series is that "we work so hard to create the space within which we can just play." Ultimately, *Broad City* is a portrait of an unconditional friendship that inspires them to ever-wilder flights of freedom. It's the kind of camaraderie between women that feels essential in a regressive political moment. By creating a space for themselves to cavort, they are also making room for all of us to experiment.

CHAPTER 8

Crime Family Values:
Jenji Kohan's *Weeds* and *Orange Is the New Black*

Jenji Kohan at work on *Orange Is the New Black* in November 2013.

Jenji Kohan's production company is nestled inside an ornate old theater building near Los Angeles's seedy MacArthur Park. A grand, tangerine-colored hallway leads to the staff's offices. *Orange Is the New Black* executive producer Mark Burley sits in back in an office decorated with an inflatable palm tree and Santeria candles featuring *Orange Is the New Black* characters. He is musing on what unites Kohan heroines such as *Weeds*'s Nancy Botwin and *Orange*'s Piper Chapman. "It is somebody who comes from a fairly normal middle-class morality set who behaves outside that morality set. Nancy and Piper are making their own morality," Burley concludes.

"I think people generally reassure themselves that they are the good guy, even when they are not," Kohan elaborates several months later. She says she is fascinated by the way that people in morally compromised situations "create codes, lines you won't cross so you can keep telling yourself you are a good person."

When Showtime picked up *Weeds* in 2004, male antiheroes swaggered across the cable landscape like malevolent gods. Jenji Kohan had a response to macho archetypes like Tony Soprano: Nancy Botwin, a suburban homemaker turned gangster whose journey would whisk her from bake sales and PTA meetings to weed dealing and standoffs with drug lords.

"I prefer the gray areas," says Kohan, who favors bright, candy-colored hair. "With *Weeds*, I was looking for a little more truth in my characters. It's actually easier to identify with people who are flawed." Kohan plunged deeper into the gray zone with *Orange Is the New Black*, a show consisting entirely of people who, on paper, ought to be utterly unsympathetic: hardened criminals and their callous or corrupt jailers. Now she was interweaving the plotlines of dozens of antiheroines, each of whom seized tiny moments of elation and enlightenment in the shadow of the prison industrial complex.

"A good deal of people in prison are serving time for the worst day of their lives or a really bad situation they were in, not because of the darkness of their soul," Kohan says ruefully. "They are spending a great deal of time in prison for crimes that took very little time to commit. I think there are those who are nuts or evil—but very few. People are more complicated than that."

———

Television is Jenji Kohan's birthright. Her father, Buz, is an Emmy-winning TV writer who hauled his family from New York City to Los Angeles when he got a gig on *The Carol Burnett Show*. Her older brother, David, went into the family business, too, co-creating the sitcom *Will & Grace*.

Dinner-table conversation was competitive in the Kohan home, with both parents being writers (her mom, Rhea, is a novelist). "They say there are book Jews and money Jews," Jenji once told the *Jewish Journal*. "We were raised book Jews; it was about intellectual and educational and personal achievement. It wasn't about accumulation."

The Kohan kids were expected to become doctors or lawyers or scientists. That held little interest for young Jenji, who won some writing contests as a teenager. While attending Columbia University in the late eighties, she landed an internship at Franklin Furnace, a downtown Manhattan haven for spoken-word performance artists such as Eric Bogosian, Spalding Gray, and Karen Finley, which came under fire from Senator Jesse Helms at the height of the culture wars. Kohan briefly entertained thoughts of being a spoken-word performance artist. Looking back now, though, she practically snorts at the idea. "I'm not comfortable onstage. I am very blinky; my voice is very nasal!" she says. So, after graduation, she returned to Los Angeles, where she cobbled together journalism internships and odd jobs.

Kohan never seriously considered taking up her dad's line of work until an ex-boyfriend negged her, saying she had more chance of "getting elected to Congress" than working on a TV show. "My impetus was vengeance, initially," she admits. "I don't like to be told I can't do something!"

While her medical-student roommate pored over anatomy textbooks, Kohan made a forensic study of comedy videotapes from shows such as *Roseanne*, *The Simpsons*, and *The Days and Nights of Molly Dodd*, then churned out spec scripts. Although her father was a show-biz veteran and her brother, David, was already making his way up the industry ladder, neither was prepared to give her a leg up: "They were like, 'Go to law school!' They wanted me to be independent." Eventually, a friend of the family handed Kohan's spec scripts to an agent who worked in his building. That led to a job on *The Fresh Prince of Bel-Air*, where she was often the only woman in the writers' room. Kohan, just twenty-two, found the *Fresh Prince* workplace dysfunctional and frustrating. Racial tensions were taut in the wake of the LA riots. She told NPR that, after they'd attended a Louis Farrakhan rally, some of her colleagues started to refer to her by a nickname: "White Devil Jew Bitch."

Talking about her ability to rub colleagues the wrong way, Kohan admits with a chuckle, "I'm a big personality, shall we say. I realized early on my path would be easier if I were in charge."

So she began writing pilot scripts every season, hoping to find a side door to success. One of her scripts got her hired on *Friends*, a job she lost thirteen episodes later, after arguing with her older bosses about the authenticity of the twenty-something characters. Rethinking her career choice, Kohan left Hollywood to hike through Nepal. But even in the midst of Himalayan grandeur, she couldn't shake the TV bug, cranking out a draft of a spec script for *Frasier* in the land of Sherpas and Buddhist monks. "That made me realize, *maybe* I'm not quite done," she laughs. Kohan went back home and wrote for *Boston Common*, *Mad About You*, and *Gilmore Girls*, but none of the jobs lasted. It wasn't until 1996, when she landed a job on HBO's Tracey Ullman sketch-comedy series *Tracey Takes On*, that she found anyone approximating a mentor.

What Kohan learned by observing Ullman up close was "how to run a healthy show," one that didn't involve bruising ego battles and soul-sapping creative conflict. Kohan also found it helpful that she could give Ullman material and she would "immediately perform it and let me know how it was." Kohan stayed for four seasons, during which she won an Emmy. Yet all the while, she kept on writing pilots—seventeen or so, among which were a couple of near misses.

In 2004, one of Kohan's creations finally made it onto the small screen. CBS sitcom *The Stones* was advertised as "from the creators of *Will & Grace*," David Kohan and Max Mutchnick. Its true mastermind was David's thirty-five-year-old sister. *The Stones* starred Judith Light and Robert Klein as a divorced couple living under one roof, tossing barbed comments at each other as their long-suffering kids looked on. ("Are you sure you're at your dating weight?" Light quips. "Watch me lose a hundred thirty pounds in one second," Klein replies, removing his wedding ring.) With low ratings and mediocre reviews, the show was axed after several episodes.

Jenni Konner, who worked on *The Stones*'s writing staff, was struck by Kohan's originality even then. "I just think network wasn't a place for Jenji. It's not even because she was trying to do extreme sex scenes or something like that. It just felt like there was this innate struggle that I hadn't seen on other shows." Part of that, Konner says, was that Jenji didn't have complete control—and, she adds, "the person who had control over her was her older brother. Who wants that? There are some people who should just have their own place in the world."

Christopher Noxon, Kohan's husband and collaborator, calls *The Stones* "a crushing experience, where she really just threw her hands up. *Weeds* was her Hail Mary," he says. "It was like, 'All right, fuck all of ya.'" Kohan was ready to give up her network-television dream and make her way in the promised land of cable TV.

Despite her background in lighthearted family sitcoms, Kohan secretly yearned to create a female antihero. Obsessed with *The Shield* and *The Sopranos*, she decided to write a series centered on a criminal. The only question was: which crime? Pot was in the news then, thanks to California's medical marijuana initiative Proposition 213, so Kohan fastened on the idea of a suburban homemaker who turns to drug dealing to support her family after her husband's death. HBO passed on her pitch, but pay cable competitor Showtime took a gamble on it.

For years, Showtime had been struggling to escape the shadow cast by the critically acclaimed HBO. At first, it tried targeting the neglected niches of America: *Queer as Folk* for the LGBTQ crowd, *Resurrection Blvd.* for Latinos, *Soul Food* for African Americans. Then, in 2003, new head of programming Robert Greenblatt (who'd been an executive producer on *Six Feet Under* and had been involved in the *Sopranos* pilot) took over. He itched to compete on HBO's challenging terrain.

So, when Jenji Kohan walked into the Showtime offices and pitched *Weeds*, the executives listened eagerly. Sitting in a lotus position on the couch, Kohan told vice president Danielle Gelber that the idea was inspired by the mother of a high school friend who dealt pot. While visiting her friend's house one day and looking for an after-school snack, young Jenji opened the refrigerator crisper and found marijuana instead. The mom, Kohan recalled, wore a blazer with secret compartments stuffed with pot. Gelber sensed that Kohan, if unleashed, could make a lot of noise for Showtime.

"*Weeds* felt really fresh and different," says Burley, a Brit with a bone-dry manner who was quickly hired as a producer. "Marijuana is now legal in some states and may be legal in all the Blue states in a few years, but at that time it felt *out there*." *Weeds*'s tone was also unorthodox: it was a half-hour series that mixed black comedy and soapy drama. The word *dramedy* had been coined in the late eighties for shows, such as *The Days and Nights of Molly Dodd*, that slipped dark subject matter into the traditionally light-hearted sitcom format. The genre requires actors who can operate on several levels simultaneously. In true comedy, a happy ending is assured; in dramedy, a character might be making people laugh while disaster enfolds her.

Kohan wrote Nancy Botwin to be "human, relatable, flawed," and she needed to find an actress who could make all those qualities come to life. Stage and screen actress Mary-Louise Parker had won a Tony for the play *Proof* and an Emmy for her role as a hallucinating Mormon in *Angels in America*; she'd recently come off a run playing feminist Amy Gardner on *West Wing* and gravitated to the edgy suburbia Kohan had conjured with *Weeds*. A single mother herself, she found the show's relatively brief commitment (thirteen half-hour episodes) appealing.

"There were other TV shows offered to me at the time, and people were like, 'You are really going to do a show on *Showtime*?' It was like I was saying I was going to do a show at Duane Reade!" Parker says, sitting in a banquette at the Beverly Wilshire Hotel, dressed in drapey black layers of fabric. In the flesh, she seems to vibrate emotion as viscerally as she does on-screen.

"*West Wing* lived within its framework. There are things you just can't do on *West Wing*. But there was almost nothing you couldn't do on *Weeds*," she says, exhaling deeply. It was a show where plot twists "bumped up against moments of sweetness and humanity—that's what made it difficult to pinpoint as a comedy or a drama."

The pilot suggests that *Weeds* might be a sly swipe at American hypocrisy. Setting recently widowed Nancy Botwin against the backdrop of a conservative suburban community, it opens with her standing before a PTA meeting. None of her fellow parents has any idea that while the Botwin kids are at school, Nancy commutes between her gated community and the kitchen of her drug supplier, Heylia (Tonye Patano). Nancy tries hard to prove to Heylia and her extended family that she's not a "dumbass white bitch" slumming it in the ghetto, but she keeps giving herself away, such as when she hands over money for the week's weed supply in a cute ribbon-tied package, as if it's a crafting project. A lot of the show's laughs, and its uncomfortable edge, come from the way that Nancy doesn't fit in in either of the worlds she moves through.

Weeds had wicked fun tampering with the wholesome, all-American ideal of the soccer mom: While watching her son Shane play a match, Nancy slips city councilman stoner Doug (ex-*SNL* star Kevin Nealon) a magazine containing his stash. She is employing the kind of housewifely pluck that once led women to become Avon ladies—except she's peddling a whole other brand of escapism.

By the middle of the first season, however, it became clear that Kohan had something altogether more deranged in mind than satirizing suburbia. Intoxicated by danger and fueled by caffeine, Nancy begins seeking ever-wilder thrills. Instead of being intimidated by a rival local drug dealer, she screws him in an alley in broad daylight. Similarly, when she realizes that her new fling (indie film favorite Martin Donovan) is a DEA agent, she marries him. Not only won't he turn her in, he busts her competition. At every turn, she uses her beauty as a weapon or a shield, eventually working her way up the illicit-drugs chain until she is romancing Tijuana mayor Esteban Reyes (Demián Bichir), whose public office conceals his secret identity as a narcotics kingpin.

Nancy is a complex, towering antiheroine, and Parker imbues this ruthless character with a crumbly fragility. You can see emotions percolating under the surface of her ivory skin, as if she were mustering all her energy to maintain that deadpan composure.

"Nancy doesn't think ahead very much, doesn't really put other people ahead of her. People who have a sweetness about them—they get away with a lot of shit," Parker says, her lips turning up in what could be a grin or a grimace. "I love that character, and I love how Nancy is ultimately a very charming woman used to things going her way." That self-belief powers her self-reinvention from forty-something wife and mother to canny entrepreneur, cooking up a succession of businesses. There's a baked-goods shop, grow houses, a potent strain of pot dubbed "MILF weed," in honor of the then recently coined slang, and in a flash forward to the near future, a chain of legal marijuana stores so successful that Starbucks wants to buy them. She is a paragon of American start-up success.

As deliciously brazen as Nancy Botwin is, there are always a half-dozen other brilliantly drawn characters orbiting and abetting her: her brother-in-law, Andy (Justin Kirk), a slacker who teaches Nancy's sons important lessons (such as how to masturbate effectively) and emerges as the unlikely moral compass of the series; the aforementioned Doug, who becomes Chong to Andy's Cheech in their own personal stoner comedy; next-door neighbor Celia (Elizabeth Perkins), Nancy's nemesis, who's put through the ringer with cancer and prison. And of course, there are Nancy's two young sons: Silas (Hunter Parrish), who retains an essential goodness, and Shane (Alexander Gould), who blossoms into a fine young sociopath.

While she leverages her sexuality and thrives on risk, Nancy strives to be a good mother to her boys. But her job continually puts her family in jeopardy; even worse, it becomes clear that she finds playing for high stakes way more fulfilling than living her stable old life as wife and mom. Her TV precursors Roseanne Conner (who barked insults at her kids but provided a bedrock of affection and support) and Lorelai Gilmore (who fed Rory a diet of junk food but devoted her whole existence to her daughter) were lousy parents only when measured against an impossible maternal ideal. Nancy veers perilously close to becoming the one thing that TV audiences had never accepted from a woman: an actively bad mother, someone who puts her children in harm's way while also eroding their sense of right and wrong.

Even Botwin "family time" sometimes results in rather warped scenarios. When the boys' grandmother Bubbe, hooked up to a life-support machine in her home, begs to be allowed to die, Nancy makes a graceful elegiac speech and shuts off the respirator. Yet Bubbe's body stubbornly breathes on. As the camera pulls outside into the dark night, as if withdrawing from a scene too awful to contemplate, you can hear Nancy's dry command: "Shane, get Mommy a pillow." We never see Bubbe again.

Although Showtime encouraged Kohan's imagination, Burley recalls some early concerns about increasingly edgy plots involving Nancy's sons. "There were strong discussions about whether [the kids] should be smoking pot or selling pot," he says. "But Jenji would stick to her guns, and after a while they stopped asking. They were a little afraid of her." And what about the child actors themselves, Hunter Parrish and Alexander Gould? Jenji confesses to feeling guilty sometimes about giving the boys such "rough material." She says, "I hope they can pay extensive therapy bills with the money they made on the show."

Battered by the network sitcom system, Kohan had long dreamed of creating her own work environment: a sane, balanced place for the hatching of unbalanced characters.

Parker's relationship with Kohan, however, became a tense battle of wills between two detail-oriented women with strong visions. "She's very used to getting her way, and this was my baby," Kohan told an audience at the Writers Guild in 2010. "There was a lot of push and pull." Eventually, producer Lisa Vinnecour became a kind of liaison mediating between the showrunner and the actress. A "diva whisperer" (as Kohan once called her), Vinnecour went on to run the *Orange Is the New Black* set, where she made the sprawling cast feel like a tight-knit family. Vinnecour shrugs off the word *diva*, however, protesting, "These are artists."

Like Shonda Rhimes, Kohan swore by a "no assholes" hiring policy. This became even more of a priority when she gave birth to her third child on the night of the *Weeds* premiere in August 2005. She brought in Roberto Benabib (a filmmaker who had written for *Ally McBeal*) to help run the writers' room. At first it consisted largely of men (several of them playwrights); as the series progressed, Kohan hired more women, but she believed that hiring ought to be gender-blind and color-blind. "I think it's really limiting to say that only women can write women or black people can write black people," she tells me. "It's an exercise in imagination!"

Exercise their imagination the *Weeds* writers did. Every time the series seemed to be settling into a groove, Kohan and company yanked the carpet out from under it. After three successful seasons set in the upper-middle-class suburb of Agrestic, California, Kohan says, "The writers were getting antsy and talking about projects they wanted to write in the off-season. I said, 'What do we have to do here to bring all the creative energy back into the room?' And they basically said, 'We're sick of suburbia.'"

Kohan unleashed a radical solution: she burned down Agrestic and relocated the action to a beachside town, bringing in new characters and eliminating some old favorites. This became a pattern: whenever the show seemed to be stagnating, Nancy and her drug-peddling clan moved elsewhere—to Mexico, across America, and eventually back to a rebuilt Agrestic. "We write ourselves into a corner, we all go away and relax, and then we come back and say, 'How do we get ourselves out of this mess that we made?'" is how Kohan explains the Botwin family's trademark restlessness.

Her craving for change even manifested itself in the show's theme music. She had chosen the acerbic, anti-suburbia folk song "Little Boxes," by Malvina Reynolds, from the outset—in fact, when she was struggling to write the pilot script, she typed the song's lyrics just to fill up the first page. Christopher Noxon, initially the show's music supervisor, says they quickly started thinking about using cover versions of the song, because they were bored with the original. "That is the story of *Weeds*," Noxon says. "Jenji just didn't want to do the same thing again." Soon they were barraged by requests to cover "Little Boxes," and went on to air versions from dozens of musicians, including Elvis Costello, Death Cab for Cutie, Angélique Kidjo, and Regina Spektor.

Ultimately, *Weeds* accomplished exactly what Showtime had hoped. It reframed the cable network as a creative daredevil in the scripted-television arena, a brash upstart nipping at HBO's heels. To solidify its image as a home for dangerous women with attitude, Showtime launched a string of shows created by women: Ilene Chaiken, Michele Abbott, and Kathy Greenberg's *The L Word*; Lucy Prebble's *Secret Diary of a Call Girl*; Liz Brixius and Linda Wallem's *Nurse Jackie*; Diablo Cody's *United States of Tara*; and Darlene Hunt's *The Big C*. At a time when HBO had no series by female creators on the air, flawed heroines became Showtime's signature. By the end of 2009, the pay cable network had increased its subscribers by more than 25 percent.

Yet *Weeds* itself never quite got the respect it deserved. Was it because it was a half-hour dramedy rather than an hour-long drama? Was it because its protagonist was a middle-aged mom? Or maybe because the show kept remaking itself?

A year after *Weeds*'s debut, another series about an ordinary person who turns to drug dealing to support the family premiered on AMC. *Breaking Bad* featured a mild-mannered high school science teacher named Walter White who, like Nancy Botwin, deployed charisma and cunning to penetrate the closed circuit of the drug underworld. Vince Gilligan, *Breaking Bad*'s creator, confessed that he hadn't heard about Kohan's show when he pitched his own series. "If I had known of *Weeds* weeks or even days prior to that meeting, it's likely I wouldn't have had the will to go on," Gilligan told *Newsweek*. But because he didn't subscribe to Showtime, he wrote and sold his tale of a geek turned sociopath.

Walt represented the domesticated middle-aged American Everyman whose suppressed masculinity would burst through if truly tested—an alluring fantasy for suburban drones everywhere. Nancy also held the promise of self-transformation through accessing hidden depths of reckless courage and ruthlessness—but this was not something a mainstream audience necessarily enjoyed seeing in a middle-aged mom. By *Breaking Bad*'s finale, there was no doubt that Walt had become monstrous—yet he finished his life on his own terms, without ever going to jail. Nancy, on the other hand, gets her comeuppance. In season seven, we see her dressed in shapeless green prison garb at the conclusion of her three-year sentence in a Connecticut federal prison.

Just as Nancy Botwin was leaving behind prison life, Jenji Kohan's jail time was beginning.

———————

While Kohan was working on the final season of *Weeds*, a friend gave her a copy of Piper Kerman's memoir *Orange Is the New Black: My Year in a Women's Prison*. Kohan thought it would make a perfect next project, but when she pitched it to Showtime, she was stunned to hear them turning her down.

"I had your hit show for eight years, and you don't want my next thing?" she marvels, her voice quivering with anger even now. But it wasn't just Showtime that was skeptical about the appeal and viability of a show involving a multiracial cast of female criminals. "HBO passed," Kohan notes sourly. "A lot of places passed."

Amid all this disappointment, Netflix swooped in. An online movie-rental store, Netflix had grand ambitions to create and stream original content. So far, it had bought only one series, a political drama called *House of Cards* that hadn't yet aired. It needed Kohan to lend it creative credibility and nab the public's attention, as she had helped do for Showtime. So Netflix tempted Kohan with an enticing offer: the chance to make thirteen hour-long episodes, with no test pilot required and minimal network interference.

While the *Weeds* scribes worked on the Botwins' final season, Kohan brought in a new group of writers to work on *Orange Is the New Black* in the same building at Universal Studios. "*Weeds* was her baby, so those of us on *Orange*, we kind of felt like we were the redheaded stepchildren living in the basement," says Sian Heder, who wrote for the show's first four seasons. "We were the new kids. And we had a pretty daunting task, because there was no pilot." Kohan had originally cowritten a script with *House* producer Liz Friedman, but the partnership had not worked out. "There was a pilot that she wasn't happy with, and we weren't allowed to see it, so we just talked about the book and what the show could be," says Nick Jones, a playwright who moved to Los Angeles to work on the show. "I was surprised at how unstructured it all was. We seemed to spend weeks just getting to know each other and going on walks and just talking about issues." They also met former inmates and visited a women's state prison.

Orange's author, Piper Kerman, is a college-educated Brooklyn woman who ended up in jail for a youthful stint as a drug dealer. Her memoir offers a personal view of the dynamics among female prisoners. A few figures stand out, such as Pop, the Russian mobster's wife; Morena, a Latina prisoner with crazy eyes; and Pornstar, a mustachioed prison guard. Kohan quickly realized that, for legal and creative reasons, they'd have to change some characters and invent others. She deemed the blond, fictional version of Piper her "Trojan horse," explaining to an audience at a 2014 live event, "If you go into a network and say, 'I want to do a show about poor Latinas and black women and their issues,' it's not a big selling tool. The *Private Benjamin*/white girl/fish-out-of-water conceit is familiar, and it's an easier sell—but it was never my intention to just tell Piper's story; it was a gateway to all the stories."

With no model to work from and no actors yet attached to the series, the writers were flying blind. For instance, they knew Kohan wanted a transgender character in the fictional Litchfield Penitentiary, ideally to be played by an actual trans actor, but that was pretty much all they had to go on. So, when Heder wrote the script for *Orange*'s third episode, which gave viewers Sophia Burset's backstory, she had to keep an open mind. "I thought, *This could be a working-class white person, this could be an African American person*," Heder says. "I just had to create a great story and be adaptable with the dialogue or that person's mannerisms."

Kohan wanted to base *Orange* in Los Angeles, where her three kids were happily ensconced in school, but the studio preferred New York, for tax reasons. As a compromise, they resolved to split the production: filming would be done at Kaufman Astoria Studios, in Queens, with Lisa

Vinnecour supervising the actors in Kohan's stead, while the writers' room and postproduction would stay in LA with Kohan and Burley. This was an unorthodox choice, separating the showrunner from the show, but it would end up being a huge advantage in terms of access to talent, since many of the women they ultimately cast were New York–based theater actors with little or no TV experience.

Kohan asked *Girls* casting director Jennifer Euston to help her assemble a large, star-free cast. What the showrunner had in mind for *Orange* surpassed even the diversity of Shondaland's shows: a cast composed of women of all racial backgrounds but also all ages and sizes. Rhimes had nudged color consciousness to its limits on network television, but her spot at ABC meant she could push only so far past mainstream ideas of beauty. Jenji wanted to steer *Orange* into cinema verité territory: having the "Hollywood pretty" Piper character at the show's center would only accentuate *Orange*'s realistic depiction of the other women's bodies.

"Unknowns, all women—and so many minority women? I was like a kid in a candy store!" Euston recalls of the casting process. She had so many favorite actresses who, because of their color, size, age, or unconventional looks, could never get more than bit parts. And here was Kohan, promising possible series-regular roles for these great stage and character actresses.

Euston didn't have much material to work with for the initial auditions. For the role of an inmate named Taystee, she had just a single line—"You got those TV titties, all nice and perky!" Taystee says admiringly of Piper's breasts in the shower room—but actress Danielle Brooks exuded a joyfulness that fit the part. Uzo Aduba was on the verge of quitting acting to go to law school when she read for the character of Jenae, a former track star. A runner herself, Aduba arrived for the audition with her hair tied in knots and a white tank top to show off her arms. Kohan later watched the tape and said, "I want Uzo for Crazy Eyes!" Euston was baffled. "I said, 'Who is Crazy Eyes?' She wasn't even in the script at that point. But Jenji took the pool of people that I showed her, and if she liked them, she would just find them a part."

Although most of the roles went to unknowns, Kohan drafted several familiar faces, such as Kate Mulgrew, Laura Prepon, Taryn Manning, and Jason Biggs. The role of Piper went to Taylor Schilling, who had starred in NBC's medical series *Mercy*, and Kohan brought over a few actors she'd worked with on *Weeds*, including Pablo Schreiber (who would play the creepy corrections officer nicknamed Pornstache), Michael Harney (the slightly less creepy prison counselor Healy), and Natasha Lyonne.

Lyonne was playing a small part on the final season of *Weeds* when she got a hold of the *Orange* script and nearly jumped out of her skin with excitement. She quickly started trying to convince Kohan and director Michael Trim that she was a perfect fit for the role of tough-talking, sweet-hearted junkie Nicky Nichols, using her own public struggle with smack as a guarantee of authenticity. "I know you're thinking, *How could this girl have had a tough life?*" Lyonne recalls telling Kohan and Trim. "Google it. I have a criminal record to back this show up!" Lyonne, a native New Yorker known for roles in *Slums of Beverly Hills* and *American Pie*, worried that the plum part would go to an ethereal twenty-something waif. But her "I'm a junkie, honest!" pitch did the trick.

Sitting in a booth at a Los Angeles diner, Lyonne holds forth in her brassy New York accent, sounding more like a bawdy old Jewish man than the petite thirty-seven-year-old actress she is. Beneath those wide eyes and waves of red hair, Lyonne says she feels a kinship with the kind of hard-veneer 1970s male characters played by Robert De Niro, Harry Dean Stanton, and Gene Hackman. The part of Nicky Nichols, an ever-shifting mix of loyal friend, lesbian lothario, brittle fuckup, and relapsing addict, plays to her strengths.

Like Lyonne, many of the actresses on the show had struggled for years in the business, too oddball to fit the kind of cookie-cutter roles that generally presented themselves. But now, with *Orange*, they finally had a chance to shine.

"A lot of the women in the show are too distracting in their originality," Lyonne suggests. "So we are blown away that the secret all along was:

Dorothy, be yourself." She tugs at her white-and-blue-striped sweater as if there's something crawling inside it, and finally pulls it off, revealing a delicate black lace camisole underneath. "The actresses were all past the time where it was do-or-die for them—they were just over the hump of whatever life horror it was that didn't break them. So they were willing to bring all that to the table and access it without having it destroy them."

Laverne Cox is a transgender actress who was performing at the East Village drag bar Lucky Cheng's when she auditioned to play Sophia Burset. "Laverne is a great example of someone who for sure was bringing aspects of her personal journey," says Lyonne. Cox embraced the role of Sophia, a former fireman who winds up in prison after engaging in credit card fraud to finance her transition. At the time, there had been very few recurring transgender characters on episodic television, and the broader conversation about trans identity and rights hadn't yet reached mainstream America. (Caitlyn Jenner came out as a trans woman nearly two years after *Orange* premiered.)

Determined to make Sophia Burset realistic and sympathetic, Sian Heder interviewed a number of transgender people before writing the season-one episode that detailed Sophia's life before prison. The result was a character who was "kind of selfish in some ways," not to mention a criminal. Heder was worried about the potential for backlash, she says, "but I think trans people were so relieved to have a three-dimensional person on-screen, warts and all."

The episode suggests Sophia has escaped the jail of gender only to be incarcerated once again. We catch a glimpse of Sophia's troubles within the prison system, which declines to pay for the female hormones she needs. And we hark back to her transitioning in the years before she's sent to Litchfield: trying on tacky girl's clothes in front of wife Crystal—"You look like Hannah Montana," Crystal teases—and dealing with a young son who is angry and embarrassed by Sophia's metamorphosis.

"The big problem with that episode was that we had to have scenes where she used to be a man," says co-executive producer Lisa Vinnecour.

Although Cox was game, the facial hair just didn't look right on her, so the search began for a male look-alike. "We were really struggling, and then Laverne mentioned, just real casual one day, 'You know I have a twin brother?' We had no idea!" So Cox's twin, M. Lamar, swept in and played the part so well that many viewers didn't realize they'd used a double.

Less than a year after the show's premiere, Laverne Cox appeared on the cover of *Time* magazine, won a GLAAD Award, and became the first transgender actress nominated for an Emmy. "What's revolutionary is not that there's a trans character, or even that a trans character is being played by a trans actor, although that's a big deal," Cox told the *New York Times* in 2014. "But it's written in such a profoundly human way, so that audiences are connecting with this person that they didn't expect to connect with."

That's true of so many of the inmates, castaways on an Island of Misfit Toys populated by women rarely seen on American TV, unless it's on reality shows or the news. They are Latina or black or Asian, elderly or sickly, overweight or skeletal, and all of them carry backstories of emotional trouble, or crippling poverty, or sexual abuse, or drug addiction. Out of the pandemonium of clashing personalities and ethnic rivalries, an aria gradually emerges: broken lives converge into a ragged and unruly sort of harmony.

"People are living in more and more insulated worlds, in feedback loops," Kohan says earnestly. "So if I can introduce something new to familiarize those people with others or the Other, and to help recognize parts of yourself in people you never thought you would, I feel like that is part of my job."

A whirlwind of buzz met *Orange Is the New Black* almost as soon as Netflix made all thirteen episodes available in July 2013. It wasn't just critics raving. Fans binged and tweeted and Facebooked and Instagrammed and created memes—all those digital modes of expressing enthusiasm and exuberantly arguing about a show's merits or defects that have become integral to TV viewing in the twenty-first century. The first series to really benefit from

Netflix's approach of releasing all of a show's episodes at once, *Orange* depended upon social media as a form of promotion, since it didn't have weekly time slots around which an audience's reactions could be synchronized and unified.

The network encouraged interaction with blooper videos and fan art, while the show's stars offered up pictures of themselves palling around on set and supporting one another's projects off set. It wasn't just a publicity ploy, either; many of the actors had grown very close. In order to cultivate intimacy among the sprawling group, Lisa Vinnecour organized outings while shooting the first season. They might walk across the Brooklyn Bridge en masse or go for a drive to visit a haunted house in Connecticut. A few weeks after the first season premiered, Vinnecour invited everyone to her birthday party at a joint in Manhattan's West Village.

"I started noticing other people surrounding us and whispering and pointing. Next thing you know, there's a line forty people deep to get in," Vinnecour says with amazement. "People are calling their friends, saying, 'Get over here, the cast of *Orange Is the New Black* is here!' That was when I realized, 'Whoa, this show is much bigger than I expected it to be.'"

Shooting with such a massive cast (sometimes as many as eighty speaking parts in an episode) is challenging, but it eliminates any possibility that the writers will get bored, because there's a kaleidoscopic array of personalities to probe. As Kohan promised, Piper acts as a stand-in for the average white upper-middlebrow viewer. She exudes unconscious white privilege from every invisible pore. "I'm gonna read everything on my Amazon wish list and maybe learn a craft!" is how she imagines she will make the most of her jail time, before she actually goes inside. Through Piper's eyes, we learn the internal politics of this minimum-security prison, where women congregate in tribes based on ethnicity. Guards vacillate between well-meaning ineptitude and sadistic cruelty; earnest prison administrator Joe Caputo spends his downtime playing in a bar band called Side Boob.

The show is structured so that viewers can't help but see past the khaki prison uniform to the human being inside. Each episode includes flashbacks that focus on a particular character's backstory, complete with the miseries and misdeeds that set her on the path to incarceration. We glimpse self-possessed Taystee as an orphan who found a mentor in a charismatic neighborhood drug dealer, and learn that tough mother hen Gloria Mendoza (Selenis Leyva) committed food-stamp fraud in order to escape an abusive boyfriend. Often, our preconceptions about the characters are totally upended. In her flashback scenes, for instance, elderly Miss Rosa (Barbara Rosenblat) morphs back into the thrill-seeking sex-bomb bank robber she once was.

Possibly the supreme example of *Orange*'s trick of flipping the viewer's assumptions involves the flashback story for Suzanne, the poetic, mentally troubled African American inmate nicknamed Crazy Eyes. Unlike some of the other inmates of color, who emerged from grim poverty and violent homes, Suzanne turns out to have grown up within the pampered security of an upper-middle-class white adoptive family. Sian Heder says this backstory wasn't at all premeditated: Kohan inserted this detail into one of the scripts on the spur of the moment, detonating a little story bomb. "It was almost like a joke shot: 'Cut to Crazy Eyes sitting with two white people, calling them Mommy and Daddy.' But you create one little detail about the character, and it ripples through to the rest of the season. Every writer has to continue to build a world around that idea."

Kohan had originally asked Jen Euston to fill even the most minor roles with powerful actors, so "if the part got bigger, they could nail it," says Euston. Indeed, as time went on, characters who lurked in the background for whole seasons moved to center stage, and inmates who initially appeared to be one-dimensional thugs (at least to Piper's eyes) were given intricate shading. One of those cartoony villains was Tiffany "Pennsatucky" Doggett (Taryn Manning), a squirrelly looking, racist meth addict with lank hair and rotten teeth who'd been arrested for a shooting at an abortion clinic. When antiabortion supporters write her letters in prison, she assures them, "I'll be out before the Rapture."

Set up as Piper's nemesis, she unexpectedly evolves into a thoughtful, sympathetic young woman forged by a childhood of malign neglect. Her mother's advice that she should passively accept whatever men sexually inflict upon her shapes Doggett's relationship with a new prison guard, Coates (James McMenamin). He seems like a gentle guy, and their outings in the prison van feel like joyful flirtation, an escape for both of them from their assigned roles as captor and convict. But then the true power imbalance reasserts itself, culminating in a heartrending rape scene in the van's backseat. The camera bears witness, staying focused on Pennsatucky's face as Coates forces himself upon her. Stoically withstanding the attack, just like her mama taught her, Pennsatucky makes no sound. Despite her best efforts to dissociate herself from her body, a single tear escapes from her eye.

"Taryn had been told that her character, because of her past, just shuts down when she gets violated," Vinnecour recalls of shooting that painful scene. "So she was in shutdown mode, and then one tear came out of her eye—it was perfect. I went over to tell her, 'That was so beautiful!' but she just said, 'I am *so sorry*. I know I'm not supposed to have an emotion. It just came out!'" Vinnecour creates a safety bubble for the actresses that allows them to make themselves vulnerable. That means clearing the set for sensitive sex scenes and keeping an eye on how the women's bodies look, so they won't feel self-conscious.

Kohan says, "The biggest problem we have with being graphic [on the show] is actors balking at it. I understand, they are the ones who are vulnerable and who are being freeze-framed and used for masturbation fodder! But I keep trying to push it, because our sexual drives aren't deviant; they are human."

At Litchfield, Piper is reunited with her drug-smuggling college girlfriend, Alex (Laura Prepon), and the charged sexual liaisons between these conventionally attractive women (in supply closets and showers) became fantasy fodder for *Orange Is the New Black* fans of all genders. Sometimes sex is played for laughs, as when butch lesbian Boo (Lea DeLaria) challenges Nicky to see who can seduce the most inmates. Other times, it carries heavy emotional weight, as when Poussey (Samira Wiley) tries to kindle a romantic relationship with her resolutely straight best friend, Taystee. After a failed attempt at a kiss between them, Taystee offers, "Maybe we could cuddle for a minute?" They lie silently spooning, a look of restrained misery on Poussey's face. And then, of course, there is sex with a power differential, between inmates and jailers, whether forced (as with Doggett) or chosen (as between a young inmate impregnated by a romantic guard). Kohan creates a microcosm of the outside world, with all the tiny pleasures and social horrors played out in captivity.

Vaginas come up as a topic in the writers' room "approximately 62 times a day," *Orange* writer Lauren Morelli has written—"much to the chagrin" of the staff's handful of male writers. Unlike *Weeds*'s mostly masculine lineup, *Orange*'s room was female-dominated from the start.

Kohan coaxed the writers to share the intimate details of their lives, and Morelli realized, while writing about and discussing Piper's sexuality in season one, that she herself was gay. "In Piper and Alex, I'd found a mouthpiece for my own desires and a glimmer of what my future could look like," she wrote in a 2015 essay for *Mic*. She left her husband and began a relationship with one of the show's stars, Samira "Poussey" Wiley. In 2017, the two women got married.

Working on a show with not just a mostly female cast but also a mostly female crew was a disorienting and novel experience for many involved. "I really had to abandon this idea I had that I'm the kind of girl that doesn't really get along with girls," Natasha Lyonne says, laughing. "It's a very interesting case study, because there are so many of us and we're all different, and yet there is enough space for all of us." Lisa Vinnecour similarly marvels at *Orange*'s unprecedented femaleness: "You look around, and the amount of women sitting on set at any given moment, on camera and off—it's epic." She recalls looking around Video Village at a certain point during the production of season four: "Every single person—hair, makeup, wardrobe, lighting, script—was a woman."

Yet imbalances persist. One enduring sore point for Kohan is pay disparities in the entertainment industry, with men at the same level of their careers as she is earning significantly more. "I am sick of not getting paid as much as I think I should've been for many, many years—particularly on *Weeds*," Kohan tells me. "It was just embarrassing, and it remains a thorn in my side." The only recourse for women, she says, is threatening to walk and being prepared to follow through, as Amy Sherman-Palladino unsuccessfully did on *Gilmore Girls*. "Ultimately, it comes down to: Are you willing to kill the baby? Maybe it's harder for women to do that, but it's really the only power you have."

Kohan admits that she has often chosen creative license over money. With *Orange*, that meant the luxury to conjure up a cornucopia of female characters, probably employing more women of color in major speaking roles than all the non-Shondaland network prime-time shows combined. That was evident when the enormous ensemble gathered onstage to collectively accept their 2015 Screen Actors Guild Award for Best Ensemble: crowded around Uzo Aduba, who gripped the statuette, was a collection of women right out of a "United Colors of Benetton" ad, beaming and hugging one another in disbelief.

Yet the show's treatment of race set off alarm bells for some critics. In the *Nation*, Aura Bogado argued that *Orange* was just the latest instance of white people exploiting the suffering of African Americans. Putting Piper and her white-girl problems at the center of the first season didn't help shore up the show's racial dynamics. Over the following seasons, though, Kohan and her writers opened up the *Orange* universe: racial caricatures often deepened into compelling characters who wielded stereotypical behavior mostly as a shield or a taunt. Black Cindy (Adrienne C. Moore), for example, starts out as a sassy quip machine, but by the third season, she's an idiosyncratic wonder. What started as a passing joke about being Jewish (so she can get the better-quality kosher food in the cafeteria) grows serious as she begins to study Judaism in order to convince the prison rabbi she is sincere. The religion's constant self-reflection appeals to her: "If you do something wrong, you got to figure it out yourself. And as far as God's concerned, it's your job to keep asking questions and to keep learning and to keep arguing." She cries when the rabbi agrees to her conversion. The final step, a *mikvah* (a ritual immersion in water), is completed during a spontaneous prison break after inmates notice a gap in the fence. Cindy jumps into the forbidden lake outside the prison and, for a moment, floats blissfully.

The tone of the series has grown bleaker over the years. In season one, "there were moments that felt too light, too frivolous," says writer Sian Heder, as if the women were bunkmates at summer camp. "Often, I would write a super-intense scene, and Jenji would write what she called a funny 'treacle cutter' at the end of it. And at first, I was like, 'God, we can't just let anything land without a joke?' But what it gave us was the idea that there is no moment so intense that you can't laugh in that moment, truly."

Increasingly, *Orange* has interspersed that humor with glimpses of the oppressive machinery behind the prison industrial complex. Most of the women at Litchfield committed relatively minor crimes out of desperation, habit, or foolishness, yet the prison embroils inmates in bullshit schemes, such as a mock job fair, rather than actually training them or helping them get work that pays a living wage when they return to the outside world. Things grow more harrowing still when Litchfield's management is taken over by a private corporation called MCC, whose sole interest is in making money. The new regime of cost cutting and profit making results in dangerous overcrowding; an influx of brutal, barely trained guards; and a general breakdown in the fabric of prison life. As one inmate notes, "We ain't people now; we bulk items."

Kohan couldn't resist having a little fun with the situation, sending Caputo to CorrectiCon, a dystopian prison-management convention featuring panels with titles such as "Shanks for the Memories: A History of Prison Weapons." But, in season four, that satire was set against a dire, serious portrait of disintegrating prison conditions. Sophia is thrown into the chasm of solitary confinement, aka the SHU, for her own "protection." Litchfield's racial factions, which coexisted somewhat peacefully in previous seasons, grow treacherously polarized (and more broadly drawn) as a new population of hardened prisoners pours into the prison. Piper, who has developed a black-market business selling aromatically infused panties worn by her fellow convicts, allies herself with a newly arrived bunch of neo-Nazi women to shore up her power against competition from a rival Dominican gang. After she rats on the Dominicans to prison guards, they retaliate by branding her arm with a swastika.

"The animals, the animals / trapped trapped trapped till the cage is full"—that's how every episode of *Orange* opens, with Regina Spektor's propulsive theme song. In the season-four episode that takes "The Animals" as its title—directed by Kohan's friend, *Mad Men* creator Matt Weiner—the inmates stage a nonviolent but chaotic protest in the prison's canteen against Litchfield's increasingly inhumane policies. The implicit message is "We are *not* animals." But the canteen becomes a killing floor when Poussey, one of *Orange*'s most beloved personalities, perishes at the hands of a poorly trained, panicked corrections officer.

"I can't breathe" are her last words, a deliberate echo of those of Eric Garner, whose death at the hands of police helped catalyze the Black Lives Matter movement. The guards leave her corpse lying for hours in the cafeteria—just as the Ferguson police did with Michael Brown after he was shot down in the street—while they pull together a cover story. Speaking to the press, Caputo treats the death as a generic occurrence. Taystee, incandescent with grief and rage, shouts, "They didn't even say her name!"—a rallying cry in the aftermath of Sandra Bland's unexplained death in a jail cell.

———

Fractious debates had erupted in the writers' room about which character should die. Kohan felt strongly that they needed to choose Poussey precisely because she was such an endearing, sensitive, and optimistic figure: "She had a future, she had potential, and that is going to be more devastating than losing other characters." Natasha Lyonne compared the epic nature of filming that scene to *Spartacus*, such was the intense coordination and rehearsal required. The entire cast was on set, a massive ensemble simulating chaos. "It has to feel like . . . it's an accident," Matt Weiner pointed out to *Vanity Fair*. "But, of course, the whole story of the episode is that nothing is an accident. This entire environment has been created because of the corporatization of the prison."

Actress Samira Wiley ran around between takes trying to cheer up cast-mates traumatized by her brutal on-screen demise. After the fourth season premiered in June 2016, many equally distraught fans protested with the hashtag #PousseyDeservedBetter. "Disgusting how you could do this to the one beautiful, strong and (finally) happy black lesbian character," one fan complained on Twitter. Others were disturbed by the show's decision to include a sympathetic flashback for the young white corrections officer who killed Poussey, a move that seemed to diminish the guard's culpability for this senseless death.

"There's something too facile about 'The evil guard kills the good prisoner,'" Kohan argues. "It's messier than that. They are all people, and they are all making mistakes and acting in the moment. There's that tension of: Are you the actions you commit? Are you separate from those? I don't want the easy way out. I want people to struggle with the material and argue with it and be affected by it."

Wiley herself told reporters she felt proud to contribute to this consciousness-raising moment: "Some people who love *Orange Is the New Black* don't know what Black Lives Matter is. They don't have a black friend and they don't have a gay friend, but they know Poussey from TV and they feel just like you said—you feel like you knew her." In a conversation about the show at the political website ThinkProgress, criminal-justice reporter Carimah Townes argued that the season's narrative was ultimately deeply resonant: "This is the black women's 'We have nothing to lose but our chains' moment. And the story line is so timely. There are prison protests (labor and hunger strikes) happening all over the country, with people saying, 'Enough is enough' with slave labor, solitary confinement, and inhumane living conditions."

Kohan is well aware that *Orange* offers her a privileged cultural perch. "A huge part of my goal for the show is to start conversations about things," she told a live audience in 2014. "It is, to a certain extent, my soapbox—I'm not secretive about my political agenda. It's great that the themes of the show have entered the national conversation and international conversation, and that people are talking about issues that they were never talking about before, and seeing the prison industrial complex in a different light and seeing prisoners in a different light."

The private penitentiary industry flourished in the early years of the twenty-first century, but there were signs of shifting attitudes. Hillary Clinton had called for an end to the for-profit prison sector, and in August 2016, two months after season four of *Orange* premiered, President Obama's Justice Department announced that it would begin phasing out its contracts with corporate prisons. A month later, one of the largest jail strikes in US history erupted all across the country: at least twenty thousand inmates from twenty-three states refused to report for their prison jobs, which paid them little or nothing. "A call to action against slavery in America," the organizers dubbed the strike, whose demands included fair pay, improved living conditions, and better educational opportunities.

"People are realizing that, okay, we might have made a bit of a mistake here with the war on drugs, that it was really a war on people," says executive producer Mark Burley. "Mass incarceration is now seen as a failure and an expensive one at that . . . and it doesn't hurt that people are watching a television show that humanizes those people." Just as *Weeds* might have helped changed attitudes toward legalizing marijuana a bit, *Orange* humanized the prison population—though, with the election of Donald Trump, federal policy on marijuana prosecution and private prisons is moving violently in reverse, back to the bad old days of "just say no" and mandatory minimum sentencing.

Struggling to think of a television series with comparable ambition and breadth, Natasha Lyonne settles on *The Wire*. David Simon's show circled Baltimore, stealthily building a stratum-by-stratum geological mapping of an urban landscape of corruption and inequality, tracing the economic pressure points and social fissures that have created an effectively symbiotic arrangement in which drug gangs and police forces have an interest in things staying the same. Crack-empire kingpins, young street dealers, cops, politicians, defense lawyers, prosecutors, and even journalists and teachers—all are implicated in a system that perpetuates itself even as it keeps on failing.

"The scope keeps growing, and suddenly you're telling me the entire story of the universe of drugs and the impact that it has," Lyonne says of *The Wire*. "It feels like that is what is happening with our show." *Orange* weaves together the stories of individual women with the systemic dysfunction of the prison industrial complex, the justice system, and society's frayed safety net. "We are starting to flesh it all out and see the entire story of what it's like being in prison."

———

The writers' room of *Orange Is the New Black* feels like preschool, stocked with toys (clay, coloring books, puzzles) so that people can keep their bodies and brains engaged, even when they're delving into uncomfortable emotional territory. It's not easy to keep dozens of narrative threads in motion, and Kohan uses a delicate balance of collaboration and discipline to keep things heading in the right direction. "There is a control freak side to me," she says, laughing. "I'm not trying to change things just to pee in the corner but to keep the tone of the show constant."

Stephen Falk, who went on to create the series *You're the Worst* after working on both *Weeds* and *Orange*, declares Kohan to be the bravest storyteller he knows. "She has no fear of putting the most dramatic thing up against the most comedic. That's a lesson I have taken from her and used to fortify my timid little heart when I get nervous about doing something." The two take frequent walks around the Silver Lake Reservoir, during which he continues to absorb her advice and admire the way she speaks truth to Hollywood power. "By being very unafraid to stand her ground, she can sometimes put executives off balance. She is unafraid to piss off the powers that be"—or to burn down the town, for that matter.

In *Weeds*, Kohan set out to create a mesmerizing woman who could stand alongside Tony Soprano. With *Orange*, she went one step further: In a show with no fixed center, men are mostly pushed to the margins. It's the women who take up emotional space within the walls of Litchfield. Joy, misery, humor, rage, jealousy, mischief, lust—nearly all of it is aimed at and reciprocated by other female characters, in defiance of or to evade the men who would restrain them. All that matters is women talking and laughing and telling one another stories.

Kohan says she approached *Weeds* with the old sitcom attitude that people don't change: "There is no growth or epiphanies. On *Weeds*, everyone just becomes more and more of who they are." On *Orange Is the New Black*, though, a completely different mind-set was required. In this least promising of environments, characters grow emotionally and forge unexpected alliances across seemingly unbridgeable chasms of race and class and sexuality. Human potential flowers against all odds.

"These women in prison, as a group—they are just lumped together and charged and treated accordingly," Kohan says. "It was a real opportunity to say, 'Take another look! There is more to this person than what crime they committed.' The more you dig, the more you find. So we just keep digging."

CHAPTER 9

Body Politic:
Jill Soloway's *Transparent*

Jill Soloway confers with Jeffrey Tambor (as Maura)
and the cast of *Transparent*.

Stepping inside Paramount Soundstage 14 is like landing on an alien planet that has painstakingly reconstructed twenty-first-century upper-middle-class life in Los Angeles.

Under sky-high ceilings sprouting massive shiny silver ducts, I walk through a maze of corridors lined with furnished rooms seemingly transported wholesale from elsewhere in LA. Down one hallway is a perfect simulacrum of a Jewish community center meeting room, complete with dilapidated carpet, ceiling tiles mottled with water stains, and tossed-aside menorahs. A few twists and turns down a claustrophobic tunnel, and I am inside a dark bedroom swathed in velvet fabric, cluttered with carefully chosen beauty products and family photos that reveal this to be the inner sanctum of Davina, a character who serves as a spirit guide for Maura Pfefferman, the trans parent of Jill Soloway's *Transparent*. Launched in the fall of

2014, the show won five Emmys that first year for its depiction of a family transforming along with its patriarch.

An unmarked door in a giant wall is the gateway to Pfefferlandia. I emerge into a thicket of trees that surrounds the façade of the Pfefferman family's modernist house. The kitchen looks ready to entertain, complete with a fresh Trader Joe's baguette and an array of cheeses. The cast and crew of the show spill out from the kitchen and onto the terrace. They are listening intently to a small figure at the center of the room, show creator Jill Soloway, as she discusses the scene they are about to shoot: a birthday party for Maura that will bring together nearly every character in the series. Judith Light, who plays Maura's ex-wife, Shelly, tries out dialogue about her character's new obsession with Twitter (her handle is @ToShellandBack). "I am coming out—as a brand!" she roars tipsily in character, and the crew laughs with her.

While the actors shuffle off to get into costume, Soloway ambles over to the cluster of seats and video monitors just outside the dining room windows, hanging her red baseball cap on the side of her canvas chair. She's directing this season-three episode, "To Sardines and Back," which she cowrote with her older sister, Faith, a member of the show's writing staff. "It's a little more of a frivolous episode for us," says Faith, relaxed in her dark hoodie, wavy hair pulled back in a ponytail. "But it is one with a serious revelation, which is that this is when Maura tells her family she wants to have [gender confirmation] surgery." The "sardines" of the episode title is a real game that Faith says the Soloways played when they were kids, an inversion of hide-and-seek, in which everyone ends up crammed together in a hiding space.

Inside the spacious dining room, crew members futz with table settings and wires. The room is strung with colored party lights that look dazzling from where we are sitting. Soloway snaps a picture of it on her phone for her Instagram page and calls long-haired director of photography Jim Frohna over to see the lights refracting through the windows. "What could we do with this?" she asks. "Maybe we could use it for the dentist scene?" he says, thinking about a psychedelic moment later in the episode. Soloway's face lights up, and she leans back in her chair, rumpling her close-cropped hair.

Eating salad from a big porcelain bowl, Soloway watches intently as the cameras roll on a scene in which members of the Pfefferman clan arrive for the party. Shelly and her bearded boyfriend, Buzz (Richard Masur), arrive by motorcycle, clad in leather. They push through the front door, Shelly shouting, "*Hullo*! What did you kids *do*?" as she looks over the changes her adult children Josh (Jay Duplass) and Ali (Gaby Hoffmann) have made to the house. Soloway never calls "cut," but darts into the house set regularly to confer, changing the camera's sight lines, suggesting tiny alterations in the dialogue, testing every syllable and movement for realness.

Instead of Shelly and Buzz simply taking off their motorcycle garb, Soloway looks for ways to use the entrance as a moment of character definition for this elderly, conventional Jewish woman who is envious of her family members' ongoing self-reinvention. "You need a place for us to put our *leathers*!" Shelly scolds gleefully, simultaneously making a joke and a fuss. Soloway also sparks a jarring but tender physical interaction between Josh and his mom's boyfriend, suggesting that Josh "stop and make a meal" of Buzz taking off the chaps. "I really want you to do the *undressing*," she says. "I want to see a real moment. Make a big deal of his chaps removal."

In the next take, while Shelly banters with her daughter, Josh kneels down like a courtly knight and unbuckles Buzz's chaps, revealing bare elderly legs and a pair of khaki dad shorts. "You should see him in chaps in the bedroom," Light ad-libs saucily at one point. Each time the actors come together, there is a palpable crackle of affection. Between takes, they gather in a corner of the room, chattering like the ersatz family they are. When the little children who play Maura's grandkids arrive on set with their screen mom, Sarah (Amy Landecker), the boy walks up to each person in Video Village (including me) and gives us an affectionate hug. Waiting for their cue, Landecker tells the kids to make sure to notice how pretty Maura looks.

The dialogue seems to change with every take, and I ask Faith if this improvisation is typical. She hands me the script. "Most of it's there," she says, shrugging. She's right, but each time the actors say the words, they seem different, like evolving organisms. As Ali, Gaby Hoffmann, dressed in a bright-green sleeveless romper that elongates her tall, slim body, resembles a sprite, clapping and dancing and jigging. At one point, she does a little twirling dance with arms aloft that inspires Judith Light's Shelly to riff on her daughter's unshaven pits. This gets incorporated into an exchange in which Shelly warns, "You're never never never going to get a man like that," only to have Ali reply, "I don't date men anymore."

Jeffrey Tambor had been dressed in a casual shirt and pants in the morning meeting, but now, an hour or so later, he quietly appears as Maura, in a demure beige dress, tan flats, and a flawless silvery blond wig, accompanied by Anjelica Huston, who plays Maura's lover, Vicki. The clamor is realistic as they arrive at the dinner party, with side conversations and voices crisscrossing. Soloway gathers them briefly, to give each moment a focus. She asks Duplass to make note of the sleek new hairstyle Maura is sporting and requests that "Maura and Shelly have a moment in the center," choreographing the actors' movements so that the chaos suddenly has a smooth grace. Shelly's fleeting attempt to take an iPad selfie with Maura for her new Twitter account barely registers, until Soloway suggests Shelly get in Maura's face: "I want you to have a little more fun with the comedy of it." Although the show is categorized as a comedy, *Transparent*'s iconoclasm lies in the way it slips and slides somewhere unclassifiable among drama and comedy, family soap opera, and political-affairs lecture. In fact, you might say that Soloway has created a trans genre perfectly suited to the fluidity of her subject.

When the food cart arrives for lunch, Soloway goes over and surveys the array of cold cuts, shouting, "Meat on the set!" And then Tambor and Light perform the scene the way Jill has modeled it. Maura says quietly and flatly, "Do not put my picture on there. I do not want to be on strangers' computers." Shelly, the unstoppable Jewish mother, ignores Maura's protests. "It has a filter. You look stunning!"

It feels like a cat's cradle of skirmishes and connections, each character allowed to shine in all his or her neurotic glory. Gaby Hoffmann compares Soloway's style of showrunning to psychoanalyst D. W. Winnicott's concept of "the good enough parent."

"You create an environment where the child is safe and then you let it discover itself on its own," Hoffmann offers. "And you don't step in and show them how to do it unless they are about to kill themselves—that is what Jill does as a director. She loves to say directing is the easiest thing in the world, but it is incredibly difficult. She makes you feel like, *Oh, this could be art*. We are making art together."

Transparent snuck into pop culture through a side door and collided with the Zeitgeist. Just as Jenji Kohan had helped put Netflix on the map a year before with *Orange Is the New Black*, *Transparent* would instantly establish Amazon as a quality digital network and supporter of a more experimental type of TV. The online behemoth had become something of a dirty word in artsy circles, where it was often accused of trying to wipe out small bookstores and publishers. But with the single half hour of *Transparent*'s opening episode, the company created an irresistible pitch to culture snobs to shell out for an Amazon Prime subscription.

Soloway had never intended to be a digital trailblazer; in truth, she pitched the idea of *Transparent* to everyone else in town. After many years of working on cable TV series such as *Six Feet Under* and *United States of Tara*, and of seeing her own projects go nowhere, Soloway was frustrated. She had some nibbles of interest from prestige cable execs but knew "it would've taken a few years, and it might never have ended up on the air. HBO just didn't need it the way Amazon did." And Amazon would give her the freedom to make a five-hour independent movie sliced into half-hour segments.

The show's full first season premiered in September 2014, just as rumors were beginning to seep into the tabloids about the transition of Olympic hero turned Kardashian patriarch Bruce Jenner into Caitlyn Jenner. *Transparent* wasn't entirely breaking ground by featuring a major trans character—*The L Word* introduced a transgender character in 2006, and *Orange Is the New Black* had recently made transgender actress Laverne Cox a *Time* magazine cover girl—but it was the first mainstream show to put a trans character at its center, and with Jenner in the news, suddenly *Transparent* seemed like a crystallization of a momentous cultural shift.

For Soloway, it was a shock. As she told *IndieWire* in 2015, "We thought we were making a smallish show for a smallish group of people that was going to resonate with queer people and maybe with Jewish people and feminists." Instead, says the show's executive producer Andrea Sperling, "We tapped into something that was brewing in our society." She muses that the show may even have influenced Jenner's public coming out, since she was in the midst of transitioning when *Transparent* premiered. "The time was right."

Jill and Faith Soloway grew up in Chicago in the late sixties and seventies in a racially integrated community of brick town houses near the South Side, attending a mostly black school. Their mother, Elaine, worked as a teacher and helped put her British-born husband, Harry, through medical school. After Harry became a psychiatrist, the family moved across town to a Gold Coast condo and sent Jill to a private Jewish school. Even so, the Soloway household was secular, with television the closest thing to a family religion. Soloway's parents each had their own sets, indicative of their somewhat separate lives. Every night after dinner, Soloway ate ice cream and watched such seventies fare as *The Mary Tyler Moore Show* and *The Brady Bunch*.

Obsessed with fame, Soloway wrote fan fiction about movie stars and chased after rock bands with her girlfriends. She also spent hours performing and making videos with her sister. After graduating from college, she returned to Chicago, where she produced commercials and worked on a documentary. She began to fantasize about making a documentary of her own—about what it feels like to have been on *The Brady Bunch*, to *be* actress Eve Plumb. Instead, Jill and Faith ended up turning the idea into an over-the-top live stage show at the Annoyance Theatre, a Chicago fringe performance space. (Faith was already a fixture on the scene as musical director of Second City and co-creator of Annoyance Theatre's long-running musical *Co-Ed Prison Sluts*.)

Premiering in the summer of 1990, *The Real Live Brady Bunch* featured future stars Jane Lynch and Andy Richter as Carol and Mike Brady. Once a week, clad in thrift-shop flares and hideously patterned shirts, the cast reenacted episodes of the original series verbatim—to such acclaim that the show eventually had successful runs in New York and Los Angeles.

Suddenly, Hollywood producers were interested in the sisters Soloway. They cowrote a pilot called *Jewess Jones* for HBO, about a superheroine whose frizzy hair alerted her to danger and whose special skill was knowing how much food to order in a restaurant—but nothing came of it. Faith soon moved to Boston to pursue life as a folk singer, and Jill drifted into a bohemian existence in rural California, writing unproduced pilots and becoming a single mom. In need of money, she got a staff job on *The Steve Harvey Show*, followed by writing jobs on a number of short-lived sitcoms. She continued to perform and write for her own sanity, placing a short story called "Courteney Cox's Asshole" in the literary journal *Zyzzyva*. A hilariously meta riff on fame, it imagined the personal assistant to the *Friends* star dealing with rumors that her boss bleached her anus.

Soloway's agent included the story in a submission to *Six Feet Under* creator Alan Ball, and it impressed him enough that he hired Soloway to write for the second season of the show. In a tribute to her in *Time* magazine, Ball recalled that within that very short story, "Jill managed to convey the very real pain of a soul yearning to be authentic in a completely inauthentic world, as well as that soul's eventual success in achieving desired authenticity."

On *Six Feet Under*, Soloway explored ideas and themes that would recur later in her work: the very first episode she wrote for the HBO series included a moonlit hippie party, a woman acting on her sexual impulses at work, a teenage boy deflowered by an older woman, and a female rabbi whose consultation with Nate Fisher leads him to suggest, "Maybe God's a woman." In her last *Six Feet Under* episode, she wrote a scene in which matriarch Ruth Fisher drunkenly proposes to a table full of friends that they create "a land of no men" (except when they are needed for child care).

Soloway says that her experience in the *Six Feet Under* writers' room was absolutely formative, with Ball serving as a great mentor. "He taught a very receptive style, where he didn't really have an agenda. He let things flow and let the conversation of the room guide the story," so that the writers felt that they were tapping directly into the Fisher family members' psyches. There was also a compulsion to share personal hijinks and traumas, providing building blocks for emotionally realistic characters. The *Six Feet Under* writers' room mantra was "Feed the machine!" she says. "You'd start telling a story—'Hey, this crazy thing happened to me this weekend'—and everyone would be like, 'Feed the machine! Feed the machine!'" she chants, pounding on the table.

After *Six Feet Under*, Soloway briefly worked as a consulting producer on *Grey's Anatomy*, but she found that Shondaland was not a good fit. "I guess I just always really wanted to be in charge," she says, sighing deeply. "So, any time I was in a consultant position, I felt like I couldn't do my thing, and got frustrated." Rhimes soon let her go. The situation at her next gig, *United States of Tara*, was entirely different: Diablo Cody had been given creative control of this Showtime dramedy about a woman with multiple personality disorder but didn't feel comfortable wielding the power. "I needed to take control and steer the ship," Cody says now, "but I couldn't do it, so I just watched people fighting over the wheel."

Soloway took over showrunning duties in season two and vowed to help Cody make the show her own. "Jill completely changed the dynamic of the writers' room," says Cody. "She has this really amazing maternal feminine energy. It suddenly became a really warm, creative place." Among Soloway's new hires was playwright Sheila Callaghan, who had written a play called *That Pretty Pretty; or, the Rape Play*, a dissection of media misogyny. "At the center of *Tara* is a girl with multiple personalities who was sexually abused as a child, so basically Jill was looking for somebody with a feminist sensibility who could write rape funny. I like to say she googled 'rape,' 'playwrights,' and 'feminist' and she got me."

Soloway had just given birth to her second child, and when she found out Callaghan also had a baby, she created a nursery in the garage of the writers' bungalow. "She really wanted to establish a workplace that was female-friendly, not just for her own interests but generally, as a statement," says Callaghan. That female-friendliness extended to the working spaces: "Jill ran our room like a womb. Lots of maternal energy." Soloway also encouraged Cody to follow some of her more unorthodox instincts—the two women wrote an episode about a Christian hell house—that didn't always please the network.

When asked whom Soloway conflicted with, Cody chuckles. "Everybody! We had the best season ever, and we scared the shit out of everybody in charge . . . so they fired her."

By 2011, Soloway was between jobs, with two children to feed. Her Chicago friend Jane Lynch set her up to meet with Ryan Murphy about a job on his smash hit *Glee*, but it fell through; Murphy had apparently heard through the grapevine that Soloway was "difficult"—the second-ugliest word for a woman in Hollywood next to "unrelatable." She started to develop a series for HBO with Zooey Deschanel starring as sixties groupie Pamela Des Barres, but Deschanel took a job on *New Girl*. Even more frustrating, she watched as twenty-five-year-old Lena Dunham swan-dived into her pool, first with the low-budget movie *Tiny Furniture* and then with *Girls*. After spending decades being told by executives that her characters were too unlikable or neurotic, Soloway was stunned to watch Dunham make those things an unapologetic virtue.

"The reason HBO picked up that show instead of mine was because they can see her voice," Soloway said in a speech at the Directors Guild of America. She recalled telling her husband, music supervisor Bruce Gilbert, "No one can see my voice. All I am is that girl who used to write on *Six Feet Under*." Rather than continue to play handmaiden to someone else's vision, Soloway finally showcased her own. The 2013 indie film *Afternoon*

Delight, which she wrote and directed, was a broken buddy movie, a collision between different versions of femininity. In it, a dissatisfied LA mom (Kathryn Hahn) takes a teenage prostitute (Juno Temple) under her wing, hiring her to be the live-in nanny. The narrative offers no pat answers, and the film's tone is so uneasy that Soloway dubbed it "funcomfortable." *Afternoon Delight* went on to win Soloway the directing award at the 2013 Sundance Film Festival.

While Soloway was creating the alternative family of *Afternoon Delight*, she was also processing some family drama of her own. Her seventy-five-year-old father called to let her know he was coming out as trans: Harry Soloway would henceforth be known as Carrie Soloway. Her children would now call Carrie "Moppa," a name halfway between "Mama" and "Poppa."

This news obviously had strong potential as the basis for a script, but Jill let the news percolate for a long while. It made her retroactively question everything in her life, from her father's distant and depressive behavior to her own sexuality. Faith had come out as a lesbian in her twenties; Jill was married with children but had long identified with queer culture and disdained girlie accoutrements. As she began to create *Transparent*, Jill Soloway also re-created herself.

She and Faith kicked around the idea of making a documentary about being the children of a trans parent, but the idea soon morphed into drama. After spotting actress Gaby Hoffmann in a brief role on the TV series *Louie*, Soloway knew she wanted to involve her in the project. They met up at Sundance, and Hoffmann says she was entranced by Soloway. "We sat down, and five minutes later we were both crying—well, I'm not sure that's what actually happened, but that is what it felt like. There was no chitchat; we were just in deep." She told Hoffmann about Carrie's coming out and that she wanted to make a TV show about a family coming to grips with this experience. Hoffmann was excited but dubious. "In my mind, I was like, *If anyone ever* lets *you do this . . .*'" she mutters.

Over the next few months, Hoffmann says Soloway would send her "little scenes here and there, and we started playing around with it." They began to shoot some material with Jim Frohna, the director of photography who had done *Afternoon Delight*, even as Soloway also worked on a different idea for a movie with Hoffmann. Soloway's agent pitched the script for what would become *Transparent* all over town, and HBO agreed to develop it—but Soloway had been down that road before. Development might result in a series several years down the line, or it might end in tears. This project was too urgent and personal to chance it. So, instead, she sold it to Amazon's fledgling streaming network, which would let her shoot the pilot immediately, with minimal interference. And if the pilot wasn't a success for Amazon, it would let her sell it elsewhere.

Soloway knew she wanted Jeffrey Tambor to play Maura Pfefferman, the role inspired by her own Moppa. A cisgender male actor best known for his comedic roles in *The Larry Sanders Show* and *Arrested Development*, Tambor reminded her of Carrie pretransition. Early on, Soloway asked Rhys Ernst, a transgender filmmaker who serves as a producer and trans consultant on the show, what he thought of casting Tambor. It was a potentially inflammatory move, but Ernst says he believed that occasional cisgender casting, "if done for the right reasons and done responsibly, makes sense." Tambor fit those criteria for him "because we are all meeting this character pretransition, we are seeing this character through the adult children's eyes, still as the father, so it makes sense to start with this actor. And [Jill] always talked about how Jeffrey reminded her of her parent, so it seemed like a responsible exception."

Judith Light, whose career spanned soap operas (*One Life to Live*), eighties sitcoms (*Who's the Boss?*), and Broadway dramas (for which she won two Tony Awards), was cast as Shelly Pfefferman, the brassy and sometimes clueless alter ego of Soloway's mom, Elaine, after the two bonded by Skype over their devotion to LGBTQ activism. Amy Landecker, who, like Soloway, came up through the Chicago theater scene, initially turned down a chance to audition for the role of Sarah, the oldest Pfefferman child, because she was uncomfortable with the graphic nudity involved. But she reconsidered after watching *Afternoon Delight*, understanding that Soloway approached sexuality from a different perspective than most other directors. *Afternoon Delight* star Kathryn Hahn was tapped to play Rabbi Raquel, who brings a touch of poetic Judaism into the secular family's life.

Hoffmann says Soloway has a genius for casting—or, as she puts it, "for gathering energies." Laughing self-consciously at her hippyish phrasing, Hoffmann describes it as "an ability to tap into something that feels like it was already there and let it be. The way that Jill cast the show and put it all together is the same way that she now directs it: it's all from the pussy, as she would say. It's all instinct and heart." The core cast smoothly fell into place, except for the character of Josh Pfefferman, Maura's hipster son. Sitting at an LA dinner party next to indie filmmaker Jay Duplass, Soloway became convinced that he was the man for the part, but he protested that he wasn't an actor and was already at work co-creating a series with his brother, Mark, for HBO (*Togetherness*). Undaunted, Soloway excitedly texted Hoffmann a photo of him after the dinner. "The first time I saw Jay, it was like a bolt of lightning," Hoffmann says. "But we had to convince him to do it, right up to the last second."

Just as she had "gathered" her actors, so Soloway intuitively amassed a team of writers with varying levels of experience and gender identities. Among them were Bridget Bedard, a cisgender straight woman who had written for *Mad Men*; Ali Liebegott, a gender-nonconforming novelist and poet from San Francisco who had been working at a supermarket to pay the bills; and Micah Fitzerman-Blue, a cisgender straight guy who had cofounded the Silver Lake group East Side Jews with Soloway and Jenji Kohan. Then there was sister Faith, who commuted from her home in Boston to work on the show, living in an apartment above the writers' room.

Soloway's initial instruction was for the writers to get to know one another. "We cried for two days," Liebegott recalls. "It was like, 'What is your life?' Everyone just told all their stories."

None of the writers was trans, however. So Soloway brought in trans artists/filmmakers Rhys Ernst and Zackary Drucker to act as consultants (and later producers); trans comedian Ian Harvie; and Jennifer Finney Boylan, an author and professor who transitioned late in life and helped inform Maura's character. They shared stories and answered questions for cast and crew, and educated Jeffrey Tambor in preparation for the role. Tambor also embarked on field trips in character, including a crucial outing to a trans bar in the Valley.

"Jeffrey had never actually stepped fully into Maura," recalls Ernst. "He'd been fitted for wardrobe and makeup, but he hadn't been out in the world." Ernst, Drucker, Soloway, and Frohna met Jeffrey in his hotel room in Santa Monica one night: "We sat around and got him into character slowly over a couple of hours. We all told personal stories about our lives and everyone's experiences of gender—even cisgender people in the group, like Jill and Jeffrey." Walking through the hotel lobby "turned into a really significant moment for Jeffrey," says Ernst, "because it was the first time he ever experienced walking in those shoes and being in public and not knowing how people were seeing him as heads turned."

Tambor held on to the sense memory of that walk through the hotel lobby, the feeling of living inside Maura's skin. "I kept telling myself, 'Remember this. Don't ever forget this,'" he told *Vanity Fair*. "'You're an actor. You must understand what is going on here and bring it to this performance.'"

Soloway had spent two decades in television waiting for her chance to make something of her own. She had long talked about fomenting a feminist revolution—even way back in 2005, in her book of funny autobiographical essays *Tiny Ladies in Shiny Pants*, she called for "an unarmed yet mighty revolution, secession into an all-female state, with a big ol' newfounded land . . . ruled by me, yes me, until the patriarchy is toppled and a global matriarchy run by me, yes me, is installed." She named her production company Topple.

Once ensconced at Amazon, she proceeded to unravel all kinds of rules. While other showrunners struggled to get female directors approved by the networks, Soloway decided that all *Transparent* episodes would be helmed by her or other female and trans indie film directors she admired, such as Andrea Arnold, Marta Cunningham, Nisha Ganatra, and Silas Howard, who could not get a foot in the door of TV studios. (The one exception: an episode directed by cis-male director of photography Jim Frohna.) She calls those directing slots "golden tickets," just like the ones found in Willy Wonka's chocolate bars—except these were shortcuts to a career in television rather than entrance to a candy paradise. A directing slot on *Transparent* would make it easier for them to get other TV jobs in the future.

Soloway also developed what she called a "transfirmative action program," actively seeking out trans personnel for the crew and even leading a trans screenwriting workshop to train new writers. Out of the latter process, she plucked Our Lady J, a singer-songwriter who ended up joining the *Transparent* writers' room in the second season. "There's a difference between laughing at somebody and laughing with somebody," Soloway notes. "That gets taken care of if you have a trans man or woman in the writers' room."

She also forged emotional bonds on her set by bringing in Joan Scheckel, a kind of director whisperer who had worked with Soloway on *Afternoon Delight*. Scheckel runs a filmmaking lab and serves as a coach, teaching directors and actors how to tap deep into emotion. She engaged the cast and crew of *Transparent* in something that sounds a bit like primal scream therapy, stripping down to raw emotion and coaxing the actors into physical improvisations that brought a quick intimacy to their relationships. Amy Landecker described it as "a huge acid-trip emotional exploration of the script." Scheckel taught Soloway and her cast to be alert to shifts in motivation and feeling that pulse behind every word and movement on-screen.

"I think it is group therapy," Soloway tells me, sitting in the red kitchen of her Silver Lake house one December morning. Exploring scenes in that way, she says, creates a sense of unified understanding. "It's like, *Oh!* That *is what the scene is about*. So, as a group, we can all feel together, *Now we are going to go* there." Which is maybe an abstract way of describing the very real thing I witnessed on the set: actors who are so embedded inside their characters and so tethered to one another that they now instinctively inflect each line and movement with the unpredictable magic of reality.

Gaby Hoffmann recalls shooting a scene in which the whole clan is gathered at the house eating leftovers. Her character storms off in anger and then returns later—but Hoffmann kept missing her cue to reenter. "I was just so enthralled, I kept forgetting that I was supposed to be in the scene. The way that Jay would dip his spoon into the coleslaw and the way that Jeffrey would turn his nose up just slightly," Hoffmann says. "I remember sitting there and thinking, *God, they are* so good."

Soloway's personal experiences have seeped into the series—translated into fictional plotlines, of course. All three Pfefferman children seem to derive slivers of their personality from Jill, but also from Faith. Jill's mother, Elaine, the loose inspiration for Shelly Pfefferman, is getting ready to leave when I arrive at the Soloway home. She repeatedly gives her daughter a report on her plan to take an Uber across town, and Jill repeatedly offers to pay for it. In the other room, Jill's son Felix watches TV, restlessly summoning his mom several times while he waits for his babysitter to arrive. Meanwhile, Jill is expecting a call from Eileen Myles, the downtown New York poet with whom Soloway fell in love while working on *Transparent*, and who was the inspiration for Ali's dyke poet paramour, Leslie Mackinaw (played by Cherry Jones).

So, while creatively everything was coming together on *Transparent*, Soloway's personal life was as chaotic as her characters'. Her Moppa's revelation had blown up her universe. She had always felt straitjacketed by conventional femininity, and this new information freed her up to question her sexuality. Like Sarah Pfefferman, Soloway separated from her husband (the show's music supervisor, Bruce Gilbert) and began to sleep with a woman; like Ali, she was experimenting with what it meant to be genderqueer.

"The series is just a couple of years behind real life, so [Faith and I] have been living it with my parents' lives and our lives, riding on the coattails of this real emotional experience." She takes off her designer version of a plaid flannel shirt. "First season, it's all about the secret. And then it's: What does it mean? And what do I not understand about myself that I would've understood had I known my parent was gender nonconforming when I was born? Who would I be?"

Looking out the window into her backyard, Soloway says softly, "What a moment! For me to have my parent come out as trans, for me to be really ready because I had just made my first film, and to have found Amazon, [which has] this business model that's giving me artistic freedom. We are working really hard, but we are doing so from the place of what is artistically exciting, not to make a person from the network happy."

When *Transparent*'s pilot debuted online along with four other potential adult series in February 2014, viewers were encouraged to vote for the show they wanted Amazon to produce. Although *Transparent* didn't necessarily get blockbuster numbers, those who liked it seemed to like it passionately. The full season began streaming in September 2014 and quickly became a critical darling. *New York* magazine's review headline proclaimed, "Amazon's *Transparent* Is Damn Near Perfect." Filmmaker Darren Aronofsky tweeted, "I gotta hang @jillsoloway #TransparentTV next to the best of Philip Roth."

The pilot dares us to hate Sarah, Ali, and Josh Pfefferman. They are the kind of spoiled cosmopolitans that heartland America loves to loathe, yet all their vulnerabilities and contradictions are splayed before us. Stay-at-home mom Sarah Pfefferman hands off a roast to her housekeeper before hustling her kids into an SUV, where she turns on that seventies feminist anthem "Free to Be You and Me"; younger sister Ali tells best friend Syd (Carrie Brownstein) of her plan to get rich with a novelty book that would be a cautionary tale about "slutting around"; brother Josh is busy photographing two bleached-blond hipster waifs, musicians with his record label.

The trio of siblings is brought together by a mysterious summons from their father. They agree it must be cancer. "He should start gifting us twelve thousand dollars a year now," Josh crassly suggests. "For tax purposes." Soloway leaves no room for illusions but lots of space for squirming. When the kids arrive for their dinner with Dad, retired professor Mort Pfefferman is dressed in a pale pink gingham button-down, his gray hair in a loose ponytail. He is dying to unburden himself of his secret while they eat barbecue, but his kids are convinced he is sick. "Stop! I don't have cancer!" he roars, his face smeared with sauce like a small child. "I'm selling the house," he declares instead—at which point the kids start arguing over which one of them deserves to inherit it.

As soon as his children leave, Mort shuffles around his house, pulling off his clothes. Moments later, he reappears wearing a caftan, pulling his hair loose from its ponytail. This is how we meet the real Mort: Maura Pfefferman.

Later, at a trans support group, Maura, dressed in a demure lavender wrap accessorized with a diamond ring and bracelet, complains about her kids. "They are so selfish. I don't know how it is I raised three people who cannot see beyond themselves." This is one of the leitmotifs of *Transparent*: How do you connect to others when you are so consumed by hiding who you are? And how do mistakes and horrors, whether it's the Holocaust or sexual abuse or social pressure, perpetuate themselves in the generations that follow?

Soloway draws a personal-historical thread through the series. Flashbacks transport us to various points in Maura's life as she struggles with her identity: secretly buying dresses that she can never wear, trying to convince loyal wife Shelly that his wearing women's underwear is just a sexy game, visiting a vacation camp for transvestites. One third-season episode even revisits Maura's childhood; sweetly embodied by a trans child actress (Sophia Grace Gianna), young Mort/Maura chafes at having to play little league baseball and makes an oasis of the family's bomb shelter, wearing her mother's nightgowns as she twirls around to pop music.

Pulling back even further in Pfefferman family history, *Transparent* pops up in 1930s Berlin, as Maura's grandmother is trying to whisk her two children away from the looming threat of Nazism. Maura's uncle Gershon has become Gittel (played by trans actress Hari Nef), a glamorous trans woman living at the Institute for Sexual Research. Although it resembles a set from *Cabaret*, the institute is based on a real place founded by Dr. Magnus Hirschfeld, a Jewish-German physician, researcher, and activist dubbed the "Einstein of sex" in his day. Author Christopher Isherwood (whose writing inspired *Cabaret*) actually lived next door; the institute was seized by the Nazis in 1933, and many of Weimar Berlin's "sexual deviants" rounded up. "You want to know what happened to your uncle Gershon?" Maura's grandfather threatens when he catches his grandchild dressed in a frilly nightgown, late in season three. "He burned to death in the oven . . . because your mother and your grandmother let him run around in a skirt!"

This might have been a didactic moment if *Transparent* hadn't already spent three seasons evoking the privileged twenty-first-century life of the Pfeffermans, who take their freedom for granted. By taking a giant step back, Soloway builds a context for the fear of Maura's Jewish father, who is desperate to assimilate as a matter of survival, and tries to excavate the lost legacy of trans and gay ancestors. The Pfefferman children know nothing of Gittel's history. All that remains of her is a pearl ring, passed around as a tainted heirloom. "Your father tried to propose to me with that *farkakte* thing," Shelly tells Ali dismissively; she insisted he buy her something fancier. Josh proffers it to his pregnant girlfriend, who rejects the ring (and Josh) and proceeds to have an abortion. Finally, Ali, who has begun to research the fate of Jews and queers in Nazi Germany, takes possession of it, sensing it is a key to the family legacy.

Soloway wrote in 2005 that her own family tree included "a hell of a lot of freaky Jews. We had them all: gays, lesbians, bisexuals, asexuals, some of your early versions of transgender." But she didn't set out to write about the Holocaust in *Transparent*. A throwaway line about "Tante Gittel's ring" in season one led the show's writers to think about the Pfeffermans' predecessors; Weimar Germany offered some startling parallels to twenty-first-century America. "There was an underlying sense back then that the world was going to end tomorrow," Hari Nef said in a 2015 *IndieWire* interview. "In that sort of half-nihilism, half-exuberant feeling emerged this amazing permissiveness and this experimentation and this collapse of binaries that was maybe holding the old world together."

In September 2015, *Transparent* was nominated for eleven Emmy Awards and won five, including Soloway for Best Director of a Comedy Series and Tambor for Best Actor. When Soloway took the stage in a black-and-white polka-dotted suit to accept, she made a point of thanking a female Almighty: "I promised the Goddess I would thank her. And Amazon. Goddess first, Amazon second."

During the ceremony, she also made reference to "male gaze" theorist Laura Mulvey. Like Lena Dunham, Soloway was determined to inhabit a female gaze, through the way she wrote and directed. "Knowing how it feels to be *inside* a woman instead of what it's like to look *at* them—it's simply the inverse of what [directors] have been doing," she tells me. During filming, she discusses with director of photography Jim Frohna the feeling characters should be evoking before the camera rolls on each shot. But for Soloway, the female gaze (a term she means to include anyone who identifies as female) is not just an aesthetic tool. It's a political one that encourages empathy in the viewer. What does it feel like to be a trans woman learning how to live in the world as a female, to be a young woman exploring her sexuality or an older woman having an orgasm?

Transparent tries to answer these questions in quiet ways. Maura gets tutored in the rules of femininity by trans friend Davina. (Pushing Maura's knees closed, Davina teases, "Can we just close up shop here a little bit?") And she experiences sexual pleasure for the first time as Maura with someone who sees her as she sees herself, new girlfriend Vicki (Anjelica Huston). Ali embarks on sexual adventures, seeking communion via threesomes and trans men and lesbians, with the same volatile energy she brings to every-thing else in her life. Sarah, as her marriage crumbles, has wild sex with her ex-girlfriend Tammy, and finds violent relief at the hands of a dominatrix. But we also find her standing stark naked in front of her kitchen micro-wave one night after a bad PTA gala, shoulders slumped, an exhausted middle-aged woman with an imperfect body being herself.

And then there's Shelly. Like most older women on television, she is assumed to be asexual, a Jewish menopausal eunuch who cares only about nagging her children and fattening them up. Soloway decimates that as-sumption in one startling season-two scene, when Shelly coaxes ex-husband Maura to give her a hand job in the bathtub. "You know that thing you used to do with your finger?" she says coyly. "What did we used to call it? Flicky-flicky thump-thump." Maura obliges impassively, almost as if her hand were disconnected from the rest of her. (In a sense, it is: "flicky-flicky thump-thump" is the property of Mort.) But the camera is in thrall to Shelly, lingering on her ecstatic face as she comes.

To film that bathtub scene, Soloway cleared the set almost entirely, personally depositing bubbles in the water to make actress Judith Light comfortable. "When I saw it in the script, I said, 'I can't do this,'" Light says tremulously. "What I meant was: I don't know how I'm going to get myself to this place. But I knew how important it was in the grand scheme of things. How many times in television have we been told, 'Nobody wants to see that'?" Before they began rolling, Soloway held hands with Light, Tambor, and Frohna, and said, "We ask that this be received in the way we are giving it," Light recalls. "She was thinking of the much larger context. It took my breath away."

Soloway says she encouraged Light not to think of a moment like this one as a nude scene but as part of a revolution: "We are showing things that no one has ever seen before, and you are going to get to share with the entire world what everybody is afraid to see, which is Mom having pleasure. I say the same thing to Amy [Landecker] as she is standing in front of the micro-wave naked: we never see women look like this on television, and yet every woman is going to understand the feeling."

Sitting at her kitchen table, Soloway wipes tears from her eyes. "Nobody ever shows this stuff, because whether or not we are conscious of it, we are always trying to make things that satisfy man's desire. It makes me cry to think about it."

For all of this seriousness about feminism, *Transparent* routinely tips its sacred cows. Soloway made a cameo appearance in the show as the professor of a women's studies class being audited by Ali. Clad in a shapeless smock and huge red eyeglasses, she delivers a lecture on the patriarchal nature of punctuation, particularly warning against exclamation points, "which are in and of themselves small rapes." After class, Ali tells the professor admiringly, "I loved your TED Talk on rape culture and breast-feeding."

Ali soon embarks on a love affair with Cherry Jones's iconic poet Leslie Mackinaw, a lesbian rake who has a thing for young teaching assistants. "I guess that Leslie harbors a little disdain for the aging female body," one of her housemates confides to Ali. While the poet keeps aging, her girlfriends "all stay twenty-one."

Leslie's character was loosely modeled on Eileen Myles. The poet's name had come up in the writers' room, and Soloway developed an art crush after reading her work. That feeling accelerated when the two met in the flesh at a museum event in San Francisco. "I went to the San Francisco museum planning to seduce you," Soloway confessed to Myles in a 2016 onstage discussion. Soon the two were a couple, and in addition to *Transparent* featuring her poetry and a character inspired by her, Myles showed up in several episodes as part of Leslie's entourage.

"Jill is very open about the fact that a lot of this stuff is coming from her life as she is living it right now," says Hoffmann. "So yeah, we talked about Eileen on set, and we met Eileen, and Eileen was there talking about Leslie being Eileen." She pauses and giggles. "Jill has recognized that not only can her life be her art, but her art can be her life—and her therapy."

As Soloway immersed herself in LGBTQ culture, the series deepened its portrayal of the alliances and clashes between feminism and LGBTQ circles. These tensions and cross-purposes were explored in one of *Transparent*'s most striking episodes, season two's "Man on the Land," written by Ali Liebegott. Having decided she is gay, Ali persuades Sarah and Maura to take a road trip with her to the Idyllwild Wimmin's Music Festival, a fictionalized version of the legendary Michigan Womyn's Music Festival. While many jokes are cracked at the expense of earnest wimmin—sample activities include a tampon-making workshop and a "Drumming Away Racism" session—the sense of liberation unleashed by swarms of seminaked lesbians dancing joyously is *real*. So is the sense of darkness that descends when Maura realizes that the festival is open only to "womyn-born womyn." Suddenly what looked like freedom feels hostile.

Waiting on line for the Porta Potties, Maura is suddenly surrounded by womyn yelling, "Man on the land!" They are warning of male maintenance workers arriving on site, but Maura cannot help but take it personally, and walks off alone into the woods, as if on a revelatory acid trip gone bad. Later, a festival veteran explains to Maura that the exclusionary policy began with a simple idea: "that we women could have one goddamn safe space in the world." When Maura tries to argue for her right to be there, the woman bristles. "I don't give a shit about your goddamn penis. It's about the *privilege*." Does the fact that Maura is privately suffering inside that male body and doesn't experience it as privilege obviate the fact that she has accrued societal benefits from being seen as male for the first seventy years of her life?

The series constantly circles the messy ways that gender, sexuality, class, and race define and empower (or disempower) its characters—that a person who feels oppressed according to one axis of identity politics (gender, say) might simultaneously belong to the class of oppressors in other areas of their existence (through being white, or rich, or feeling a comfortable fit between their gender identity and the body they were born with). There is even a term for radical feminists at odds with the transgender community:

TERF, short for trans-exclusionary radical feminist. So combustible are these issues that the real Michigan Womyn's Festival ended in 2015, after decades of debate over what defined womynhood.

Liebegott volunteered to write that episode, having performed at the real Michigan event in the past. She says she was dismayed by the division in the queer community between trans and cis women and felt immense pressure to represent the scene in all its complexity. "There's not a lot of actual queer characters on TV, so I want it to be done right. At the very least, you don't want to do anything offensive. At best, you want to show the most complete version of something as you can."

Sometimes it seems as if everyone on *Transparent* is lost in the woods. All the central characters are in transition, in one way or another. Maura's announcement sets off a chain reaction in the family, and over everyone topples, like a set of dominoes. Sarah leaves her husband to marry Tammy, a woman she dated in college, but then ditches her, too. Josh starts coming to grips with the fact that he was sexually abused by his babysitter in his youth, and that he has a son he never knew he'd spawned. Shelly pours the secrets of her own life into a one-woman show called *To Shell and Back*, which is played for laughs, until she performs it live on a cruise ship and it becomes beautifully serious.

And Ali—well, she embraces the confusion. In the first season, she instigates a drug-fueled threesome with her African American trainer and his roommate. (Amazingly, Gaby Hoffmann was heavily pregnant and had to watch from the sidelines, baby kicking inside, while a body double played out the most graphic parts of the scene.) Similarly, when Ali goes on a date with a teaching assistant trans man named Dale (played by trans comedian Ian Harvie), the camera shows us what Ali sees: a super-macho guy who drives a pickup truck and lives in a rustic cabin with a Pabst Blue Ribbon sign in his living room. Dale demands that she call him "Daddy" and orders her to lie down on his coffee table so he can shave off her bushy pubic hair. But after their attempt at sex in a public bathroom goes awry (with Dale dropping his prosthetic penis on the floor), Ali returns to his place and sees something very different: a thoughtful guy with a Prius and a modern LA house. "Want some tea?" he asks gently, making us wonder how much of the earlier scenes was real and how much Ali was projecting her own fevered fantasies onto Dale.

It was a provocative way to probe Ali's sexual-adventurer stance, as a privileged white girl taking a vacation in someone else's exotic other-ness. But the scene upset some trans critics, who felt the episode mocked Dale's masculinity. Harvie, who had served as a consultant on the show and whose personal stories had inspired the writers to create a character for him, defended the ambiguous plotline. In an interview in *The Advocate*, he argued that the episode poses deep questions that sit at the heart of the series—"Will you love me if I'm not who you thought I am? . . . Will you love me if I'm struggling with my own gender experience?" Harvie continues. "Will you love me if I . . . drive a Toyota and not a Ford?"

Rhys Ernst admits that when he first read the Dale scripts, "I was in-trigued to see them be kind of messy and complicated and unsatisfying. They were nonaffirming, awkward moments." But once the episode aired, he realized that they had tried to move too quickly. "What we missed was that this was the first time in history that a trans man had ever been represented on TV played by a trans man. We were trying to jump to a future level of messiness when everybody else felt they needed positive affirmation first."

So, while women on television are fighting to be allowed to be antiheroes and screwups, other marginalized groups are at a different point in the process, craving an idealized or, at the very least, less denigrated version of themselves. As the first mainstream series focused on a trans character, *Transparent* bears enormous pressure to fulfill a whole community's expectations. As Ali Liebegott points out, "You could have ten trans people in the room, and they would not necessarily agree on what they want to see. You would never ask that of a straight white guy: [to represent] all straight white guys."

The Dale story line was not the only thing that upset the LGBTQ community about *Transparent*. The casting of cis-male actor Tambor as Maura caused major controversy, something that deeply saddened both Soloway and Tambor. Accepting his second Emmy for the role in September 2016, Tambor made a speech asking Hollywood to "give transgender talent a chance," and solemnly declared, "I would not be unhappy were I the last cisgender male to play a female transgender on television." In a guest column for the *Hollywood Reporter* decrying the trend for casting cis actors in trans roles, GLAAD's transgender media director, Nick Adams, called Tambor "the rare exception where the casting fits the story being told—that of an older trans woman who is just beginning her transition," and lauded Soloway's "deliberate decision to bring in many transgender people behind the camera and in front of it."

In season three, the writers fleshed out characters such as Davina and Shea, two of Maura's trans friends. Both are played by trans actresses. Shea, a conventionally attractive yoga teacher, is conjured with great sweetness by Trace Lysette. A romance blossoms between Shea and Josh, but he backs off the moment he learns she is HIV positive. "I'm not your fucking adventure! I'm a person!" she shouts at him. "Grow up!"

Growing up is a tall order for the Pfeffermans. Like her kids, Maura has a knack for projecting her needs and ideas onto others. The third season opens with a stylistically startling episode that yanks us out of *Transparent*'s usual upper-middle-class havens. Volunteering at an LGBTQ hotline, Maura screws up a suicide call from a trans teen and races out to try to track down the girl at a crowded South LA shopping center. The only white person in a maze of dark faces, Maura makes assumptions based on her biases: in a wig store, she spots some Latina trans women and asks if they've seen this girl "on the streets." The women recoil at the implication, pointing out that they are nursing students. Fainting from heat exhaustion, Maura gets carted away in an ambulance—to a public hospital, much to her horror. Soloway has called the episode an "intersectional fairy tale," but there is no happy ending here, just the understanding that being transgender is but one facet of Maura's identity.

Soloway knew from the start that she wanted a series structured around all five family members, the narrative encircling them like a "ring of light." She largely used the process she learned from Alan Ball and Alan Poul on *Six Feet Under*, which is to fill big grids with sharply detailed story lines for each character in every episode, a kind of antidiscrimination policy that keeps the main characters in play and forces viewers to regularly shift their sympathies. Like Soloway, Ball was a fan of *General Hospital*, and he elevated that soap structure into a finely woven tapestry of voices.

The writers' room of *Transparent*, tucked inside a Paramount Pictures building named after golden-age starlet Carole Lombard, is surrounded by whiteboards broken into grids by episode and character. There are also vertical columns of colorful Post-its with tiny writing mapping out possibilities ("Ali's first nitrous trip. She hears the voice of God" or "Shelly getting diddled") and papers tacked to the wall reminding the writers of the bigger picture, like: "Maura WANTS to control her own transition, but NEEDS to conquer shame."

The intimate connections among family members fuel the series' action, which means the writers must find ways for the characters to come together regularly, such as at funerals, weddings, and birthday parties. *Transparent* also relies on religious rituals: in season one, the family gathers for Shabbat, during which Maura says the prayer reserved for the matriarch; in season two, there's a spotlight on Yom Kippur, with Ali throwing a fast-breaking party to celebrate her new interest in Judaism; and season three culminates in an impromptu Passover Seder on a cruise ship. Jewish-American newspaper the *Forward* dubbed *Transparent* "the Jewiest Show Ever"—which is not saying all that much, since generations of entertainment industry Jews internalized the saying "Write Yiddish, cast British," as we saw with Amy Sherman-Palladino's WASP heroine Lorelai Gilmore, who drops Yiddishisms as if she were to the shtetl born.

The funny thing is that the Pfeffermans are not a religious family; for them, Jewishness is mostly about matzo ball soup and lox. Shelly is a member of the temple's board, but probably less for spiritual reasons than for the sense of community. The same goes for Sarah, who enlists the help of Rabbi Raquel in throwing social events aimed at young creative Jews (much as Soloway herself did with LA's East Side Jews events), but puts little thought into the God stuff. Raquel, the still, ethical center of the series, finally loses her patience with Sarah's half-assed Judaism. "Can you clarify for me really fast what spirituality is for you, Sarah?" Raquel demands. "I can tell you what it's not. It's not changing your mind whenever you feel like it. It's not following your bliss. It's not finding yourself by climbing through your belly button and out your own asshole and calling it a journey"—a line that seems as much internal self-questioning by the show's writers as a rebuke to the spiritually foggy Pfeffermans.

Despite Soloway's attempts to forge an inclusive, trans-affirmative workplace, *Transparent* became enmeshed in controversy in the fall of 2017. Allegations surfaced that Tambor had sexually harassed his transgender costar Trace Lysette and his former assistant, Van Barnes, leaving the show's future in limbo when this book went to press. Former *Transparent* writer Micah Fitzerman-Blue told the *New York Times*, "It's just incredibly sad that that happened in the midst of something that felt so revolutionary." And yet the very fluidity of Soloway's approach might allow the show to make something of this culturally chaotic moment.

———————————

When Soloway talks about the skills needed to be a director, she starts to get angry at the ways the industry has convinced women they are unqualified. "I always understood directing as something I didn't know how to do. There's all this equipment and you need to know lenses and rules and math and . . . 'Don't worry, women, we've got this!'" she shouts in a deep mock-macho voice. "It's all very militaristic, with long shooting days and talk about attacking things like it's an invasion."

Soloway suddenly sits back in her chair and smiles, explaining her own very different way of doing things: "I recognize that actors are artists who use their bodies to feel things and that I am filming those feelings with a camera. So I privilege the emotions, I privilege the actors." If a crewperson says there's a problem with the focus, Soloway doesn't call "cut" if the scene is working. One of her techniques, inspired by *American Honey* director Andrea Arnold, is letting actors ease from rehearsal into being filmed without shouting, "Action," which allows her to capture fresh, awkward emotions. "I'm a bit of an evangelist around helping women recognize that a lot of things that come very, very naturally to them actually make them better directors."

Jessi Klein, the head writer on *Inside Amy Schumer*, who worked on season three of *Transparent*, extolls the way Soloway "creates a feeling before the cameras are even rolling." Trusting her actors, Soloway is confident "that if there is something that is felt strongly, there will be a way for it to make sense on the screen," says Klein. That sometimes leads to long hours, staffers note, as Soloway follows her instincts.

Looking for a leadership style that felt comfortable, Soloway considered guys such as Adam Sandler, Zach Galifianakis, and Jack Black, who all "seemed like they had access to their voices in a way I was jealous of, who were just *playing*. I think that's a really great way to be in power as a woman: hire your friends, surround yourself with people who inspire you in the same way that Lorne Michaels and Judd Apatow have been doing all these years, and then tell everyone, 'It's not brain surgery. We are here to have fun.'"

She wanted to tap into the natural comfort these white guys exuded, the feeling men have had "since they were born that it is their job to take up space and run shit," as Soloway quips. It's something she thought deeply about as she began creating a second series, *I Love Dick*. Adapted by playwright Sarah Gubbins from the 1997 experimental autobiographical novel by Chris Kraus and staffed with an all-female writers' room, *I Love Dick* plunges into the brain of a married female filmmaker (played by Kathryn Hahn) erotically obsessed with a dickish academic named Dick (Kevin Bacon). "The whole series is about why women have so much self-hatred when it comes to demanding their right to lead and see as a filmmaker,"

Soloway explains to me a few weeks before the premiere of the series, an unabashedly feminist artwork dropped into the middle of Amazon's mainstream marketplace.

This is an emotional and intellectual journey for Soloway, whose ideas about women, and gender generally, transformed between our first interview and when I finished the book. In 2017, Soloway came out as gender nonbinary, indentifying neither as a woman nor as a man, and answering to the pronoun "they" rather than "she": "One of the evolutions that I have experienced in the past two years is the notion of not wanting to label myself as a 'gender essentialist,' someone who would say, 'Women are X and men are Y.'" For many years Soloway spoke as a cheerleader for womankind with exhortations such as "Women can hold space because they have babies." But, Soloway continues, "I can't really say any of that anymore. It doesn't allow us to have the trans and gender-nonconforming and nonbinary people in this conversation, who also do this work beautifully."

The primary criterion now is finding people who can immerse themselves "in the friction of emotions" and live in the fluidity of the moment. Soloway compares the way they shoot *Transparent* to a documentary, one that yields constant surprises: "I sometimes watch *Six Feet Under* now and I see the rigidity with which we approached the work. I feel like I have discovered these keys to the kingdom now: it's all about not knowing if something will work and showing up to watch it unfold."

EPILOGUE

In 1975, Gloria Steinem imagined how aliens from outer space trying to decode America based on TV and movies would see women: as a marginalized servant class who slept in false eyelashes and full makeup. If those same aliens watched television today, they would glean a very different picture.

Contemporary television quakes with women's sound and fury. Since 2015, a torrent of series created by and revolving around women has shot forth with the explosive velocity of a champagne cork. A very partial inventory includes *Insecure, Unbreakable Kimmy Schmidt, Jessica Jones, UnReal, Crazy Ex-Girlfriend, Queen Sugar, Fleabag, Difficult People, Another Period, Grace and Frankie, One Mississippi, Good Girls Revolt, Chewing Gum, Underground, Divorce, Great News, Supergirl, I Love Dick, Harlots, Better Things,* and *Glow.* The subject matter spans sexual exploration and sexual abuse; female camaraderie and artistic emergence; depression and cancer. Among the protagonists are journalists, prostitutes, wrestlers, superheroes, and, in *My Crazy Ex-Girlfriend*, a lawyer with a tendency to turn female troubles such as heavy breasts and period sex into musical extravaganzas.

Some shows, such as British writer/actress Phoebe Waller-Bridge's brash, booze-sozzled "traumedy" *Fleabag*, grab you by the throat. What starts out looking like an updated British version of single-girl sexploits (the series opens with a 2:00 a.m. booty text) quickly mutates into something much more barbed and anguished. "Either everyone feels this a little bit, and they're just not talking about it, or I'm really fucking alone, which isn't fucking funny," the main character, Fleabag, utters darkly at one point.

Other recent series, such as *UnReal*, flip the script on TV itself. "We threw out the word *likability* really early on," *UnReal* creator Sarah Gertrude Shapiro told me of her show about two female producers at the helm of a reality TV franchise. Shapiro had toiled miserably as a producer on *The Bachelor* and wove elements of her own divided consciousness into *UnReal*'s Rachel Goldberg (Shiri Appleby). A feminist producer on a reality dating show, Rachel finds her job involves manipulating female contestants into compromising situations to satisfy the public's sadistic gaze. "The first time we see Rachel, she's wearing a THIS IS WHAT A FEMINIST LOOKS LIKE T-shirt," Shapiro points out. "I really wanted people to know: This is not a lark spoofing reality TV. This is about somebody who lost their mind because they are totally living against their ideals." The primary love relationship in the series is between Rachel and her brassy, older boss, Quinn (Constance Zimmer): two women in the entertainment industry trying to figure out how to exert their power without being demonized or marginalized.

Shapiro says she struggles with those quandaries on a regular basis— from being told to be nicer to crew members to getting pushback on hiring female directors. "When we were talking about hiring a director for the pilot, I would say a name, and there would be this weird silence. It was women who had done incredible work, but people would say, 'I've heard she's *tough.*' What does that even mean? We just hired an asshole guy who went five million dollars over budget, so should we not ever hire another *man*?"

Even as women carve out space for themselves as showrunners, direct-ing on television remains a mostly male milieu. Despite directing several independent films, Nisha Ganatra struggled for years to get a foothold in television. "It's like a catch-22: You can't do it unless you've done it before, and nobody will let you do it!" she says, laughing. It was only after an in-tervention by Jill Soloway, who hired her to collaborate on *Transparent*, that Ganatra's television career took off.

Soloway describes the TV industry as an ecosystem in which men in power traditionally surround themselves with writers and directors who share their basic worldview and make them feel comfortable. "You can picture the older male director who hires the freshman director," says Soloway. "They are both wearing baseball caps, and he's got his arm around the kid, and they know how to do this because they've both been on teams and they know how men mentor one another. So they are going to be chosen above a woman or a person of color or a queer person or a trans person. If you are a white straight guy who's lived in the Pacific Palisades for the past twenty-five years and you bring a young trans director of color onto your set, you are not going to get to have that relaxed feeling of 'Let me throw my arm around you and show you how things go.' You are going to be forced to confront your privilege."

Breaking these patterns means dissolving cozy networks; every female or minority or trans hire is one less job for the boys. "You can't just make more space," Soloway argues. "So you are asking men to not hire the people they know and trust, people that make it easy for them because they have a shorthand. That is a pretty big ask for a lot of men who don't consider themselves racist or sexist but have comfortable systems in place for their professional and personal relationships." This is why a number of showrunners, such as Soloway, *Queen Sugar*'s Ava DuVernay, *American Horror Story*'s Ryan Murphy, and *Jessica Jones*'s Melissa Rosenberg have tried to even up the playing field by publicly vowing to hire female directors for half or more of their series' episodes.

Increasing the number of female directors or showrunners isn't going to fix big American problems like the wage gap, and developing more series with female protagonists won't defeat the assaults on women's reproductive health, either. We need a grassroots activist onslaught to achieve that. Yet cultural representation is no small thing. Growing up in a world where you don't spot versions of your experience reflected in the culture makes you feel small and invisible. It tells you, and all those around you, that your voice is not important. By reflecting the reality of women's lives, the television creators in this book arguably have helped provoke the current political backlash. That means they could play a prominent role inspiring the resistance.

There are no fairy-tale endings here. When I began writing this book, Hillary Clinton was sailing toward the White House, assisted by Shonda, Lena, Amy, Abbi, and Ilana. When I finished it, Donald Trump was sitting in the Oval Office emitting misogynist tweets, and Republicans were once again waging war on women's health and reproductive rights.

Less than a year into the presidency of a man who once bragged he liked to "grab them by the pussy," though, monstrous revelations about movie producer Harvey Weinstein in the *New York Times* triggered a kind of mass symposium on sexual misconduct, leading to the ousting of serial harassers and predators throughout the journalism, political, and entertainment industries (among them Louis C.K. and Kevin Spacey). *Time* magazine made female "silence breakers" its "Person of the Year." It was as if the squalid underbelly of the patriarchy had suddenly been exposed, and the experiences women had silently suffered were brought into the open in a #metoo moment of painful but cathartic recognition and solidarity.

History is a giant tease: it jerks around our hopes and assumptions, it ebbs and surges and doubles back on itself. The long arc of history may bend toward justice, but when you're living through a reactionary period, it feels as if progress were being forced treacherously backward. The fact that forces of repression are now emboldened and energized makes the need for a cacophony of diverse and unconventional voices on television even more vital and urgent.

"I think the big breakthrough we had the past couple of years comes from the proliferation of all the venues [showcasing] all these original voices that networks wouldn't touch," suggests Lynda Obst, the legendary movie producer who has executive-produced TV series such as *Hot in Cleveland* and *Good Girls Revolt*.

The major broadcast networks (ABC, CBS, NBC, and Fox) have not made consistent strides in terms of gender parity. (The CW is an exception, with a majority of series run by women.) A recent analysis in *Variety* found that of the new scripted shows being made for the 2017/18 season, just 29 percent of the broadcast showrunners are female and only 35 percent of the lead actors are female. Yet the old network system's dominance is over, as hundreds of cable and streaming networks lure away viewers. Even Rhimes turned her back on the old network system in 2017, leaving ABC for a multi-year production deal with Netflix.

The death of network primacy is a manifestation of the shattering of consensus in American culture as we retreat into belief bubbles and demographic niches. Cable channels and streaming services are open to taking more risks and courting viewers who have been neglected by the old network system, all of which means more chances for women to steal the show. Jenji Kohan's *Orange Is the New Black* helped bring attention to Netflix's programming; Netflix went on to deliver *Unbreakable Kimmy Schmidt*, *Jessica Jones*, *Grace and Frankie*, *Lady Dynamite*, *Glow*, and imports *Fleabag*, *Anne with an E*, and *Chewing Gum*. Amazon followed its *Transparent* success with pickups for *One Mississippi*, *Good Girls Revolt*, *Z: The Beginning of Everything*, *I Love Dick*, and Amy Sherman-Palladino's series *The Marvelous Mrs. Maisel*. Traditionally sedate female networks made room for more challenging fare (*Queen Sugar* at Oprah's OWN network, *UnReal* at Lifetime), and executives at Hulu showed staunch support for female showrunners.

Even cable network HBO, which had a historically grim record of airing series created by women, stepped up its game and made a home for its first female African American auteur with Issa Rae's *Insecure*. A Stanford grad and aspiring screenwriter, Rae was frustrated by the lack of black sitcoms on the twenty-first-century airwaves. "When *30 Rock* started, I really appreciated it because Liz Lemon is awkward, and I identified with her," she told *New York* magazine. "But it was frustrating that there were no characters like her that looked like me." Like Lena Dunham and the *Broad City* duo, Rae snuck into the industry through a side door, writing and starring in lo-fi Web series such as *The Misadventures of Awkward Black Girl* before attracting mainstream Hollywood attention. After a fizzled collaboration with Shonda Rhimes, she created *Insecure*.

Melina Matsoukas knew she was the right visual storyteller for *Insecure* from the moment she laid eyes on the pilot script. It mirrored Matsoukas's own life "as a young black woman having to navigate through worlds where we don't always fit in," and evoked friendships between women that resonated deep in her bones.

"We are telling stories about women and people of color on the show," Matsoukas says, "so that diversity on-screen should lead to more diversity behind the camera as well. It's really about being in charge of that gate. I'm like, who's allowed to come through that door? We have a small grip on that handle now."

———————————

Imagine a Los Angeles restaurant dining room filled entirely with women, clustered around ten tables, as if at a wedding banquet. Only, they're not dressed in glitzy gowns; they're dressed for work. These women call themselves the Woolf Pack, and they are some of Hollywood's most powerful showrunners.

Fledgling *UnReal* showrunner Sarah Gertrude Shapiro has planted herself next to television empress Shonda Rhimes at a table that also features *Vampire Diaries* co-creator Julie Plec and Liz Tigelaar, showrunner of *Casual* and *Life Unexpected*. The conversation at this particular table occasionally veers toward kvetching about things such as how difficult it is to hire female directors, but Tigelaar finds herself rapt in astonishment. "I was so struck by the fact that we could all sit there and complain that we should be getting more or should be further," she admitted later, "but what everybody at this table has accomplished is amazing. It just feels so nice to know that you're with women who are showrunners, who are doing this crazy thing that you're trying to do, too."

The Woolf Pack (the name a tip of the hat to Virginia Woolf and her quest for a space for female creativity, aka "a room of one's own") has been meeting sporadically for the last several years under the aegis of the non-profit Humanitas Foundation, which presents prizes to television and film writers who nobly explore the human condition. After being nominated for an award for *The Big C*, Jenny Bicks suggested getting more women involved in Humanitas, and a posse of female showrunners began to meet.

Bicks says it began as a small, informal gathering: "I remember women, one by one, getting up and telling their stories, and it was incredibly liberating because, as showrunners, directors, anything in charge, we spend so much of our time trying to play by rules that were not set up by us. We have very few people we can trust, people we can turn to and say, 'This isn't okay, right?'" As the group expanded by word of mouth, Bicks continues, "We shared our fears and our anger and our projects." They also raised money for the Hedgebrook women's writing retreat and traded tips on mentoring and hiring. "Very few of us had female mentors. If you are a showrunner who started when I did, there were a few women, like Diane English, but it was pretty much all men."

Bicks recalls a Christmas lunch at which she announced, "If this place got bombed, there would be no more female showrunners." She adds, "Which would probably make a lot of people happy."

DeAnn Heline, co-creator of *The Middle*, says that at her first Woolf Pack gathering, each woman took a turn answering questions such as "What was your greatest victory?" or "What was the craziest thing an executive ever said to you?" It was a rare moment when she was able to compare notes with her peers, she says. "You can ask Shonda or another showrunner, what did *you* do in this situation?"

Although the stalled statistics suggest there's still a steep climb ahead for female showrunners, Tigelaar sees an industry in which an increasing number of women *are* finding a foothold. "Looking at the numbers, maybe it seems bleak and like the uptick hasn't happened yet. But the feeling of being in it is real," she says, her voice vibrating with optimism. "I think it's a great time to be a woman in television, and I look around at that [Woolf Pack] lunch and, I'm like, look at what my friends are doing: they're all badasses! I think doors are being kicked open."

ACKNOWLEDGMENTS

Writing a book is a deeply solitary experience on one level, requiring thousands of hours alone in front of a computer, begging words to arrange themselves on a page. But writing this book was also a communal experience. I spent many happy days driving to Pacific Palisades and Sherman Oaks and Echo Park to listen to creative women talk about what they do and how they do it. I could not have written this book without the many interviewees—more than a hundred—who took the time to speak to me on and off the record. Not everyone I interviewed made it into the book by name, but all of their wisdom contributed to the finished product. I'm also appreciative of the many publicists and assistants who made these interviews happen. Alison Rou, Erin Kellgren, and Christina Brosman all went the extra mile for me, as did Lisa Vinnecour.

I also had a lot of help from my friends and colleagues. I want to thank Alice Short, Martin Miller, and Elena Howe, editors who assigned me related stories or otherwise supported me at the *Los Angeles Times*, where I worked when this book was born. Thanks also to Meredith Blake, Amy Kaufman, Greg Braxton, Gina McIntyre, Rebecca Traister, Deborah Vankin, Emily Ryan Lerner, Lisa Jane Persky, Tom Ceraulo, Yvonne Villarreal, Carolyn Kellogg, Mary McNamara, Liz Brown, Sarah Schrank, Christopher Noxon, Amy Reiter, Laura Miller, Danielle Nussbaum, Sharon Mizota, Oliver Wang, Sarah Hepola, Ivy Pochoda, Michelle Dean, Colleen Conway, and Jason Grote for providing me with contacts, title suggestions, or other vital aid.

I am so lucky to have Rakesh Satyal as the editor for this book. As well as being a great prose-smith, he is a true TV devotee who seems to have perfect recall of plot twists in many of the shows documented here. I cannot imagine a more ideal reader; the finished product owes much to his interventions.

At Atria, I am also grateful to have the support of Judith Curr and Peter Borland, and the aid of Loan Le and Paul Olsewski.

Thanks to my agent, Daniel Greenberg, who instantly understood what I wanted to achieve with this project and helped me shape the idea and find a home for it.

Finally, thank you to my family—to Tasmin Press-Reynolds, who joined me in my viewing research and delightedly watched series like *Roseanne*, *Murphy Brown*, and *Gilmore Girls* for the first time; and Kieran Press-Reynolds, who patiently watched me secede from domestic life for weeks on end as I sat hunched over my laptop. And to my husband, Simon, love of my life, who urged me to step off the treadmill of journalism and into the long-form space of this book; served as my first editor; offered guidance on every stage of this book; watched ridiculous amounts of TV with me; and cheered me on, even when the election results threatened to send us all into a permanent depression. I began this book and finished it thanks to him.

PHOTO CREDITS

INDEX

Page numbers of photographs appear in italics.

ABOUT THE AUTHOR

Joy Press has been writing about TV for more than fifteen years. In the 2000s, she was the chief television critic at the *Village Voice*. She later served as entertainment editor of *Salon* and then as pop culture editor at the *Los Angeles Times*, where, in addition to commissioning television coverage, she wrote and reported features on the medium. She has contributed to publications such as the *New York Times*, *Slate*, *New York*, *Salon*, and the *Guardian*. She lives in Los Angeles.